3
RN

Maya: Statuette of a Man.
Courtesy of The National Gallery of Art, Washington, D. C.
(Robert Woods Bliss Collection)

THE ART MUSEUM
IN AMERICA

by

WALTER PACH

62 ILLUSTRATIONS

PANTHEON

The reproduction on the title page of a Greek amphora of the late sixth century B.C., showing a foot race, was made with the permission of The Metropolitan Museum of Art.

Printed in United States of America

Photolithographed by
The Murray Printing Company
Wakefield, Massachusetts

LIST OF ILLUSTRATIONS

PREFACE AND ACKNOWLEDGMENTS

THE NEED for a book such as the present one transpired in a conversation, a few years ago, between an eminent European scholar-diplomat, who was visiting the United States for the first time, and Henry Allen Moe who told me of the occurrence.

"I was somewhat prepared for what I saw here when visiting your hospitals, libraries, and universities," said the ambassador. "But while I found them immensely beyond what I had expected, both as to extent and quality, there was one thing I discovered here which I had not expected in the least, and that is what you have done with your museums. The fact is that I had not known that there were any of importance or even of interest; now I find that they are everywhere, that they are magnificent, and that they are doing things for people that our museums do not so much as attempt. Perhaps I should blame my ignorance on Europe's chronic idea that America is a materialistic place, but on the other hand, the fault is partly your own: there ought to be a book from which we could learn what has taken place in your country. We have known, of course, that Americans have bought and carried off great numbers of masterworks from all parts of the world, but how could we know that so many of them have been given to the public?"

The question — a challenge, indeed — formed part of Mr. Moe's thinking for years and, because of his contacts with the Latin-American scholars and artists who have been coming to us in steadily increasing numbers, he first suggested my writing a sort of handbook in Spanish to make such visitors aware of what they might see in the various cities they would visit. Further discussions convinced us both, however, that the people who most need such a book are our own people: they are all too often victims of the error confessed to by that ambassador, who had accepted the legend of the "dollar land" as one unable to take time for the deeper thoughts which find their expression in art. Hence this volume is dedicated to a wider knowledge of America's handling of the force which has been a chief cause of action in all countries and periods — even more than the record of those times and places, a thing for which art has always been recognized. It is hoped that a translation of the book for our friends beyond the southern border of this country may follow in due course; and among the important encouragements I have received, it is a pleasure to recall that of Francis Henry Taylor, who said that the work ought to appear in all the chief European languages.

Though I had had very unusual opportunities to know our art resources, from the Atlantic to the Pacific, a new study of them and renewed contacts with the men who are building up those resources appeared desirable before writing on our institutions, their history, and the problems they look forward to. For this purpose The Rockefeller Foundation made a generous grant-in-aid, enabling me to visit certain collections which I had not known before, and to confer anew with museum men and women throughout the country. To list them and give an idea of the thought and effort they are giving to their splendid task would be to add too many pages to this book. People who know our institutions, however, will be sure to realize that in speaking of the Fogg Museum at Harvard, I am alluding to the work of Edward W. Forbes and Paul J. Sachs, and to my conversations with them; the great work with the classical collections at the Metropolitan carried on by Gisela M. A. Richter from the earlier contributions of General Cesnola and Edward Robinson, is so well known that the sources of my information from those scholars will again be manifest; the same is true with regard to the help I have received from Fiske Kimball as to the development which the Philadelphia Museum has had at his hands; Laurence Vail Coleman, director of the American Association of Museums, was also most generous in taking time for discussion of his present activity, and in recalling the results of the six years he gave to the monumental reference book which I refer to in later pages; James Johnson Sweeney, of the Museum of Modern Art, very kindly read the chapter on the work which especially interests him; W. G. Constable, of the Museum of Fine Arts in Boston, Mr. Taylor of the Metropolitan, again, and Dr. William R. Valentiner who, from the three American museums where he has served, has exerted so wide an influence, all have read parts of the book, and have given me invaluable advice. I cannot forget the day in Chicago when Daniel Catton Rich began in the morning to continue earlier talks about museum problems, carried on through lunch, and finished only when his secretaries came in with the letters he needed to sign before closing time. But already I am launched on the list I said would be too long — and there are still numbers of people, like Grace McCann Morley of San Francisco, who have offered me deeply appreciated assistance.

Even so, one more source of the help I have received is of such importance that I must still record it, if only as an assurance to the reader that this book has had the benefit of the most expert counsel to be secured anywhere. That is only a moderate statement as to the history and attainments of Henry W. Kent. When I say, therefore, that every page of my manuscript (save for this preface) has been read — and in many cases reread several times — by Mr. Kent, when I say that he has been unsparing of his time, his information, his impersonal correction as well as his always generous encouragement, it will be understood that not only I am indebted to him, but that the debt extends to every one interested in my subject. To him, then, as to all who have aided me, directly or through their work in our museums, I beg to offer my most sincere thanks.

W.P.

TABLE OF CONTENTS

INTRODUCTION

GREAT WORKS of art in museums, like the masterpieces of literature and music, are things we think of when pondering what are called "permanent values." Some of these objects have lasted for centuries or even for thousands of years, and the ideas they offer us have a faculty of renewal that makes them as true today as at the time when they were created.

But the museum is not in the same class as the objects it contains. A modern phenomenon, it changes in response to the needs of the age, and thus vitally expresses it. We have just passed through a war which left a barrier between the old world of the past and the new world of the present. The conditions under which we are living are so different from those we knew before World War II that we recognize them as an earnest of a new world.

Those last two words have long been used, especially when printed in capital letters, to mean America. In writing my last chapter, *The Museum of the New World*, I had in mind two aspects of the term. The earlier sections of this book tell of the history, achievements, and problems of the art museums of the United States. The final section, though not neglecting our own museums, also refers to American countries outside our borders, and to the art of the Western Hemisphere before the coming of the European, who, as will be seen, has been notably changed by "Americanization."

Everyone knows how different the American of European descent is from his cousins in the various parts of the Old World: his appearance, his speech, his philosophy, in a word, his whole way of life — all have been modified by the character of the great double continent he has lived in for over four centuries. Yet, few people have thought of American art as anything but a provincial form of European art. The difference between the two is usually regarded as one of accent, the thing which distinguishes the speech of a Chicagoan from a Londoner's, a French Canadian's from a Parisian's, and a Mexican's or Peruvian's from a native Spaniard's. But more than accent enters the question; for we think American far more than we talk American, as everyone will agree after comparing life in the Old World with that in the New. And just as life has been changed here, art is bound to be different too, for art is that which tells most fully and intimately about life.

1

The claim made in these pages is not for any newly created forms: even those of our most original works in architecture are closely related to European forms. Neither do I believe that the great indigenous cultures of America will ever dominate modern American art; true, the glorious pre-Columbian arts of this hemisphere have never ceased to prove their perennial vitality, but European contributions to our thought prevent their renascence without material modification. Also, modern European art is still too powerful an influence for us to exorcise it, if, indeed, a complete break were desirable — which is at least open to question.

With European and purely American elements thus united, the two senses of the term *New World* tend to merge into one. As man, or Western man (for I cannot speak of the Orient) works out the form of civilization under which he is to live, the role of America must become more and more important — perhaps dominant. At all events, it is in this hemisphere, unscarred by World War II and by the worst of those hatreds which bred it, that the character of the New World is bound to assert itself most clearly. And in achieving an understanding of that character, no source of insight can surpass the museum.

Marshal Joffre, addressing a group of American students of art, said that if they wanted to know the secret of France's survival in 1914, they could read it in her museums. There her nature and destiny are registered. The great old soldier spoke as much of the past as of the present. He could as confidently have spoken of the museum in terms of the future.

For the museum, which to many people seems to look only backward, is in reality one of our chief means of looking forward. Its final teaching is that spiritual values transcend material ones. A period of enormous scientific, military and economic development forgot this truth — and World War II resulted. We need to see that the infinitely extensible enjoyment of the arts (including, of course, literature and music) is not only an ideal but a possible goal, whereas the enjoyment of material possessions, being limited by the resources of the soil and of the machine, must lead to competitive strife. This may be a necessary instrument for mankind's ascent; but when the very existence of the human race is threatened, as it was in World War II, the moment is ripe for laying emphasis on those elements which we have mastered. Since they are embodied in the arts, the museum is necessarily called upon to play a great part in making them familiar to us. A moment devoted to considering matters dealt with by our museums will show the immediacy of their relation to the life of the average person.

1. First Home of the Metropolitan Museum, New York, 1872.
    Courtesy of The Metropolitan Museum of Art.

It is a privilege for anyone to see the pyramids of Egypt, the Partho non and the other temples of Greece, the cathedrals of France, and the great monuments of ancient India or of ancient Mexico; but it is not necessary to see them in order to realize that the world is a different place from what it was when they were built. We no longer produce works of such impressiveness: our tallest skyscraper or our most over-grown city is a poor substitute for the beauty of Chartres or for the unique personality to be felt, let us say, in Siena or Toledo. Arguing from such a premise, some people have interpreted the change as decadence. But instantly our achievements in the social and physical sciences reassure us that we are still tapping, if in other ways, those quenchless sources which gave us the great things of the past. It is when we try to copy these things that we make our failures: to see the academic imitations of Greek sculpture, for example, is indeed to be tempted to look on human genius as hopelessly diminished, whereas an airplane tells us that we have succeeded where Icarus, Leonardo da Vinci, and many another great mind of the past failed.

The difference between the modern airplane and its forerunners, as they existed in the vision of the old-time dreamers, may be pursued a step further. Our miracle of flight is not due to individual effort, how-ever much certain devoted men may have contributed to it by their observations and inventions. It is the collective effort of thousands of theorists, experimenters, and mechanics that has permitted us to cross the Atlantic at a speed equalling in an hour what Columbus did in a week, and to do so with all but mathematical certainty, as contrasted with the old navigator's mere faith, sublime though that faith was.

We are considering, then, the difference between what is accom-plished by man acting singly and man acting in groups, often over wide areas and long periods of time. It is this latter type of activity which produces the most impressive results — the pyramids, temples, and cathedrals in the past, and, in the modern age, the conquest of plagues, of ignorance, and of distance. If disease still offers immense problems, we know at least that it can be checked by science — we no longer attribute it to the whims of evil divinities. If education is still to be developed from what are even now its earlier stages, we have instruments like the printed book and the limitlessly reproduced images of photog-raphy to carry a maximum of enlightenment to the masses of mankind — which the past barely considered; and if our saving of time by modern inventions has not brought with it a knowledge of what to do with that time, the wonders of the telephone, the telescope, and the airplane still rank with the wonders of the ancient world.

It is at museums that we become aware of such questions as I have just raised, and there are few bigger ones. They are, today, of the most fundamental importance to us, for we need to feel that we are worthy of our past, in facing a future never more beset with difficulties. The New World is heir to enormous problems from the Old. We must radically change our attitude toward human affairs, or move, and doubtless move rapidly, toward destruction and chaos. Against these auguries of evil, we can confidently advance the heroism, faith, and achievement of the modern world. I have mentioned some of its conquests in the world of science, but humanity needs other things besides, and it has other things to show. At the art museum some of them appear, and if, at the museum, we are once more faced with the difference between Egyptian, Greek or Gothic achievement and our own, I will make bold to say that all the advantage does not belong to the past.

The museum is itself a collective work, in many ways comparable to the pyramid, the temple, or the cathedral. Those monuments drew upon the accumulated knowledge and aspirations of man, and we can parallel that effort when we collect in our museums the material expressions of the thought and feeling of the ancients. We know, of course, that the greater part of man's past accomplishment has been destroyed by time, as far as visible evidences are concerned, though there are survivals in our thought, sensibility, and instinct. And without the work that our museum men have done, much of what remains of our greatest tangible heritage would have been lost.

But there is infinitely more to the museum than its role as a preserver of old values, though it was this aspect which most interested the pioneers in its development. A far greater role is its capacity for clarifying — almost for creating — our conception of art. Starting as a picture gallery or a sculpture collection, the museum now embraces ceramics, arms and armor, laces, textiles, and the other applied arts. From the European peoples it has reached out, successively, to those of other continents, even — in our more enlightened museums — including the ancient works of the American continent. Similarly, museums have extended their range in time, and are now coming to realize that their biggest problem, as well as their biggest opportunity, resides in imaginatively dealing with the present.

Europe has temporarily solved the problem of coverage by creating museums of the older arts, of modern art, of decoration, and of ethnography. Perhaps, considering the vastness of the Louvre, the British Museum, the Museum für Völkerkunde in Berlin, and other collections abroad, the dividing up of the subject may afford a permanent solution for Europe. It appears less satisfactory for America. For, while Rome, Florence, Paris, Bruges, and many other European cities are, in effect, museums themselves, with their wealth of architecture and sculpture, American cities often contain only the fewest edifices designed for permanence and even fewer that can be considered works of art.

To give a comprehensive survey of all forms of art is obviously beyond the scope of any conceivable gallery. Yet, our people do look to their museums for guidance on all artistic problems, and, to an increasing degree, they are getting it. But just as we turned aside from the conception of the museum as dealing solely with ancient material, so we must now turn away, and even more decidedly, from the museum as a kind of scientific or social instrument. It should serve essentially, whether the politician, the educator, and the moralist like the conception or not, to give the highest type of pleasure — a peculiarly intense pleasure to those able to experience it. Their number is rapidly increasing, and America may have a hundred persons (or, who knows, a thousand) for every one it had a generation ago, who can testify from their own experience to the truth which made a line of Schiller's a household word for millions, in Europe. When the poet wrote the lines to be read at the dedication of a new theater, and included in them his now proverbial "Ernst ist das Leben, heiter die Kunst," he expressed something already deep in the consciousness of all men — that life is earnest, art is joyous.

The theater, the opera, the ballet, and the concert affirm to us the indissoluble relationship between life as a thing of purposeful directing and life as rendered for the eyes and ears in terms of nobility, beauty, and grace. So also, in the realm of the museum, we may — at any visiting hour of any day in the year — see people under the spell of enchantment which (having not the slightest need to do so) they cannot describe or analyze. They recognize it by instinct. That faculty tells them that the magic has come down from dimmest prehistory, when man first detached himself from the lower animals by giving body to his thought and aspiration in works of art. He alone can produce them.

2. Façade of the Central Part of the Metropolitan Museum, opened in 1902. Courtesy of *The Metropolitan Museum of Art*.

CHAPTER I

ON ART MUSEUMS

FROM TIME to time all ideas may be restudied to advantage. If in even so exact and demonstrable a science as mathematics the axioms that constitute the foundation of all reasoning are proved to be not completely valid, we feel no surprise when the less exact sciences are found to be in need of revision. Coming to the more controversial fields of thought, we expect even such pivotal concepts as justice, government, philosophy, and religion to demand re-examination in the light of changing conditions. And so a book about art museums needs no apology if it begins by saying why its subject demands consideration. To those who love museums and their contents such an offering of reasons may seem as irksome — objectionable even — as telling why we love our country, the faith of our fathers, or certain persons.

The museum stands quite apart from these. Far from being in the sphere of individual faith or choice, it is — and increasingly so — the community's. Beginning as the delight of princes temporal or spiritual, or of rich men, the museum changed its character, a century and a half ago, when the French Revolution took the Louvre away from the kings whose sole possession it had been for hundreds of years, and gave it to the people. Since then, under the impact of a number of forces hardly conceived before (imperial conquest, democracy and its concept of the common man, science and its ever-widening frontiers, aesthetic innovations undreamed of in the past and other elements besides), the museum has been developing beyond recognition. More, it has become so thoroughly accepted as one of the institutions essential to civilization that most people look on it as having a kind of foreordained value, and — though they may criticize it and want to change it — they would no more challenge its position in human affairs than they would attack the position of the ballot, the school, or the church.

Like those three centers of activity, again, the museum needs periodic re-appraisal of the work it performs, or is supposed to perform. Like them, it can be a living thing or, falling into a rut, obstruct the path of the spirit, for which it was created. Part of our task will be to inquire into that creation, and to compare results with cost. The latter item is not easy to calculate even in terms of money; for if an estimate were made of the outlay for the works of art in our museums, plus all the expenses connected with buildings, installation, and related items, we should still have to add a sum beyond calculation for the art objects acquired by Americans under the impression — mistaken or not — that they were buying things of museum value. In several cases that have come to my notice, single individuals have bought a thousand or more paintings and sculptures, not one of which has stood the test of time — even quite short periods of time. The reason for this may have been fraud practiced by dealers in "ancient" art, but more often it is the result of the conviction that good judgment in business matters, law, finance, medicine etc. would automatically translate itself into good judgment in art. In the estimate of what museums have cost this country, the spending of such persons is also to be entered — under the rubric of trial and error.

Multiply it as often as you like to get a figure for the outlay of the numberless persons who have bought one or two pictures of no value and of the institutions that have collected small groups of such things, and the sum will still be less than what Europeans, generally, would suppose it to be. There are, indeed, Europeans who realize something of the real wealth of our museums; but they have also seen so many unskilled and gullible American collectors that the idea of a desert of trash here, relieved by an occasional oasis of fine things, is widespread. If the trash were as the sands of the desert both in quantity (which it is not) and in sterility (which it is), it still would not be too early for an affirmation that our mistakes are immeasurably outbalanced by the value of our positive achievement.

To realize that achievement in its entirety, one must visit hundreds of museums, not to mention a multitude of private collections. According to Laurence Vail Coleman's book, The Museum in America, the number of such institutions in 1939 had reached twenty-five hundred, though this includes museums of science, industry, etc. (Often, especially in the smaller cities, all public collections are housed under one roof. Mr. Coleman is careful, however, to particularize as to the galleries wholly devoted to art). More significant than even the surprising number of our museums is the rapidity of their increase, for they had more than quadrupled in thirty years: in 1910 there were only some six hundred. Still more remarkable is the development in terms of financial resources. The investment in buildings rose from $36,000,000 in 1910 to $180,-000,000 in 1939, while the increase in income again almost doubles this proportion, going from $2,000,000 in the earlier year to $18,000,000 in the later one. As Mr. Coleman remarks, "Already this country has perhaps a quarter — surely a fifth of the world's museums."

Crassly quantitative as all these statements must appear, and open to some discussion because of the lack, in certain cases, of accurate European statistics, these figures have, nevertheless, a very genuine meaning. But first, in order to avoid misunderstanding, it may be well to state quite formally a thing which might be passed over as too obvious for mention: that our fifth of the world's museums does not give us a fifth of the world's art, nor a fiftieth of it, nor a five-hundredth of it. But since we are here approaching the contents of museums, it is only fair to say that the progress in the quality of our possessions was far and away more notable, during the thirty years described, than the material advance expressed in those statistics.

What, then, do those statistics signify? Simply this: America believes in the museum. It believes in health, and seeks it; it believes in education, and makes a vast effort to attain it. If we have done the startling thing of creating out of nothing a fifth of the world's museums, the reason is that we want them. Someone may say — some do say — that we are wrong to want them, and that my reasoning is no better than it would be if I tried to prove a supernal value in the tulip because the hard-headed Dutch once went mad about the flower. "People tell me this is the art of my period," said Ingres; "but suppose my period is bad?"

Suppose that the museum as a goal is bad, that the people who built it up were as wrong as the Dutch people at the time of their tulip craze. We need all sorts of things — hospitals, for example. Many a man, and not necessarily a foolish one, has said, "If we want art, let us go ahead and produce it, instead of paying fancy prices for a lot of stuff, mostly foreign, that may mislead us as to what expresses our thought here and now. You say America wants these institutions, and has proved that it does by the effort and money it has given to them; you say they are a chief expression of our period. But suppose our period is bad in its reasoning at this point, and that the future is going to steer clear of our record here as it will steer clear of any number of errors we are now making. What then?" The question, paraphrasing that of Ingres, is one that he never would have asked; for — to a degree reached by few other men — he understood the museum as the embodiment of all that is best in humanity.

Justifiably, then, the American people want the museum. Do all of them want it? Practically all, even though only a few realize it, just as slum dwellers are generally unaware of their need for fresh air, baths, books, and the other things they should have. We say, with no sense of presumptuousness, that they should have these things because people

3. Project for the Reconstruction of the Metropolitan Museum in the near Future.
Courtesy of The Metropolitan Museum of Art.

we all consider wise and good have decided that these are not luxuries but necessities, if men are to live fully.

Such a definition of the museum's role is surely close to that in the minds of the really superior Americans who have for so long, and with such self-sacrificing effort, and with such intensive thinking, above all, given to this country its extraordinary if still insufficient opportunity to know art. The history of their labors goes back to our earliest times. It is a truly representative history; for if the staff of a museum must be formed of specialists, if the trustees are men who have, as a rule, art collections of their own and are in the great majority of cases persons enjoying special contacts with art, the membership of our museums — people who contribute money, perhaps in very modest sums, and those who function solely as eager visitors, form quite an appreciable fraction of our population. Yes, from the dreamers and idealists who started things to the big public of today, America believes in the museum.

A man, whose lifetime of effort in the Boston museum gave him a right to speak with authority on his calling (though his best title came through his temperament and intellect), Benjamin Ives Gilman, in his invaluable *Museum Ideals*, lists various accusations against the institution. One of the wittiest is that of a German writer who describes a museum of art as a place "where every separate object kills every other and all of them together, the visitor." And, indeed, numbers of people have played on the similarity of the words "museum" and "mausoleum."

Yet, a fairly wide acquaintance with Americans quite convinces me that even the people who have never set foot in a museum, and who have no intention of so doing, willingly acknowledge the great service offered by the museum. There are hardened cityfolk who will concede anything you like about the beauties of country life — if you do not ask them to go in for it. General Grant may have been thinking of his position as a military man, or even as a politician, when he disclaimed any connection with music, saying he knew only two tunes, the one that was "Yankee Doodle" and the one that wasn't. But few would claim that he was disparaging the art which meant so little to him.

Robert Henri was asked by an anxious father, "Should I make an artist of my boy?" The wise painter and teacher replied, "Why not make a man of him?" He expressed a typically American point of view: first things first. If others were to be added on, well and good; if not, one had done right, anyhow. Part of the problem of the museum, as we shall discover, is to be attractive when people feel like turning to it, but not shrilly to solicit attention from those who are busy with useful and absorbing affairs of their own.

A little later, I shall have much to say about the businessmen, bankers, lawyers, and other laymen who have contributed in large measure to the organization and support of American museums; to an overwhelming extent it will be a favorable opinion, indeed a grateful and admiring one.

But in considering our subject logically, the people of immediate interest are those on the museum staff. Like other persons in scholarly pursuits, they have only in exceptional cases had personal fortunes at all commensurate with the work on which they were engaged, and never enough wealth to build up the great public collections. Also, they are rarely fitted to manage vast sums of money, reach crucial decisions, enter into contracts, and make political arrangements with some branch of the government, local or national.

Yet, if such matters loom large in American life generally, it is our pride that we have, from our beginnings, been unsparing of the honor given to clergymen, teachers, scientists, and philosophers. We have been slower about recognizing and rewarding poets and artists, but there is no mistaking our public's good will toward them, even if its busy "practical" life has cut pretty deep into the leisure which, at best, we have reserved for the difficult problem of art and letters. In passing, one may note that Europe, in the same thirty-year period, differed from America not so much because it gave more time to aesthetic matters as because, opportunities in Europe being so much more widespread (they have been so for centuries), the average European starts off at a point far in advance of the average American's. Our people's disadvantage is, of course, being rapidly reduced — above all, by the museum.

The consciousness of participating in its splendid work gives to American directors, to curators, and, indeed, often to the humblest members of museum staffs a sense of mission akin to the one felt by our clergymen and teachers, scientists and philosophers. Also, since much of museum work still lies in uncharted regions and must discover its principles by pioneering experience, there is the stimulus coming from new fields of study: the Far East, remote antiquity, and the wealth of early America, as well as methods of making the public a full sharer in the benefits of the institution.

Most important of all, considering the nature of the exhibits that museum men collect and handle, their success in understanding their problem is largely dependent on their entering into the ideas of the artists whose work they preserve and display. Indeed, from the time of that admirable painter Charles Willson Peale, one of the earliest museum directors in America (like John Vanderlyn, his contemporary and peer, the creator of a museum), many of the best workers in our collections have themselves been artists.

And, still basing my case for the museum on the fact that people want it, I come now to the class that speaks with final authority on the subject. As the artist does his work primarily out of an urge toward such activity, even if, in well-balanced periods, he has also got his livelihood from it at the same time, so his collecting and the showing of his possessions has been for the love of the thing, and without thought of gain. Rembrandt, indeed, spent his way to bankruptcy, in his enthusiasm for art, and it is an exceptional man, in the profession, who does not acquire some ancient or modern examples of his craft and its neighbors. The art objects in his studio may be as much a part of his equipment as are paints and brushes, hammer and chisels. For does not Poussin tell us in so many words that he never felt so much like taking pains and going beyond his former achievement as when he had been handling some beautiful work of art? Such testimony, a thousand times confirmed by the example of artists from ancient days to the present, gives us our best key to the secret of the museum.

The enjoyment it offers is not passive; it is dynamic, it leads to acts, and not merely to states of mind, however pleasant and fine these may be. And returning to the fact of our having gone from six hundred to twenty-five hundred museums in thirty years, with more development constantly occurring, we are reminded that the character I describe for the institution does not concern the artist alone. The tens of millions of dollars that go into American museums every year are, very clearly, not contributed solely for the benefit of artists (who could live in grand style on a mere tithe of that money). The men who earned it, and who have given mature thought to its disposal, have decided that no other investment will yield such returns for themselves and their fellow citizens.

They may not have analyzed the precise method by which the museum men collect and handle, their success in understanding their haps, like that great railroad builder, Sir William Van Horne, they have themselves gone in for painting as a hobby (and any competent visitor to Sir William's house in Montreal knows that his work sometimes attained real value as art); or perhaps they merely parallel the artist by the type of thought they give to their own affairs (a financier said he liked "abstract" painting because he felt that he did something similar when calculating the curve of an investment: it was simply the movement of the market that he found interesting, and not the amount of money he would make, or even the intrinsic value of the commodity represented by the bonds and shares).

Lest anyone regard this as suggesting a new type of utility for art, I will affirm that the gentleman's explanation, exact or inexact as it may be, was not proposed as a formula for success in Wall Street, though I did once encounter a man who thought he could, without study, compose music by a comparable procedure. He made graphs of the lines formed by the holes punched into pianola records, combined these lines in formations dictated by his own taste and fancy, had the new graph punched out as a recording — and doubtless got effects that had a species of originality; I never listened to any of his "music."

Our period, with its bewildering succession of scientific inventions, and its audacities in the realm of the arts, has led to many an aberration as foolish as that of this "composer." But no wrongness is more flagrant than that which treats the classics as things of the past. The touchstone of anyone's understanding of them is his ability to recognize their actuality — their immediate application to the thought and life of the modern world. And the fact that works produced hundreds or even thousands of years ago are absolutely living today carries with it the conclusion that they will never cease to have the same vitality and significance for future ages.

That would be one fulfillment, at least, of Egypt's demand for immortality. The word may have had a different, perhaps even a material sense for the ancient people, when they placed food and other useful articles in the graves of their dead. Or again, these accompaniments of the departed may merely have been symbolic, a part of the ritualism of a people not so primitively literal in its thinking as to imagine that their bread and beer were to be consumed by the dead man as he used to do when alive. Other religions, nearer to us in time, make us familiar with a similar mingling of the material and the immaterial; so that the Egyptian idea of the afterworld may have located it, essentially, in the memory of men. If their attempt to reach eternity was so directed, they made the right move when they bred their race of artists. There are records of man's presence on the earth far more ancient than those of the historic time of Egypt, but none of them has shed upon their makers such luster as belongs, by universal consent, to the people of the Nile.

The span of their recorded existence is the longest in human history, but even such extent in time — the horizontal dimension of their life — is small compared to their vertical thrust — the height and depth attained by their art. No wonder that the men who have offered to this country its museums, as an incentive to thinking and as a measure of

4. The Metropolitan Museum: Hanging of Pictures, Old Style. Courtesy of The Metropolitan Museum of Art.

5. The same Gallery as in Plate 4, about Forty Years later.
Courtesy of The Metropolitan Museum of Art.

thinking, have laid a strong emphasis on our Egyptian collections. Our interest in Egyptology goes back a long way; and if anyone should be tempted to look on this as preoccupation with "curiosities," or with the morbid thought sometimes associated with mummies, I would refer him again to the profound appreciation of Egypt by Herman Melville, when that great American writer visited the country, about a hundred years ago.

Perhaps the earliest of "museum ideals," to use Gilman's words in a different sense from his own, Egyptian art is at least approached in quality by that of the Chaldeans; but it is only at the Louvre that one can see the mighty sculpture of the land of Sumer in anything like its full stature. Other museums, like that of the University of Pennsylvania, and that of Boston, give a glimpse of this elemental and yet highly evolved art. It is, in all likelihood, still to reveal its greatest achievement, for even the prodigious things we have are apparently less than its master-works. So that here, in the field of man's ultimate expression, one realizes that the work of the museum is as yet only fragmentary. Inviting research into things five thousand years old, like the Chaldean, or into the not less mysterious mind of today, or into great matters anywhere between the two extremes, like the older art of the American continent, the museum has so much "unfinished business" that men accustomed to order, organization, and clarity in their own affairs have responded eagerly to its challenge. As we shall see, much of the significant investigation and restoration of our time has been the work of Americans.

A score of lifetimes would not offer the years needed to know art; and our glance at material so incompletely represented as that of the Chaldeans illustrates only one type of the mysteries that we encounter at every turn in our course through the museum. Surely, one would say, this will not be true when we come to the Greeks, after all the centuries during which their order, organization, and clarity have been regarded as the master models of those qualities. But then we see that mysteries can result from a wealth of knowledge, quite as well as from a dearth of materials for study.

In 1944, the Metropolitan Museum, New York, gave an exhibition illustrating the use of color by the Greeks, and it threw new light on what is unquestionably a major problem of our classical heritage. The rich group of objects on view included that greatest of war refugees, one of the maidens of the earlier Acropolis; and she is still resplendent in color that no one could have imagined before seeing it. Accompanying the show was a booklet especially written by the curator of the department; it might well serve as a model in the educational work of museums.

For it does not obtrude itself between the visitor and the objects of his study but, read over after getting home, and inviting him to a return match with the fascinating material he has seen, it organizes his impressions into a logical sequence, directly following out the one through which the Greeks themselves evolved from simple to complex forms.

And here we are faced with another major problem, both as regards the Greeks and the later peoples, including — especially — ourselves: what is the relation, in terms of art, between the simple and the complex forms mentioned just now? A decade or two since, the more primitive styles were particularly acclaimed; then, with our study of the baroque, we turned once more to sophistication. Perhaps a new surge of interest in the great simplicities lies before us, or perhaps the ability to recognize in highly evolved periods the persistence of elemental instincts such as those which gave us the bare essentials in works like our seventh-century (B.C.) statue of a Greek youth, in the Metropolitan Museum.

But certainly, the lesson of Hellas is an anticipation of the lesson of France, as Elie Faure showed in his masterly juxtaposition of a series of photographs of works of the two great countries — a startling feature of his book, *The Spirit of the Forms*. He clarified his illustrations by his text, showing a similar evolution in the political and social structure of Greece and France, and thus explained their astonishingly parallel expression in art.

And the galleries devoted to Rome in our museum, do they bear out the words "pillagers and verbose" which Renoir applied to the men of the first world capital? Or is Brancusi nearer to essentials when he sees in Roman genius a quality which gave to architecture the gigantic sweep that made a river and a whole valley but incidents of such large-scale planning that it relegates Greece herself to the role of a perfectionist?

The list of museum problems with which the toughest intelligence can enjoy a tussle — to apply its findings to the world about us — may scarcely be even glanced at here. What of the Byzantines? Do they tell us of a decadence or of a new birth? Seeing them, doubtless, from the standpoint of that Greek perfectionism just alluded to, André Derain called them "the people who invented bad taste." But with the mission of putting into form and color the greatest romantic adventure that humanity has ever known — and that seems a none too daring definition of Christianity — Byzantium was forced to break with classical canons.

If it is only with an event as recent and as pivotal in importance as the restoration of Hagia Sophia in Constantinople that we begin to look with some confidence into the enigma of the Byzantines, there are lands nearer home where new and vital studies were needed, and are now being made. Our notions of Provence, the focus of Italian, French, and other arts, during and after the sojourn of the Popes at Avignon, have been all too vague. That eminent scholar, the late Henri Focillon, was defining another phase of French genius in his later studies. He proposed a new title for the art of western France, calling it that of the Atlantic school, since its monuments are in parts of the country bathed by that ocean. Evidently the eastern shore of the Atlantic is referred to, yet the term has its interest for Americans, since their country forms its western shore, and since much of our inspiration comes from the lands directly across the sea. And the Atlantic school carries on, evidently, into England.

But we are coming to a better understanding of other regions, some of them possibly of even greater consequence to us. To express an idea similar to the one in our proverb, "Blood is thicker than water," the Spaniard says, "Near is my shirt, but nearer yet my skin." Our museums are engaged in demonstrating that the change in America after 1492, from redskin to whiteskin, was not so fundamental as we had been led to believe. It was so in the cities, but they are mere dots on the map, after all; the "rocks and rills" remained the same, and they — with the woods, the vast prairies, the coasts, and the climate — determine the character of life for the great majority of our people, as they did for our predecessors on this continent.

We have always felt for these aborigines at least a vague kind of esteem, and in truth, they have taught us much. We are coming to realize that the Indian had more to offer us than tobacco and corn, woodcraft and games, and the kind of fighting at which we had to meet him on what was — quite literally — his own ground. Now that we know that ground more intimately and have less of the ruthless spirit of the white pioneers, we find in the soil other things than the arrowheads, cooking pots, and beadwork which stirred the imagination of our ancestors, causing them, indeed, to found for the preservation of such relics, some of our first museums.

In our Southwest, in Ohio, in Florida, all over our country, in fact, we are becoming acquainted with Indian sculpture of great expressiveness and nobility. As to the countries to the south of us, the extraordinary merit of their ancient art was recognized by a very great man, and from the first moment when he, or anyone else in the Old World, saw it. One cannot recall too often or with too much emphasis that when, in the very year of the conquest of Mexico, examples of its art were sent to Europe, they were shown to Albrecht Dürer, who wrote in his diary that nothing he had ever seen gave him more pleasure than these things from the new land. We have been slow in catching up with Dürer, but it now appears that our museums are beginning to look upon the art of early America as the supremely great achievement that it is.

In saying this, I do not consider that I am departing from my present purpose, which is merely to record the fact that this country wants the museum. At most, I am going no further than the outermost fringes of the vast question as to why that is our will. The easy answer of many people is that we have always been devoted to education; and at moments, a definition has been offered that the museum is an instrument of visual education. The words are inadequate, indeed misleading, a part of what has been called the education-disease. It is not the first business of art museums to be "educational"; and it is not their business primarily to teach; there are schools, colleges, and universities to do that.

All right then, says somebody, what do you propose that the museums do? We propose — quite simply — that the museums be. It is up to the individual to decide what he is going to do. He can begin by making another trip to the museum. I rather imagine he hasn't been there for quite a while, and he will find, if he gives the place a chance, that it will turn out to have the property of making him want to return to it oftener and oftener.

Some of its exhibits have been hinted at in the foregoing pages, but how few of them! There has not been a line about that outburst of splendor which we call the painting of the Renaissance. The word makes us think of Italy, and of men as different as Giotto, with his vitality and humanity, and Andrea del Castagno, with the grave, impersonal beauty of his frescoes. And we have not so much as glanced at the amazing extent of this painting, as it goes from the positiveness and calm of these Tuscan artists to the ineffable mystery of Giorgione's art, when his imagery and his color lead to the maturity of Venice.

This book does not attempt the criticism, explanation, or appreciation of art. Delacroix, in beginning to write on Titian, said he felt like the lawyer who drew up a memorial in favor of God. I take it for granted that you find art desirable, as I assume that you want to live; therefore I merely discuss certain aspects of an institution the human race has been evolving since the time it began to live a kind of life it prefers to that of the beasts of the field or, at best, to that of men who live "by bread alone."

But as this book will give me only limited opportunities to occupy my mind with artists, do bear with me a moment more while I correct an impression which might result from such casual references as I have made to the contents of American museums. They do possess Egyptian, Greek, and Italian works, indeed an amazing wealth of them. But in even glancing at the scope of museum work — and its significance — I cannot fail to mention the connection established between the classic lands of the Mediterranean and those of northern Europe, from the people of which most Americans are descended. The two men who chiefly represent the vital tie between the southern countries and the people once called the Barbarians are Poussin, a Norman, and Rubens, a Fleming — both of whom can be known well from our collections.

By saying this, I suggest that the museum affords us opportunity for that exercise of intelligence which consists in seeing as complementary aspects of the truth things which, to narrower minds, appeared as irreconcilables. Poussin and Rubens were, for centuries, supposed to be reciprocally destructive forces, just as, at a later time, the blind partisans of Ingres and Delacroix would admit no vestige of right in the work of the "rival" master whom they fought. To see that both are masters and both are right is to achieve that superior level of civilization which is at the farthest remove from spineless lack of conviction.

I fear I am, after all, assigning values to museum study, when all I had intended was to allude to the delight awaiting anyone who makes the right approach to the collections. For example, take the case of one master to whom our country has shown a special devotion. I refer to Rembrandt; and it is only fitting if his name leads to mention, in this first chapter, of one of the men to whom we owe most in our opportunity for a knowledge of art. More than half a century ago, Henry G. Marquand, a New York bank president, gave to his city the magnificent collection which previously had adorned his home. These pictures afforded his fellow townsmen their earliest important contact with the head of the Dutch School, and even now, with an astonishing increase in our treasury of Rembrandt's works, one of Mr. Marquand's pictures still holds a first place in our list — if I may take, momentarily, a somewhat personal point of view. I do so the more willingly since the canvas has been doubted by a leading expert — not only as a Rembrandt, but as a thing of his time, and even of his country. So, indulging in the luxury of speaking my own idea, I say that portrait of a bearded man, his face half in shadow from his broad-brimmed hat, is not only a completely authentic work, but one that even Rembrandt could not have produced before the last years of his life (the period always assigned to the picture). Then, like the old Titian, the old Frans Hals, or the old Renoir, and only then, when his experience and insight were at their fullest, could he produce a thing of such incomparable beauty.

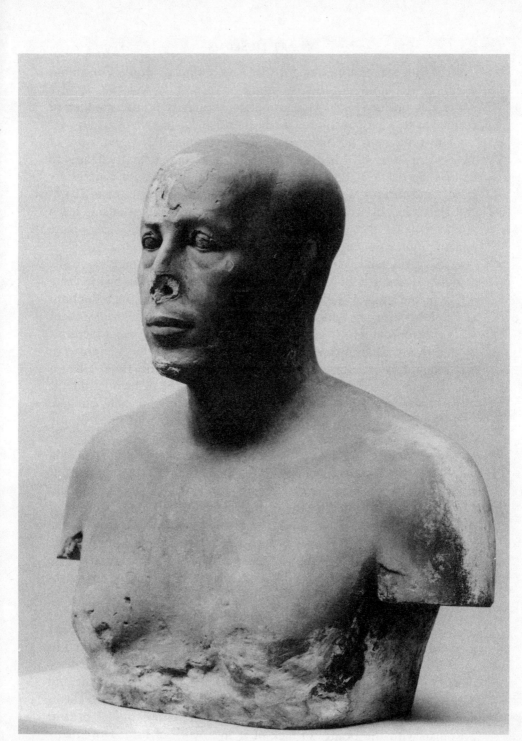

6. Egypt, 4th Dynasty: Bust of Ankh-haf.
Courtesy of the Museum of Fine Arts, Boston.

It is with malice aforethought that I write the last word. For, in our seeing of the museum and its problems, beauty is still the decisive matter, as one may say with complete awareness of the conflict of opinion as to what constitutes the beautiful.

This time I am not offering a merely personal idea when I tell of an incident in which I had a share: I am reporting, at what chances to be first-hand, a very illuminating example of the misuse of a necessary word. And thereby, as in the cases of Poussin and Rubens, or of Ingres and Delacroix, an occasion is given to see that museum problems reach out far beyond the walls of the building. (Inside it, however, there remain problems enough.)

Here is my tale — and I remember the speech it contains as vividly as if I had heard it only forty minutes ago, instead of as many years ago. On the walls of my first studio in America, I had reproductions of a number of works which had meant much to me during the student years abroad from which I had just returned. One print was a facsimile of an early Rembrandt etching, the 1628 portrait of his mother; my own first attempt at etching was a copy of it. At about this time, I had a visit from an old sculptor, a prominent member of the Academy, and one whose statues and whose writing on art are alike insignificant. He gave me a lecture (intended altogether for my well-being, I am sure) on the danger I was running into by studying that etching.

"Rembrandt," he said, "deserves his fame because of the great skill with which he worked out the problems he set himself; they are difficult ones, and he was a great man, of course. But you are a young man, and I hate to see you taking chances with getting yourself into a bad way of thinking. Because of Rembrandt's mastery, you shut your eyes to the fact that his subject is an ugly old woman. If you let such an attitude grow stronger in you, the time will come when you will not even realize whether a thing has beauty at all — which is the state of mind that gives us the work of Rodin, and the toleration of it."

When, on a few occasions, I have told this story to artist friends, it has been a signal for hilarity. But I take it seriously, for if the sacrosanct name of Rembrandt puts everyone against that sculptor who wanted to protect me from Rodin and ruin, not everyone is safe from the fallacy of treating ugliness and beauty as well-defined things, like night and day. Note how often people use the words as my exhorter used them, and generally with his own silly confusion, of the beauty or lack of it in a woman with the beauty or lack of it in a work of art. How many people will miss the point by a question-begging denial that a woman is ugly because she is old! Or, hating such insipidities as the old academician himself produced, they see salvation in departing as far from academic work as possible, not stopping to think that one can get just as far from art along "modern," nonrealistic roads as by way of the sirupy nature-faking of the school they despise.

I insist on the error of using the word "beauty" as if it were measurable and decided on for all time. A well-known critic once remarked, "It is strange that you like Géricault: his work is totally lacking in beauty." And similar charges are leveled at Picasso, to whom, on the other hand, some men have objected on the ground of his excessive devotion to beauty. In short, the term is one that calls for suspended judgment. There is never complete unanimity as to the problems of art — witness the belated opponent of Rembrandt — but, with time, we do have agreements as nearly general as that which concerns the Dutch master. That takes our subject out of the category in which the Sophists of ancient Athens placed all matters of truth, denying, as they did, that it was more than a relative question, one in which rightness or wrongness is to be seen merely as a result of one's point of view. To them, morality, religion, science, and the rest became meaningless — save for this person or that, as he attaches to them such values as suit his individual preferences.

Here again we see that art questions are not to be separated from those of life and thought in their other manifestations. But keeping to the museum's own problems, it is clear that this world within a world offers the best proof of certitude, on the one hand, and of the continuing evolution of ideas, on the other.

We are learning how to deal with this condition. France had, to a degree, shown us the way by creating two national museums: the Louvre, for works approved by long periods of time; the Luxembourg, for works still on trial. Both museums had their defects, due chiefly to the same cause: insufficient integrity in dealing with exhibits. Before the last transfer to the Louvre of works from the modern gallery, too many inferior things had been admitted. The Chauchard Collection, though it contained magnificent pictures, carried into the Louvre much that could be explained only by the financial relations of the owner of the collection and an important personage in the government. The very bad works which entered from the Luxembourg, about 1929, represented a compromise with the evil forces which had all but totally dominated official art circles, the museums, the schools, and government patronage.

To follow the French model in our country, where art has fortunately been free, or very nearly so, from control by politicians, would obviously expose us to danger. France was making progress, as her better artists acquired more and more influence; but in view of the slighter artistic knowledge of our congressmen and other functionaries, it is all too likely that we should pay a heavy price for government management — a phenomenon foreign, in any case, to our habits and preferences.

First Chicago, through the influence of the Arts Club, and then New York, with the Museum of Modern Art, proved that our old system of private initiative could deal with the situation created by the need of trying out unfamiliar forms of art. For years the older organization in Chicago, the Art Institute, has been profiting by the lessons of the more advanced group. Despite the large outlay made for the Modern Museum in New York, despite its tempting freedom as a place dedicated to a single idea, and not forgetting the rarity of trustees capable of dealing with both ancient and modern art, we may yet see an amalgamation with the Metropolitan Museum, at least to the extent of assigning to each its role in the common cause. Apart from occasional duplication of effort, as between the two institutions, it is absurd to have the public offered a museum of art and a museum of modern art, as if the two fields were separate. Many people, especially among the younger ones, have come to think that there really is an essential difference between ancient and modern art. The new work offers them more excitement and enjoyment, while the old is supposed to represent a dead past.

It is not too much to say that the Modern Museum is the greatest mistake the Metropolitan ever made, bringing about, as it did, the creation of the newer institution through intolerance of the latter-day masters. It can afford the loss of the vast numbers of visitors who would otherwise be entering its doors, but it cannot afford the loss of influence on its own thinking caused by the diversion from it of some of the strongest elements in the community. And obviously, the modern museum needs a constant checkup on the tendencies it follows. This would come automatically if visitors moved freely between galleries of later and earlier works, and had an easy means of comparing the purpose and effect of the two.

But museology is a very young study, and the record it has already made justifies abundant hope for the future. Even the question of modern art, which sometimes involves bitter tension between conservatives and progressives, is being studied intelligently; this is proof — as are innumerable other services performed by American museums — that they represent us in the best of our achievement and our aspiration.

Such matters are not to be realized through compromise, through

7. Egypt, 1490-80 B.C.: Queen Hat-Shepsut.
Courtesy of The Metropolitan Museum of Art.

concession to elements among us that are popular in the sense of being inferior. Our people saw through such fraudulence when the pictures of the older schools were submitted to the test of public approval: the inferior ones had to go. For a time the public may be fooled by the more up-to-date kind of trash, but there is rapidly increasing evidence that such things are tolerated today for a far shorter time than formerly. Later on, we shall discuss the possibilities of the genuinely popular arts, those which have the vitality of the masses, not those — the travesty of the real ones — which commercialize bad taste among the masses.

In concluding this introductory survey, suffice it to say that the museum is a place where all that our race knows of magic allows us to see the splendor of the human past, and the way that splendor continues and evolves when aristocracy of intellect is united with democracy of opportunity.

CHAPTER II

1. SOME AMERICAN HISTORY

THE CREATION and development of museums in the United States constitute an amazing story, which will probably remain unique. Nowhere, whether we look to South America, Australia, Siberia, or any other big spaces still underdeveloped as regards museums, can we see the probability of a growth paralleling that which has taken place here. The ready explanation of many people would be "American millions," the words so often cast up to Dr. Victor Heiser when he was introducing to various countries the ideas evolved by the United States for combating and preventing disease.

But the explanation is utterly insufficient. Purchases in astonishing quantity were indeed made by our collectors during the past half century, when great fortunes piled up and when people discovered that paintings and sculpture offer a fascinating means of spending or investing; but the history of American museums goes back to times considerably antedating the great accumulation of wealth, and is, moreover, the story of effort by men who, in many cases, were far from wealthy. No, the determining factor in the case is the type of men who gave to this country its special character, its ideals, and its attitude toward the great works of the past.

Childe Hassam, the painter, used to insist that it is a mistake to speak of Americans as a young people; they moved over here with a high degree of the culture that Europe had when they set forth, and their government, with its century and a half of continuity in a single form, is today one of the oldest among modern nations. On the other hand, we did come to a continent so thinly populated that vast stretches of it showed no sign that man had ever been there; it was this wilderness which we have turned into a great pattern of busy cities and thriving countryside.

What interests us here is not the land itself, but the people; this book deals with one aspect of the people, the attention they have given to art. It is a particularly American aspect of them, if we consider the way their interest was claimed by other matters. Museum-building, it is true, is characteristic of the whole nineteenth century, the Germans doing most remarkable things in it. The English, perhaps the greatest

29

of travelers and collectors, were early in the field, with the British Museum and the National Gallery. But there is nothing in all Europe to suggest the way in which the museums of America, in a democratic response to a general demand, have spread from coast to coast. In the Old World they usually represent the gathering together of material already on hand; in America, everything save collections of local relics had to be built up from nothing. Most significant of all is that the institution is ours as the gift of private citizens and not as a gathering of things forfeited to governments.

The growth of free popular education in America has been written about innumerable times, and we know well, for example, about the founding of Harvard College when the colonists were still struggling for bare existence, only sixteen years after the landing on Plymouth Rock. But how many Americans know that the cultural foundations of our museums date back to exactly the same period? Just one year after the coming of the Pilgrims, there arrived on our shores a man who, remaining here from 1621 to 1631, connects us with the love of the classics which has always been the forerunner of the museum. This was George Sandys, the treasurer of the Virginia Company. He was the author of a book of travels in the Holy Land, Cyprus, Sicily, Naples, and Rome, which went through many editions in Europe, and was translated into various languages. During his stay in America, he continued to work on his translation of Ovid, and so gave us, in our earliest days, an example of scholarship, which was to be followed by notable successors. Their share in preparing America for the development of museums will be obvious from the first glance, and it is one of the reasons for the magnificent achievement throughout the early United States when, in the first part of the nineteenth century, we contributed so signally to the Greek Revival.

Well worthy of so important a subject are Professor W. B. Dinsmoor's researches into the role of the classics in our country, and it is to a paper by him on "Early American Studies of Mediterranean Archaeology," read before the American Philosophical Society in 1943, that I am indebted for a large number of facts, including those on George Sandys. Among other such contacts with the classical schools by men who were to bring art, and an understanding of art, to America, I note the sojourn of John Smibert in Italy, from 1717 to 1720. This Scotch painter, coming to our shores in 1728, and producing many portraits of our early countrymen, brought with him a collection of engravings after famous paintings. But great difficulties faced our artists at this time (and later), so that Smibert was obliged by circumstances to dispose of

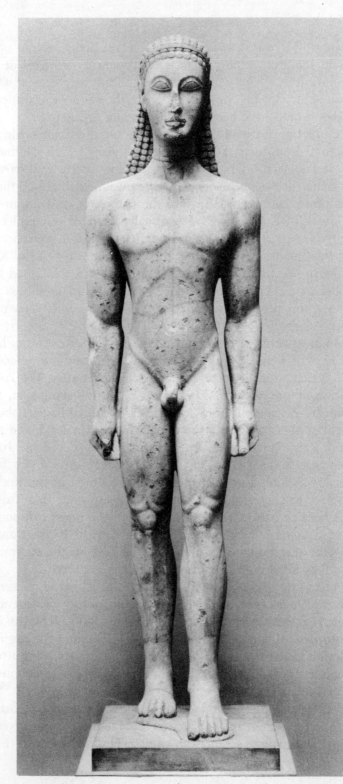

8. Greek (Athenian, probably 7th Century B.C.): Statue of a Youth.
Courtesy of The Metropolitan Museum of Art.

his engravings. He was, however, able to retain his collection of casts after ancient sculptures, the first to reach America. After his death in 1752, the inventory of his estate appraised these sculptures at £4, not a very great sum even for those days, especially when we consider how valuable they would have been for students and laymen.

Yet before the death of Smibert, Benjamin Franklin could write that "the first drudgery of settling new Colonies, which confines the attention of People to mere Necessaries, is now pretty well over; and there are many in every Province in Circumstances that set them at Ease, and afford Leisure to Cultivate the finer Arts, and improve the common Stock of Knowledge." We usually think of our philosopher as primarily interested in science and politics; but when we reflect that the above statements, from his *Proposals for Promoting Useful Knowledge among the British Plantations in America*, were published in the Philadelphia of 1743, we have proof that he — and doubtless many others among our people — already regarded the fine arts as a part of "Useful Knowledge."

If Franklin's words were prophetic, as they so often were, he did not have to wait long or look far to see them borne out. Books on antiquities were appearing in private and public libraries. We know of an exhibition of waxworks in 1749, and, in the following year, if not earlier, Harvard began collecting "curiosities." Oxford had set the pace for universities by starting its Ashmolean Museum in 1683, and so our own seats of learning were following a distinguished precedent. In 1718 Elihu Yale gave to Yale University, founded seventeen years before as the Collegiate School, a portrait of George I, painted in the workshop of Sir Godfrey Kneller. It was not until 1831, however, that Yale's art collections became part of the University's active interests, through the purchase of Colonel John Trumbull's paintings of the Revolution. The following year the Trumbull Gallery was erected on the campus, the "first art gallery to be built by a university in this country."

We must turn back, however. Without the slightest pretense to giving a complete account of the early museum history of America, we should note that the oldest of all such institutions in this country is that of Charleston, South Carolina, established in 1773 under the auspices of the Charleston Library Society. Like so many of the pioneering attempts here, it is not entirely an art museum, though important collections were early brought to Charleston.

Philadelphia claims attention again — as it will repeatedly. Gustavus Hesselius, the Swedish artist, had arrived there in 1711, and the city saw the birth of the first native American painter, James Claypoole, in 1720, as also of our first native sculptor William Rush, in 1756. The two earliest exhibitions of pictures in this country were held in the old State House, and by 1782, P. E. du Simitière of Philadelphia opened a museum in his home.

The following year, again in Philadelphia, our fine native painter, Charles Willson Peale, gave an exhibition of his portraits. In 1784, in his own house, he added zoological specimens, the collection being transferred in 1794 to the American Philosophical Society, which had been founded more than half a century earlier; in 1802, it was moved to Independence Hall. Later, some of the numerous artists of the Peale family tried to continue the museum, but without success.

In 1791, Charles Willson Peale himself had founded a drawing school which, in 1805, has as its successor the Pennsylvania Academy of the Fine Arts. William Rush joined Peale in teaching there, as did Giuseppe Ceracchi, the Italian sculptor of the well-known bust of George Washington.

Already in 1795, Peale had drawn up plans for the Columbianum, or American Academy of Painting, Sculpture, and Architecture, in Philadelphia. The English painter, Robert Edge Pine, arriving in 1784, had brought with him a cast of the Venus de' Medici. Peale borrowed it to initiate the hall of casts. "Moral scruples also affected the art school and the Columbianum failed in its turn." And this occurred despite the fact, recorded by H. G. Dwight, that in urban Philadelphia, "delicacy required that ladies be admitted to an exhibition of classical sculpture at separate hours from gentlemen." Similar difficulties attended the Boston Athenaeum in the early days of the nineteenth century, when an essay on the Greeks, read by one of the members, was objected to by another because it contained too much "nakedness."

As early as 1779, Thomas Jefferson had brought forward a bill to amend the constitution of William and Mary College, and proposed the "inclusion of professors who should instruct in the fine arts as well as in ancient languages." The contact of our country with the great art of Houdon and with classical architecture, as a result of Jefferson's deep interest in such matters, is too well known to require more than a mention here. It was he who influenced the eminent architect, Charles Bulfinch, to turn his studies toward classical works, the results being visible in many famous buildings. Talbot Hamlin's book on the Greek Revival in America, and the notable exhibition of that development given in 1944 by the Metropolitan Museum are further proofs of the vitality of early classical studies by our countrymen. They connect, very naturally, with the devotion to classical languages and literature which had so decisive an effect on the thinking and the writing of the men who founded this nation. It was natural for them to ask a Frenchman, L'Enfant, influenced by David's renewal of the antique, to draw the plans for our new capital city of Washington.

In 1760, Benjamin West, arriving in Rome, was presented to Winckelmann's great patron, Cardinal Alessandro Albani. Conducted by this arbiter of the arts, he saw the statue then regarded as the ideal of masculine beauty, the Apollo Belvedere. It drew from him the exclamation: "My God, how like it is to a young Mohawk warrior!" (In his boyhood West had had contacts with the Indians which gave him the right to speak in this vein.) He soon attached himself to Anton Raphael Mengs, the Romanized German in love with classical art. "Fifty-six years later, as the venerable president of the Royal Academy, West's evidence was one of the most decisive factors in persuading Parliament to acquire the Elgin Marbles for the British Museum." The rewards of the old Quaker were not in prestige alone; the price paid for his *Christ Rejected*, at the sale after his death, in 1820, was 3000 guineas, an indication of the material success of the "American Raphael."

Other early American artists brought home echoes, at least, of the great masters. Thus, we recall Henry Benbridge who arrived in Italy in 1764 or '65. He was followed, ten years later, by John Singleton Copley, whose vivid interest in ancient art ran side by side with his passion for the exact character of his personages. And so the letters he wrote from Rome and other places still repay a reading, if only to show this firm double basis for our first great art. The earliest American to behold Greek temples, those at Paestum, he was led by his feeling for the Greeks to paint, in the background of his portrait of Mr. and Mrs. Ralph Izard (now in the Boston Museum), figures of Electra and Orestes, and also a vase whose decoration is so accurately copied that archaeologists have been able to identify it exactly, as to its school and date (about 450 B.C.).

This incident in the career of the greatest painter among the founders of our school is evidently unusual, but it may still fairly illustrate the attitude of the long line of artists and writers who went abroad, even if they did not approach Copley in talent. Their point of view is expressed in the writings of Horatio Greenough, the sculptor (born 1805), who studies the ancient works with eager admiration, goes pretty deeply into their significance — and vigorously defends his pioneering country against European misunderstanding. His analyses of aesthetic problems are not inferior to those of many of his able contemporaries in the Old World.

But John Vanderlyn offers a far more striking example of the way that ability in the arts was inherent among the Americans of this time,

9. Greek (4th Century B.C.): Goddess.
Courtesy of the Museum of Fine Arts, Boston.

when they had so few masterworks to guide them. Greenough's talent, developing from a boy's skill at carving with his jackknife, soon attracted attention in his native Boston, and led to his getting orders for works of sculpture. Vanderlyn, born in the small Hudson River town of Kingston, might easily have gone through life without a chance to profit by his extraordinary gift for painting. Fortunately, the artistic sensibilities of an eminent American, at the very beginning of the nineteenth century, changed the young man's whole career. Aaron Burr, happening to visit Kingston, was shown some of the work of Vanderlyn, then a carriage-painter in his twenties. Jefferson's vice-president may well have learned from his chief how to value talent, at all events he promptly invited the young man to New York, and then sent him to Paris — the earliest of our artists to get his training there. A few years later, when Napoleon instituted a competition in historical painting, one that attracted over a thousand participants, it was Vanderlyn who won the medal, which Napoleon in person bestowed upon him.

The prize-winning picture, now in one of the museums of San Francisco, seems cold and stilted to most people today, even to those who can look with enthusiasm upon portraits by Vanderlyn. Indeed, like so many men dominated by David, he is at his best in them. Yet we have the indisputable fact of the rating his *Marius amid the Ruins of Carthage* was given in that magnificent art world of Paris during the First Empire. When the painter returned to America, it was with the devoted purpose of giving to his countrymen a share of the benefit he had received from that world, which had afforded him his splendid training.

The prestige resulting from his decoration by the Emperor helped him on his arrival in New York, but was not sufficient to bring permanent success to the ambitious scheme he soon started, that of endowing the city with an art gallery such as he had seen in various European capitals. Going heavily into debt for the project, and unable to meet his obligations, he was in his latter years a disappointed, even a bitter man. His experience doubtless furnishes the most regrettable example of the price paid by Americans ahead of their time in the effort which has given us our museums.

That effort, largely forgotten today, was, however, far more widespread than we realize. In 1790, John Pintard, a distinguished citizen of New York, had persuaded the Society of St. Tammany, later so prominent in politics, to found a museum. As was natural for an institution named in honor of an Indian chief, and reflecting the very general interest in the older peoples, the museum consisted largely of Indian relics. The seriousness of the enterprise was attested by Pintard's securing "all that could be found of Indian literature in war-songs, hieroglyphic writings on stone, bark, skins, etc." At first, a room in the City Hall was assigned to the collections; then followed a number of vicissitudes at the end of which the enthusiastic founder having no true successor — (he later helped to organize the New-York Historical Society) — the contents of the museum were sold to P. T. Barnum for his display of curiosities.

But our early failures are constantly balanced by new attempts that widen the field of interest. Many of these measures have a distinctly democratic quality. Thus, early in the nineteenth century, the New York City Common Council voted a recommendation that citizens visit the exhibitions of art dealers; and it gave further impetus to such ideas by authorizing the painting of portraits for a collection in the City Hall. This continued for seventy-five years, and explains the city's ownership of eleven works by John Trumbull, the great portrait of Lafayette by Morse, and pictures by Vanderlyn, William Page, and other fine artists. It is notable how, from the first, the men who represent the country at its best in every field are the ones who aid in the movement for art. Still considering the initial years of the Republic, we find Edward Livingston, one of New York's most distinguished mayors, arranging that his brother Robert, our minister to France, secure casts of great sculpture as an aid to the new aspirations of the city. A subscription was made for their purchase and, to house the statues, an academy was founded in 1803, Mayor Livingston being its first president. Napoleon and his minister of fine arts, Vivant Denon, were made honorary members, the former responding with a gift of twenty-seven volumes of engravings by Piranesi. When Philadelphia decided to add to its store of casts in 1805, Napoleon again showed his interest in American culture by calling on the sculptor Houdon to help in the work, which was successfully carried through.

As mention has several times been made of the aid given by artists in the efforts leading to our museums, it is only just that the reverse of such influence should be noticed. Thus, in 1810, a group of Philadelphia artists formed a society in opposition to the Pennsylvania Academy. The reason they gave for their action was that they considered the latter institution to be "intended merely as a museum, and consequently not likely to become of much importance, either in the improvement of artists or in correcting public taste." What they obviously wanted was the sale of their own pictures. No one can object to their desire to live by their work, the natural and proper course for all men — provided the work is worth paying for. Doubt on this last point immediately arises if we find artists setting their pecuniary reward above the principles of their profession. And that accusation holds when men who are supposed to care above all for the excellence of their painting or sculpture are so shortsighted as to look on a museum as anything but the best of means to "correct public taste," and so establish standards which really work for "the improvement of artists."

Other such cases are only too frequent in our history. On the very day of the inauguration of the Metropolitan Museum in 1872, it was denounced as a "damned humbug" by an artist who doubtlessly misinterpreted the function of a museum as so many others do: they look on it as their customer, or as a source of customers, through exhibitions of their works. The matter was stated with unconscious humor by an artist who wrote to a museum official during the great depression: "At a time like this, you have no right to buy works of art: you ought to buy our pictures." It is doubtful whether men of this type would care to see real art works purchased at any time, especially if such buying diminished their own revenue.

And yet it must be admitted that such self-interest had good effects in some cases. Aggressively going after business, the artist often launched new collectors. If the first pictures they acquired were poor ones (and indeed, in many cases, the last they acquired were no better), certain men did progress from bad beginnings, and bought fine things later on. We may regret the inferior works that went into the homes of many idealistic men, but for the better things to be appreciated, it was necessary to have numbers of collectors.

In the early times we are reviewing, art patronage ponderably increased, and not merely in the cities previously mentioned. James Bowdoin, returning from Europe in 1811, brought with him a most creditable collection of paintings and drawings. He gave it to the college which bears his name, at Brunswick, Maine, and so formed the nucleus of what is today one of the most attractive of our smaller museums. Because of its comparative isolation, it performs a specially useful work. Harvard and Yale, as we have seen, had also been pioneers in exposing students to the influence of works of art. Later on, Princeton, the University of Pennsylvania, Smith College, Phillips Academy at Andover, and other centers of learning followed these examples.

The Boston Athenaeum, beginning its work in 1807 with a library, held its first art exhibition twenty years later. It continued to do so until 1876, when its collections were placed in the young Museum of Fine Arts. How important to the city its showings were may be judged from Emerson's letter, dated 1822, in which he speaks of the beautiful collection of casts from ancient statues "which attract the eye in every corner from the tedious joys of reading and writing."

10. Greek: Fresco from Boscoreale near Herculaneum.
Courtesy of The Metropolitan Museum of Art.

Beginning in 1828 with the purchase of a Carracci, the Athenaeum went on to acquire works by Bourdon, Ruisdael, van de Velde, Poussin, Bronzino, and other masters. The evolution of a museum was thus clearly forecast.

In Hartford, Connecticut, "on December 1, 1841, Daniel Wadsworth offered the lot of land on Main Street on which stood his grandfather's house, as a site for a building to contain a Gallery of Fine Arts, the Hartford Young Men's Institute, and the Connecticut Historical Society. The next year, the Wadsworth Atheneum was incorporated and the money was raised." The Gallery of Fine Arts was opened in 1844 with some eighty paintings

In Washington, casts of ancient sculpture appear as early as 1842, and in 1846, Congress founded the Smithsonian Institute. With its varied contents, it was the biggest museum in America, and if it is only in part an art museum (following the character given it from the start), it does contain the "largest, most comprehensive collection of American aboriginal pottery in the world," to quote from Helen W. Henderson's book on our capital city. The group of works is important not only in extent, but also for the scientific scholarship which has gone into their assembling and cataloguing. Examples of sculpture from Mexico and the other countries south of us, exhibited near the productions of our own part of America, give irrefutable testimony to the cultural unity of the continent.

This latter point will bear a good deal of future demonstration, for too many of our museums fail to treat as art even the most remarkable sculpture, ceramics, and decoration of the great races who once peopled our entire hemisphere, and still do, very largely, various parts of Latin America. A notable exception and perhaps the first among our chief art museums to see the matter correctly was that of Detroit, where Dr. Valentiner pioneered in exhibiting ancient Mexican art. His example has been followed at Cleveland, Worcester, and other cities. The present-day painting of our own Southwestern Indians is so fine that it is causing a realization of their immense talent for art. But as a rule, we still relegate the work of the original Americans to natural-history museums, where it is entered under the heading of anthropology. There is, of course, an explanation for this in the history of thought, as will be apparent if we recall that the great art objects of China were at first regarded merely as curios. (For an amusing example of nineteenth-century contempt for the Far East, see Collingwood's *Grammar of Ornament*.) Similarly, the vast artistic expression of Egypt was revealed as a by-product of curiosity about a people mentioned in the Bible.

A great advance was made in the cultural standing of the national capital when William Wilson Corcoran (1798-1888) opened his gallery in Washington. It was soon enriched by other collectors who were sympathetic to the founder as a patron of American art. He is to be remembered as one whose individual effort gave a museum to his city. One of its admirable features is the collection of bronzes by Barye, which a trustee of the Corcoran Gallery, William T. Walters of Baltimore, ordered in 1873 from the artist himself. When that collector, on one of his visits to Paris, gave to Barye Corcoran's request for an example of every bronze he had produced, the great old sculptor, who still maintained the Spartan reserve with which he had faced so much adversity, was deeply moved, and said, "M. Walters, that is more than my whole country has done for me."

This incident deserves a notable place in our records, especially as this recognition of a living genius did not date from Barye's last years, but went back to the time, over two decades before, when Mr. Walters first visited him in his studio. This was the result of the admiration for the sculptor that had moved Mr. Walters' fellow townsman, George A. Lucas, for more than fifty years a resident of Paris, to bring Barye and the railroad builder together. Walters ordered, for Monument Square, in Baltimore, bronze casts of the models of Barye's decoration for the Louvre. Beginning in 1850, there grew up, in Mr. Walters' home, another of our very personal museums. For his Oriental collection, the first to be formed in America by a private individual, William T. Walters himself wrote the 1884 catalogue, covering forty-one hundred objects. Henry Walters, the founder's son, so greatly increased the wealth of the museum that its handbook can say: "It is estimated that when a proper catalogue is made, the number of items in the collection may reach twenty thousand." The estimate has proved, since the time of that publication, to be too conservative, the still incomplete count running well over twenty-two thousand.

And this quantitative measure of buying by the Walters is matched to a very great extent by the high quality of their possessions, now given to the public. Henry Walters attended a lycée in Paris at the time of our Civil War, and had as a schoolmate Paul Durand-Ruel, who, after entering the family business, became the pioneer patron of the impressionists. Though a lifelong association united the American and the Frenchman (both of them lived to be old men), Walters seems to have accepted Durand-Ruel's advice chiefly about the romantics, favored by the firm of Durand-Ruel. Henry Walters' other interests — ranging from Greek to Oriental, from medieval to Mexican art — almost always trended to the older things, splendid examples of which can be seen at

the Walters Gallery. Collecting modern art had to wait for a different
generation of collectors.

At this point, we are coming into contact with the collectors whose
buying had passed far beyond the stage reached by the earlier art patrons
of America, men like Luman Reed, Thomas J. Bryan, and Louis Durr,
whose collections are still the backbone of the New-York Historical
Society. From 1804, when this body was founded, it was the main
repository for bequests of collections until the Metropolitan Museum
offered a more specialized place for works of art. Yet with knowledge
and opportunities far more limited than those which a later day afforded,
the collectors just mentioned gave vital support to the love of art in this
country. Already many splendid works mingled with the mediocre, poor,
and fraudulent productions remembered by visitors to the Historical
Society's former home on Second Avenue.[1] By exhibiting its important
American works in galleries where their neighbors were Italian and
Flemish primitives of a high order, or later masters like Philippe de
Champaigne, Rubens, and Rembrandt, the Historical Society gave our
artists a chance to see how their work bore up when confronted with the
classics. Poorer examples were demolished, to be sure, but many a sturdy
portrait by the older Americans stands its ground — as a fine thing if
not as a world masterpiece.

It took time, naturally, for people to realize the difference between a
historical collection and one devoted solely to art. In the former, it was
quite right to assemble everything connected with our development,
showing that the first needs of colonists were for articles of use, and then
of well-being. Our mistakes belong there as well as our successes: poor
works, copies, and even forgeries as well as our fine production. Only
later, when the quality of the objects was studied, and finally made the
subject of experts, like the curators of museums, did these institutions
attain their true character, which is embodied in their privilege, their
duty of showing only the most characteristic and best examples of the
artists. In the presence of this problem, they have found out anew
the truth of the words that Hippocrates uttered, about 400 B.C.: "Life
is short, opportunity fleeting, experience treacherous, and judgment
difficult."

Glancing again at the time represented by painters like Copley and
Stuart, we are proud to find that their public contained men worthy to
supplement their effort through lay appreciation. Together the artists
and the art appreciators laid firm the foundation of American culture.

---

[1] The New-York Historical Society is now commodiously lodged on Central Park West.
Most of its record of our age of innocence is now kept in storage.

11. France (13th Century): Engaged Capital from Langon.
Courtesy of The Metropolitan Museum of Art (The Cloisters).

Thus, when our famous old fighting ship, the *Constitution*, made an extended voyage through Mediterranean waters, George Jones, the chaplain of the frigate, was well aware of his opportunities for classical study. It was with eager interest that he visited the plains of Troy in 1826, and Mycenae and Tiryns in 1827. Indeed, the captain of the ship, realizing the importance of two colossal marble statues he came upon in Greece, purchased them and brought them to Philadelphia, where one remained at the Pennsylvania Academy as late as 1937. As Professor Dinsmoor observes, it is embarrassing to report the destruction of this work, for it was broken up to avoid the expense of shoring it up. If not of the highest order of classical sculpture, it was at least good enough to throw added luster on "Old Ironsides," and on a generation including the intelligent men who sailed her.

That generation was interested not only in the art of Greece and Rome, but also in that of Egypt. As far back as 1823, at least, a mummy was sent to Boston. The first American collection of Egyptian antiquities was assembled at Thebes by Col. Mendes I. Cohen of Baltimore; after his death, it was given to Johns Hopkins University. Further accessions to our store of such art were the Lowell Collection, sent to Boston in 1834; the Egyptian pieces which went to the National Institution in Washington in 1842, and the important collection made by Dr. Henry Abbott, an English physician in Cairo, between 1832 and 1852. It contains the first known Cretan artifact, one imported into Egypt around 1500 B.C. After eight years in America, the collection was bought by the New-York Historical Society in 1860.

The Near East came also within our ken at an early date. In 1817, bricks with cuneiform inscriptions were brought to our shores, and the languages of the Bible lands were studied by numerous American missionaries. Thus, the way was prepared for the founding of the American Oriental Society in 1842. In the following year, its Journal began to appear and, from the first, gave space to archaeological studies. In 1851, William F. Williams, a missionary, arrived in Mosul. For services he rendered to the ruler of the country he was rewarded by the gift of various slabs from the great palace of Assurnasirpal, which had already furnished to the British Museum and the Louvre their treasures of Assyrian sculpture. Mr. Williams sent the slabs to America and they were distributed to centers of theological study. Thus, Amherst, Andover, Auburn, Bowdoin, Dartmouth, Union, Vermont, Williams, and Yale received works that were to stir many a New England imagination. The examples at Andover finally entered the Boston Museum, and the large and splendid pieces at Auburn were acquired for the Metropolitan

Museum. Other sculptures from the same palace went successively through the hands of Henry Stevens and James Lenox (whose great book collection was one of the basic bequests of the New York Public Library) and at length passed to the New-York Historical Society.

The westward spread of such interests is not marked in the earlier times by events of historical importance comparable to those just recorded. Having seen the role of New England's great colleges in the development of our culture, we are not surprised to find a continuation of such influence when, early in the nineteenth century, first Ohio and then other Middle Western states founded institutions of learning directed by scholars from the older universities. When no permanent center existed, there would at least be lecturers like Emerson and Agassiz who visited the provinces more or less regularly. A speaker on Egyptology, getting as far as St. Louis in the early eighteen-forties, had audiences sometimes numbering two thousand.

As so often in other phases of our history, the fascination of the Indian now helped in developing our museums. It had given to Fenimore Cooper his countless readers, not only in America, but in Europe, where the art of our early peoples was studied at a later time by such great institutions as the British Museum or the Völkerkunde, in Berlin. Fortunately our own scholars were alive to the importance of Indian collections, as we may see in the marvelous group of sculptures at the Ohio State Museum, the basketry shown at the Southwestern Museum in Los Angeles, and other groups of work — in New York, Philadelphia, Chicago, Milwaukee, and Seattle to name almost at random a few of the cities where such collections exist. As has been said, the Smithsonian is pre-eminent among them, its study of Indian culture dating back a full century.

The history of Chicago's art development is almost as old. Already in 1859, the city had a sufficient store of paintings to furnish a very extensive loan exhibition. It was organized by prominent citizens, and a catalogue was prepared. Its entries show a degree of connoisseurship, indeed, which was by no means universal at this time; for even in Europe the most famous names in art were freely bestowed on old pictures. Instead, we read here such attributions as "supposed Rembrandt," or "after Claude." There were not a few works called copies — and much of our study in early times was based on copies. But, along with the more modest Old Masters like Pompeo Batoni, we find names such as Correggio, Titian, and da Vinci — attributions we must "view with alarm."

Looking forward to the day of Chicago's important role in the sponsorship of American art, the exhibition of 1859 contained pictures by George Caleb Bingham, William Hart, Christopher Cranch, and many other painters of the day. The intrinsic value of their work is not always the essential point in the record. Many of them were teachers and all of them exerted influence, sometimes bringing people to an interest in art by the mere fact that those around the early painters felt their seriousness and purpose. Many an artistic effort by some small-town boy or farm boy has been due to the presence in his home of a picture that he could realize later (but only later) to be crude or dull. It is common experience, when one visits our Western cities, to find groups of artists doing good work because they have been inspired by some older man who will never be admired for his own production, but who could transmit the ideas he brought from the East or from Europe.

To this day, numbers of towns, all over the country, give us a picture of what our chief cities were before the founding of great museums began, seventy-odd years ago. Perhaps there will be only a single art lover in the place — but he may be very clear-sighted. Thus, from a small town in New Mexico a New York critic received an urgent suggestion to write a book on Poussin. Of course, this lover of Poussin was not a cowboy, but the mere idea of anyone in that section of the "Wild West" interesting himself in the most classical and perhaps the most difficult of French painters indicates the quality of mind that is found not infrequently in any part of the country.

Sometimes these isolated art lovers are women. In a city of the corn belt, where old inhabitants still have memories of battles with the Indians, a lady founded a reading club, some forty years ago, and led her circle to concentrate on art matters. Daughters and then grand-daughters of the original group carried on the activity, in which many men of the community participated with conviction. In time, the association raised substantial sums to purchase pictures from the exhibitions it brought to the public library, where its acquisitions were placed for all to enjoy. And many of them were worthy to be enjoyed, as one might reasonably expect. For, when I first visited this city, so far from the great museums, each member of the group had a copy of Sir Arthur Evans' book on Crete; one would read a report on a chapter, together with her added research and comment, which was eagerly followed by her associates through reference to their own study of the passage assigned for that meeting.

Thus, in the course of time, there was developed that surest foundation for a museum: an intelligent and sympathetic public. Unfortunately in this particular case the institution which crowned the labors of so

12. France (14th Century): Virgin and Child.
Courtesy of The Metropolitan Museum of Art (The Cloisters).

many years did not continue its fine preliminary work. A large money gift from a well-intending citizen somewhat outside the original group took the movement from their hands, and placed it in those of other people. A big building was erected and, though the space thus created did not exemplify the worst fate of such a vacuum, the orderly evolution of the community was destroyed.

Another case where important developments can be attributed to a woman is that of a college in Montana. The head of its art department was indefatigable in corresponding with the best authorities in the East, bringing them out as visiting instructors, if only for a day or two. Her staff made up for its small numbers by intelligence and enthusiasm, qualities that it communicated to the students (including Indian boys and girls).

Still another idealist was the librarian of a town on the Pacific coast. She made her institution the center of the community's interest in art, arranged for lectures and exhibitions, encouraged buyers (who got some fine works), and lived long enough to see the art association she had created obtain a splendid site for its museum, which bids fair to become a fine one.

Always the best results follow when the tradition of a town has prepared it for the expansion that comes with wealth. Thus Detroit, with memories of an old French culture evolved while its name really meant "the strait" to everyone, was ready for the coming of artists. They, in turn, built up a taste for a living art so that when the great industries of the city invited a new and wider development, it was based on something more significant than the little museum already existing. The studios of the painters and sculptors and their Scarab Club, quite as much as the big fortunes of the community, influenced the city's purchase of art works. All these resources were so admirably drawn upon by a great museum director that, in a few years' time, he carried the collections from insignificance to a position of international renown.

It would be invidious to name other cities where vast funds have failed to produce similarly satisfactory results. Failure must be blamed on trustees who had not been prepared to disburse intelligently the funds they controlled, either personally or by employing experts. Sometimes they would thwart the experts through sheer ignorance, and sometimes they would fail to secure truly expert personnel.

Such matters are part of the record of a country in which many places are new and inexperienced. When to these drawbacks is added the cocksureness of self-made men who see themselves as capable of solving any problem they choose to tackle, we see the explanation of the fakes which have deluged the country. An old employee at the customs house in New York used to say he could tell just how far west a picture was going by the badness of the forgery. To be sure, this amusing diagnosis dates back many years, and conditions have changed since then. Such a place as Oklahoma, whose very name suggests Indian fighting and other frontier conditions, now contains some really beautiful collections, which will undoubtedly come before the public at a later day. When we reach the National Gallery in Washington, we shall see how modern scholarship has permitted great collectors to create overnight (as it seemed) an assemblage of works characterized not merely by genuineness but by the highest quality. The foundation for further achievement along these lines is being laid in quite remote parts of the country, as understanding spreads. Yet there is no reason to blink the fact that our beginnings, away from the centers of culture, have often been marked by incompetence or even absurdity. Some museums did not contain a single genuine work by an artist of any consequence, the names of even third-rate painters being attached to reproductions of their minor followers.

In one museum of the Far West hung canvases labeled da Vinci and Rembrandt, about which the most remarkable thing was the family resemblance of the signatures — very large and legible in both cases; they were so clearly from the same hand that visitors from afar were amazed that the many cultivated citizens of this large community did not rise up and rid it of the scandal. The fact was that the museum was the pet interest of an all-powerful newspaper editor and politician. He took on jobs that would have required an entire staff of experts, buying, with equal cheerfulness and ignorance, paintings, sculpture, Oriental works, and other art objects. A responsible citizen assured me that he had seen this worthy take out his jackknife and "improve" the nose and mouth of a terra-cotta bust. I can believe the fantastic tale because the same thing was told me — and about himself — by a college president in New York. Without a smile or a blush, he related how he had "corrected" the modeling of some of the sculptures in his institution.

Yet in that Western city, there turned up a very notable collection which had quietly been formed by a man of culture; and no one can say what other such surprises are in store for us. The leading native authority on the colonial painting of Mexico, Don Manuel Toussaint, was advised to go and see the collection of it at the museum of Davenport, Iowa. The name meant nothing to him or to those whom he consulted; but finding himself in Chicago — not too far away for a flying visit — he decided to investigate. His resulting discoveries, including numerous photographs of important works, were published in the Gazette des Beaux Arts for September, 1943, with a statement of his complete conversion to the view that masterpieces might well be found in the most obscure collections.

Some years ago, meeting a member of the old French aristocracy of New Orleans, I was asked what I would like to see. My natural reply, that anything my host would care to show would interest me, was not accepted: I must name what I myself wanted to see — the great city could evidently furnish it. Finally giving in, and thinking there might indeed be a chance that one or more of the five lost Géricault pictures of the madmen could have reached the Creole capital, I asked to see paintings by that artist. None was forthcoming. But shortly after my return to New York, a dealer telephoned, asking me to come and look at a picture which had been sent him as a Géricault. It was, indeed, a very fine work; it had turned up unexpectedly among the possessions of an old New Orleans family.

The fullest insight I had into the resources of the country came when, in 1940, I was assembling the pictures for the New York World's Fair. In 1939, the Fair had drawn so heavily upon our collections that many people feared the success of the show could not be repeated. To be sure, it was not the unknown masterpieces that saved us, the second year, but they helped — and above all, by convincing the country of its achievement in collecting. For, instead of the magnificent loans from Europe which had done so much for the first exhibition, we had to depend, in that war year, upon works in America, and upon no others. The country stood the test, and as few persons thought it could.

In assembling pictures for the Fair, I went to Seattle, Washington, on the Northwest, to San Diego, California on the Southwest, to San Antonio, Texas (where a private collection furnished a splendid Greco), and to Maine, where I saw again the outstanding works of Copley, Feke, and Stuart at Bowdoin College. It was my constant experience to find masterpieces in the most unlikely places — as they might seem to many people; thus, there was a grand work by Delacroix in Portland, Oregon, and a supreme Renoir in New Orleans. Naturally, the museums known to everybody furnished many superb canvases.

To be sure, great works were usually recent arrivals in the collections. But there was every evidence of distinguished antecedents for such works — either materially or spiritually. The more remote centers, whose culture was somewhat similar to that which cities like Boston and New York had reached in the past, testified vividly to the spiritual and material foundations on which our great museums were built.

13. Spain (Catalonia, early 12th Century): Byzantine Chapel.
Courtesy of the Museum of Fine Arts, Boston.

2. OUR HISTORY CONTINUES

HAVING NOTICED certain phases of the spread westward of American interest in art, we return to the eastern cities and to the developments that preceded the great museums and the new era they inaugurate.

For some time, the public had to be turned toward art, and an important share of this work was done by the exhibitions of our artists, especially at the National Academy of Design. Founded to give to its members more freedom than did the old American Academy of Fine Arts, which we have seen receiving the casts sent from Paris by Robert R. Livingston, it eventually took over those works and early began to add others. From its foundation in 1826, Samuel F. B. Morse, the first president, was its leading spirit. Though his struggle to perfect telegraphy and spread its use took much time from the painting he practiced so admirably, Morse remained an artist throughout his life. When Yale, his alma mater, opened its art gallery in 1864, Morse donated the first new work it received, a painting by his old teacher, Washington Allston. He himself taught at the Academy and gave courses of lectures at New York University, where he continued as professor of fine arts until his death in 1872.

Meanwhile, with the growth of collecting (that great art lover, Luman Reed, beginning his work in 1830), the dealers' galleries became more numerous and more secure in their patronage. They could thus offer work of better quality, due to the increasing discernment of purchasers. Although frequently berated by artists and collectors, the dealers, by their enterprise and connoisseurship, have brought to America a large share of its possessions. Also, by stimulating public interest in art, they have done invaluable work in attracting more buyers — still one of the greatest needs of this country. Keeping up with the development of our art appreciation (or, rather, keeping just a little ahead of it), the dealers' galleries are today an Aladdin's cave for treasure.

The importance of the dealers' role may be gauged by the record of the American Art Union. That body functioned for thirteen years, from 1838, when it gave its first exhibition, until 1851, when, because of its method of distributing pictures to its members, it fell under the ban of the law against lotteries. It listed 16,000 subscribers for engravings, and an astounding estimate of attendance at its 1844 exhibition places the number of visitors at over 500,000. Besides the engravings, it distributed some 2400 other works during its period of existence. No wonder that the biographer of Asher B. Durand, the painter, states that the Union saw artists increase from a number one could "count on one's fingers" (doubtless an understatement) to "a large body of workers." The Union, like the dealers, unquestionably contributed very much to the developing of our interest in art.

Nor should we forget our great fairs, beginning with the Crystal Palace Exhibition of 1853. It took its name from the show, of the same name, held in London two years earlier. This had been followed, in 1852, by the founding of the Victoria and Albert Museum, "the first fruit of the effort to meet the problems of the industrial age." At a later time this institution had a marked influence on our own museums, particularly — and frankly — the Metropolitan.

No immediate results of great importance can be claimed for our own fair; but its collection of 675 paintings and sculptures exerted some influence none the less: art-buying increased and, as a consequence, knowledge of art spread. And it is probable that the showing affected the plans that Peter Cooper was maturing at this time. These plans eventuated, six years later, in his founding the very important Union devoted "To Science and Art." The opportunities Cooper Union has afforded to countless thousands of underprivileged people give it a secure place in the history of the United States; and its collection of decorative art objects (especially textiles, the gift of J. Pierpont Morgan), which Mr. Cooper's daughter, Mrs. Abram S. Hewitt, and her daughters, the Misses Sarah and Eleanor Hewitt, continued to develop from 1889 until their deaths, ranks very high among such monuments to the genius of the craftsman, chiefly European, especially French.

The old building where Lincoln made one of his most important speeches has a thousand other memories of lecturers, artists, and students; of William Rimmer, for example, our great anatomist, sculptor and painter, who taught there for many years. And so the museum of Cooper Union, with its school and fine library, is one of the places especially dear to New Yorkers who care for their city. It looks forward to another monument, left us by a great citizen, many years later, the American Wing of the Metropolitan Museum. There, preserving the façade of the Assay Office, a splendid building dating from old New York, Robert W. De Forest and Mrs. De Forest gave us the series of period rooms in which we may realize the good sense as well as the taste for gracious living that characterized so many Americans of Colonial and early republican days.

Let us now glance at what some of our nineteenth-century writers and scholars did to prepare for museum development. This was surveyed in a very informing study of early American art literature by John B. Montignani, of the Metropolitan, who published it in that museum's

Bulletin for January, 1941. His later researches have yielded little to be added to the bibliography he collected at that time.

Mr. Montignani found that the first book "of any importance is one which deals with the artists of our own country, William Dunlap's *History of the Rise and Progress of the Arts of Design in the United States.*" It appeared in 1834; then, in 1847, there followed Henry Theodore Tuckerman's less comprehensive book on the same subject. In 1845, Samuel Gray Ward published his translation of Goethe's *Essays on Art*; mention should also be made of Giles Henry Lodge's translation of Winckelmann's *History of Ancient Art*, which appeared in four volumes between 1849 and 1873. Clearly enough, our public was finding out how Europe had evolved ideas — and their transmission was done by our own men.

Returning to original writing, in 1850, we find Richard Henry Dana, Jr., editing a volume of Washington Allston's lectures on art, together with his poems; the painter had died in 1843. An example of current aesthetics, as furnished by an anonymous critic, writing on the New York exhibition of 1853, follows:

"Success in sculpture has always been in proportion to its reproduction of Greek subjects in the Greek spirit." This may sound a bit quaint to an age which has been able to see in its museums the marvels of Gothic, Chinese, and Mexican sculpture, but we must not forget that nearly all Europeans were, at this time, capable of remarks quite as erroneous as that of our writer.

Mr. Montignani says that it was James Jackson Jarves (born 1818) who was "the first American to write extensively in a philosophical and critical vein on the arts." It is appropriate that this should be so, for the collection of Italian paintings he formed is, of course, very high in quality, its Pollaiuolo of *Hercules and Dejanira* being one of our most superb examples of *quattrocento* painting, even today. Ranging from the thirteenth to the seventeenth century, the bulk of the 119 Jarves pictures would compare very well with many collections that Europeans were forming at the time. "Jarves is the real type of the pioneer in the field of Italian art," as Lionello Venturi has written. America was not ready for the things that this remarkable student brought back to his country; it was in vain that he offered them in one place after another, for years. Finally, in 1871, they were bought by the gallery at Yale. This was largely through the efforts of Professor Noah Porter (later the president of the University), and Professor John F. Weir, himself a noted painter and a son of the art teacher at West Point who gave Whistler, among others, admirable instruction.

14. Giotto: St. Francis Receiving the Stigmata.
Courtesy of The Fogg Museum of Art, Harvard University, Cambridge.

And so, after a hint as to the paintings themselves, we are brought back to the scholars and writers. An important work appearing in Jarves' day, and showing that this collector was not a lone voice, was Tuscan Sculptors, by C. C. Perkins, published in 1864. It was followed by books on kindred subjects containing many a passage that a "modern" can still reflect upon. Among the writers mentioned, William Dunlap, painter, theater manager, and the "American Vasari," as he has half humorously been called, lived in New York; most of the rest of this immensely useful work centered in Boston. John La Farge was visiting relatives in France, at this period, and preparing himself by contact with artists and critics (but of course by his painting, above all) for the distinguished writing on art he was to do later. His contemporary, Whistler, was also absorbing the new ideas that Paris brought forth in the sixties; a decade later, men like Thomas Eakins, William M. Chase, and Kenyon Cox were to spend long periods of study in Europe, as was J. Alden Weir, another son of Whistler's old teacher at West Point, and so a brother of the man whom we have seen working for the purchase of the Jarves pictures for Yale.

All of these artists were important influences in the period that saw the astonishing development of our museums. But the painter who did most in this respect was William Morris Hunt (1824-1879). I quote from Martha A. Shannon's Boston Days of William Morris Hunt: "Admirable as was the art Hunt displayed in the portraits and all the other lines in which he exercised his skill so successfully, we owe our greatest debt to him for hastening the recognition and appreciation of what was best and most deserving in the art of others." He was the first man of our country to own bronzes by Barye, a master who had given to the young American most valuable help with his art. Another who contributed to his growth was the painter whose work was so prominent in his collection and in those of the men he advised. This was Jean François Millet, so many of whose pictures are to be seen in Boston as a result of Hunt's influence; he considered Barye and Millet "the greatest men of their time." When accused of cramming Boston with French art, he replied that "to hold that art was confined to a school or a people was as silly as to maintain that art criticism could only be written with a quill from the great bald-headed American eagle; that it was not worth while to be alarmed about the influence of French art. It would not be mortifying if a Millet or a Delacroix should be developed in Boston. It is not our fault that we inherit ignorance of art, but we are not obliged to advertise it." Further evidence of Hunt's receptivity to great schools at a time when they were as yet little appreciated is to be seen in his early admiration for Japanese prints. As to these, Horatio Greenough, the sculptor, said, "Japanese things were not *le beau idéal* but *le laid idéal*." Mrs. Shannon comments: "He [Greenough] was, however, in the minority," and ideas like Hunt's laid the foundation for Boston's vast collections of Oriental art.

Hunt's appreciation of the most diverse work explains the sympathy he extended to different temperaments among his many pupils. Such sympathy is one of the most valuable factors in the make-up of a teacher, especially when added to solid understanding of the masters. That Hunt knew such study to be essential is proved by one of his sayings: "Nobody ever did well without learning from those who had opportunity to know what was good and great. Michelangelo, Titian, Raphael, were they self-taught? I rather guess *not*."

Balancing this reference to the past is another statement in his *Talks on Art*, a book compiled by his pupils, and which had great influence. One feels how healthy that influence was when one reads: "Art belongs to this age just as the air belongs to it. 'Classic': who would have said two thousand years ago that Millet and Delacroix would be classic? Give me the fellow that can find honey in the flower that grows. Talk about Hymettus. We have just as good material to make painters of as we have to make poets. The poets have had the libraries of the world to read, while the painters have had to expatriate themselves."

On this important point, with its direct bearing on the formation of museums in America, we may also recall the visit that Hunt, in company with another artist, Elihu Vedder, made to Emerson. The philosopher asked the two young painters to explain their ideas, saying, "Nature being the same on the banks of the Kennebec as on the banks of the Tiber — why go to Europe?" To this Vedder replied (not without a sense of his own temerity), "Nature is the same everywhere, but literature and art are nature seen through other eyes, and a literary man in Patagonia, without books to consult, would be at a great disadvantage. Here he has all that is essential in the way of books; but to the artist, whose books are pictures, this land is Patagonia."

The artists, determined to reduce the likeness of this land to the howling wilderness, in 1866 founded the Allston Club, with Hunt as president. During its short life, it was largely instrumental in raising the $5000 needed to buy a Courbet masterpiece, *The Quarry*, now in the Boston Museum. The great realist, on hearing of the purchase of his picture, is said to have exclaimed, "What care I for the Salon, what care I for honors, when the art students of a new and great country know and appreciate and buy my works!" The words sound like Courbet; and what sounds right also, though again I have no proof of it, is that another great painting given to the Boston Museum in memory of Martin Brimmer, the first president of the institution, was chosen on Hunt's advice. Certainly he was a friend of Mr. Brimmer's, and it is natural that the latter's family and associates would seek the advice of the artist who, more than any other at the time, influenced the collectors of Boston. The picture was by one of Hunt's great admirations, Delacroix, and the subject, *The Deposition from the Cross*, treated in the noble manner so reminiscent of Poussin, was particularly appropriate for a memorial. (Incidentally, this early example of using an art work to commemorate a fine American life, revived a beautiful custom dating back to the time of the Egyptians and the Greeks. It has been followed in our museums on many subsequent occasions, and is particularly fitting in a country where memorials to the dead so often take the form of works or funds to bring about the welfare or the happiness of the living).

Hunt's attitude toward Delacroix reminds us again of his constant insistence on learning from the classics, a point of view that became increasingly influential in the development of museums in America. Replying to statements that he was excessively devoted to the French school, and writing of the admiration of Géricault and other French masters for English painting (and of the inspiration that English artists have derived from the French), he said, "Those who have succeeded in art have always loved and respected one another's work."

It was such an attitude that made Hunt help a man who did much to create among Bostonians a high level of judgment. As far back as 1852, Seth M. Vose began to buy the work of one of Hunt's ideals among modern painters, Corot. By 1881, he had 165 paintings by the master. He continued to acquire them, despite the fact that in 1873, when he offered his collection of Corots for sale, not one of them found a purchaser, though not one, in that difficult time, was priced at over $1250, and some of them were masterpieces. Despite the efforts of men like Hunt, Vose, and their successors among the artists and dealers of this country, one is sorely tempted to say that the difficult time for great painters is their lifetime. When Vose vainly tried to sell his Corots, their painter was already in his seventy-seventh year. But perhaps we are yet to do better for the artists and, above all, for the public. A good painter will always go on with his work, and so loses little through neglect; but the public, which needs his art most at the time when it is being produced and when it could give men the thrill of feeling their age to be a great age, is defrauded if its true representatives are left in obscurity.

15. Hubert van Eyck: The Last Judgment (detail).
Courtesy of The Metropolitan Museum of Art.

One more quotation will show how keenly William Morris Hunt, with all his admiration for the past, understood the difficult question of the art of one's own period. To a person who compared Millet and Corot — to their disadvantage — with Claude, Ruisdael, and others, Hunt spoke of things that his contemporaries were doing (things never attempted in the past), adding, "To equal what had been done before is not enough to put a man on a level with the greatest. The best must be surpassed in some aspects." The intellectual courage needed for a statement like that was the basis of American thinking when our museum pioneers faced their innumerable problems.

Returning to the printed word in criticism and art teaching, we approach the most eminent figure in that field, Professor Charles Eliot Norton. Before considering him, however, let us round out our brief survey of early American writing on art by noting three of the attempts to provide this country with journals of a professional character. These are the *Bulletin of the American Art Union*, published in New York from 1847 to 1853; *The Crayon*, which followed it two years later, and lasted until 1861; and finally — showing again how the interest in art spread to new territory — *The Western Art Journal*, founded in Cincinnati in 1855.

It is still with a sense of pioneering that we must regard the earlier contribution of the colleges to America's understanding of art. Yale claims to have been "first in this country or abroad, to include a School of Fine Arts" in its curriculum, though Robert L. Duffus, in his study of the matter, observes that at Princeton "a species of instruction in art seems to have been begun earlier." We may pass by the question of precedence in view of Mr. Duffus's own delightful irreverence in describing the early teaching (or some of the early teaching) at Yale as "a school where young ladies prepared themselves for the responsibilities of matrimony by learning to paint china." It may be, as he suggests, that the coeducational "blight" kept the institution back for a long time: in general, in its earlier days, Yale affected a rather stern attitude toward aesthetic affairs, and willingly left them to Harvard and its "rosewater."

But it was a very true scion of the first New England stock that brought Harvard to its great distinction in art study. Charles Eliot Norton, born in 1827, is described by Mr. Duffus in these words: "There is no more striking instance of the successful grafting of the ideal of fine art to the stem of Puritan morality. Norton never got over the habits of the ethical approach." It had been his guide from the serious days of the old college of the eighteen-forties, when he had studied there; it had been his guide, after graduation, when varied occupations and travels formed his mind anew. But if "to be a good man" was his lifetime's conscious motto, for himself and his students, there simultaneously evolved the conviction that "a complete and satisfactory education could not be obtained without . . . culture of the aesthetic faculties." This was pretty strange doctrine to most New Englanders (and many other people), but not to Charles William Eliot. That great Harvard man, Norton's cousin, saw eye to eye with the latter who, in 1873, began to teach in the halls of his alma mater. Year after year he lectured on art, widening the scope of his own attainments and deepening the feeling for beauty among increasingly large — and increasingly influential — groups of young men. His fastidious nature made him express himself as "horrified" at the great number of his listeners, but nothing in his record would make us doubt his belief in the value of his influence.

For Norton's influence had behind it the authority of Ruskin, whom Norton pretty thoroughly represented in America. It was further based on his researches in medieval architecture, on which he wrote a valuable work.[1] It went back, indeed, to Dante, whom Norton had translated and edited. Nay, when the Archaeological Institute of America appeared in 1879, it was Norton who proposed it. Francis Parkman was asked to be president and, could he have assented, he would have enforced his interpretation of the word "America," in the name of the Institute, by directing its studies to the Indians, the living representatives of the earlier cultures of this country. But the great historian's age and health compelled him to let the preferences of other men have sway, and so Norton's proposal to excavate Assos, near the site of ancient Troy, was accepted. Schliemann's discoveries in the Greece of Homer were before the minds of all scholars, Crete was giving up its treasures, and General Louis P. di Cesnola, the first director of the Metropolitan Museum, had made his important excavations in Cyprus. The American School at Athens was to begin its work in 1881, and Edward Robinson, later to play a notable role in the museums of Boston and New York, was conducting his researches on classical soil. The classical tradition was therefore the logical one for Norton to espouse; the Indians had to wait for a more advanced stage in our own culture, when the scope of archaeology would include the continent we inhabit.

In directing our studies to the European classics, Norton was doing, in his way, what American collectors were doing in theirs: laying the foundations of our museums within the boundaries of the peoples we principally descend from and of those who have, like the Egyptians and the Assyrians, influenced our ancestral ideas.

---

[1] *Historical Studies of Church Building in the Middle Ages*, New York, 1880.

The Civil War had interrupted the interest in art which had been taking such firm root and spreading so widely among us, as was shown by the statistics on the powerful Art Union, on the private collections now at the New-York Historical Society, on those of the Boston Athenaeum (later transferred to the Museum of that city), and on those formed at Philadelphia, Hartford, and other places. But the conflict ended, railroads spread across the nation, manufacturing increased, new settlements dotted the West, shipping crammed the harbors of the East, — and more money than ever was devoted to the arts. The centenary of American independence was approaching and, for years, preparations were made for the great Exposition at Philadelphia. Its art exhibit is one of the landmarks in our history. But the showing, important as it was, would not have had its effect if men's thought had not been turned in that direction by events six years earlier, when the museums of New York and Boston were founded; Cincinnati, with a long record of previous effort, got under way with its permanent gallery at about the same time.

Thus, 1870 is the most significant date in our record, the American Museum of Natural History, moreover, being founded the same year. For people who think of these vast and rich institutions as they are today, it is difficult to imagine them as mere embryos in the minds of the men who conceived them, more than three quarters of a century ago. To grasp that condition, one must look back further, to almost an equal length of time before, during which every attempt to give to New York and Boston a permanent museum had died a more or less lingering death. The Athenaeum survived, to be sure, but as a library association; the New-York Historical Society, while possessing, as it still does, certain very beautiful pictures, was always essentially centered on the purpose denoted by its name; the Pennsylvania Academy, though wholly dedicated to art, existed more for its school and its annual showing of contemporary art than for the collections that it housed.

Recalling the failure of preceding attempts, there was needed a high order of intelligence, courage, and idealism for the men of 1870 to give to their country the institutions they founded. And when we speak of giving them, we need to see the record of the time in order to know how literally the word applies. One of the most significant factors in the case is that the funds to start these enterprises came out of the pockets of private individuals. Soon, it is true, there were grants of city land for buildings, and appropriations for construction and maintenance. Through these democratic measures, public money had its share in the development; but the collections of objects — the one essential of

16. Franco-Flemish (late 15th Century): *Third Unicorn Tapestry.*
Courtesy of The Metropolitan Museum of Art (The Cloisters).

museums — was not the gift of the community, but of men and women whose love of art caused them to see it as the greatest benefaction they could offer to-their fellow citizens. Other lands can show splendid contributions of the kind made by public-spirited collectors to their city or nation; in America alone are the museums wholly constituted in this way.

The list of those who have built up our institutions by contributing time and effort, or works of art (or sometimes all these donations together) could be obtained only by extreme patience from the archives of our museums. To be sure, in producing such a document, there would be innumerable moments when the searcher would thrill with patriotism as he came upon the names of great leaders of thought, of art, literature, and religion, of law and government, of commerce and finance — bracketed, of course, with contributors whose identity is all but lost. To this splendid honor roll of the men who organized our museums and sustained them through years of difficult struggle, there should be added the names of those who, within the institutions, have given devoted study to the works of art themselves, protecting the collections from the danger of imposture, seeking out essential directions for growth, and studying the means to make of the objects in their care the greatest possible source of inspiration to the public.

The present volume can linger in only the briefest way over individual records, however gratifying it would be to pay tribute to men and women who have deserved the thanks of their country, not only in their own day, but for all time. Fortunately we have, and in the case of our greatest museum, a record of its development which does justice to what may be called its human side. When Winifred E. Howe was preparing the first volume of her *History of the Metropolitan Museum of Art*, which appeared in 1913, there still lived a member of the committee which broke ground for the institution; and he could give her first-hand recollections of the meeting of 1869, when the venerable William Cullen Bryant appealed to an assembly of distinguished citizens to give to the community the museum for which it was fitted by its character, its wealth, and its culture. The admirable words of the poet (who, as a newspaper editor, was versed in practical affairs) and various speeches and writings of John Taylor Johnston, Joseph H. Choate, and other eminent men among the founders are preserved in Miss Howe's book, which also contains an invaluable account of the earlier art institutions of New York.

Her pictures of those old days, when men of great wealth were not above doing the manual labor of the museum, are most revealing. "An employee of the Park Department, who had been delegated as watchman at the new building, after watching these two Trustees for an hour as they lifted object after object from the moving van and safely deposited them in the large hall, took off his coat and helped."

But the public spirit which makes our early records so inspiring is only part of the story. We need to look again at the marvelous Frans Hals, the Poussin, Canaletto, and many other splendid works still on our walls from the Metropolitan's first purchase (1871), in order to realize the fact that the idealism of the founders was sustained by genuine taste and knowledge. This high standard of appreciation, which prevailed before there was an American museum worthy of the name, was based — at least partly — on the continuance in our country, of the tradition of the Grand Tour. It had been the accepted thing in England for centuries, and there were fairly well-defined routes to be taken by persons — usually young, but also those who repeated the journey in later life — to cover the great centers of art and culture, above all in Italy. From innumerable passages in the English writers we gain a most valuable insight as to the development of ideas, depending on whether the traveler preferred the "Golden Century" or the "Silver Century."

For our present purposes, it is important to remember that a feature of the Grand Tour, especially significant to men of wealth, was the purchase of art works — originals or copies — to mark their preference while in the famous cities of the Continent. It is to this custom that England owes the seemingly inexhaustible supply of Old Masters to be found in its great mansions, all over the British Isles. Sometimes forgotten for centuries, an unknown masterpiece — a Titian, a Holbein, or a Velasquez will reappear — to startle the connoisseurs. Before Holland was properly appreciative of her great painters, English travelers were bringing home the choicest productions of the Low Countries, many of which still remain among the descendants of the original purchasers.

In the earlier days of America, the Grand Tour was undertaken by large numbers of our countrymen, and many of them acquired art works (or, often, merely copies of art works) quite as their forebears in the older land had done. We have noted how the taste thus developed was applied in the Metropolitan Museum; we may now observe it though in relation to a later time, by glancing at a chapter in the history of our other great pioneer museum.

A Boston curator once remarked, "We are as poor as New York is rich." Taking the statement at face value, one would have to say that it would not be suggested by the appearance of the galleries. There is not, it is true, such a wealth of paintings that everyone knows to be the most costly. But what of the Oriental works? A booklet reviewing the first fifty years could say, "Our museum has a more important collection of Japanese and Chinese art than exists anywhere else in the world under one roof." But above all, there are the classical and Egyptian works. How did a group of such extent and quality come to a city so much smaller than various others in America, and so much behind them in financial resources?

The answer is again to be found in that old American interest in Greece and Rome of which New England colleges had been foremost representatives. And so Edward Perry Warren was well prepared to understand the importance of classical sculptures and ceramics when they came up for sale in Europe. He had supplemented the training Norton gave him at Harvard by various sojourns in Europe where, at a later time, he maintained a splendid residence. At thirty, he had little to fear from forgers, having learned, as he said, by purchasing their products in his earlier years and so had come to his appreciation of real things by proving their superiority to the false. As a result, in speaking of things largely bought by Mr. Warren, Furtwaengler could write, in 1904, "The collection of terra-cottas ranks not only as equal to the best in Europe, but in some respects surpasses them, a fact that is particularly noteworthy for the reason that there is no class of antiquities which offers such difficulties to collectors, as forgeries are exceedingly numerous in this domain, and often very clever. I know no museum in Europe, except that of Athens, which is so entirely free from false, restored, or otherwise 'improved' Greek terra-cottas as that of Boston." It is risky to suggest another name to so famous an authority as Furtwaengler, and I should not do so without the most serious backing; but the terra-cottas of the Louvre appear to be no less irreproachable. This tremendous commendation of our museum and its benefactor may give us honest satisfaction none the less; and far greater successes than its terra-cottas, its glorious vases, and other works of *Kleinkunst* are still to be noted. For out of the 134 sculptures mentioned in the catalogue of 1925, no less than 108 were obtained through Mr. Warren.

A man of large fortune, he was wont to buy as if for himself alone, and then let the museum select what it needed. His brother was the president of the institution for many years, and even before that, when Edward Robinson was the curator (going there in 1887, he became the director in 1902, and three years later resigned to become director of the Metropolitan), Mr. Warren could be sure that his purchases would be taken over by the museum of his city and, at a later time, by that of New York.

17. Piero della Francesca: St. John the Evangelist.
Courtesy of The Frick Collection, New York.

Associating with him the great English connoisseur of classical art, John Marshall, Mr. Warren built up an organization about which a leading authority wrote, "As the result of many years of effort, he had obtained complete control of the market in classical antiquities. Almost anything that was good, whether a new find or an old, came to him for first refusal. Competition had all but ceased. The chief private collectors in Europe were dead, or had withdrawn from the field. The museums were comparatively sluggish. The British Museum could do nothing; Berlin could do nothing. The Louvre did nothing." What counts most in the foregoing statement is not that Mr. Warren happened to come at a time when European collecting had turned to other fields; the essential point is that he saw the need of our galleries for that art on which, more than on any other, all later arts are founded. Having made this discovery, he went systematically about providing his countrymen with the things of greatest importance.

Beside Boston and New York, Providence and Bowdoin were among Mr. Warren's beneficiaries; and his association with the great European scholars who delighted to honor him led him to present splendid material to the Ashmolean at Oxford, to the Louvre, and to Leipzig University.

In our next chapter we shall reach some of the most striking examples of development in the classical field, when we observe the actual contents of our museums. It suffices to say here that when Mr. Robinson went to New York, it was the signal for the Metropolitan to resume its effort to extend those collections of ancient art so extraordinarily launched by the first director, General di Cesnola.

Having noted typical examples of our museum development in New York and Boston, we may turn to a different phase of the history, as shown by the experience of Chicago. Its Art Institute had grown to a very considerable size when, around 1920, this country was becoming convinced of the validity and importance of the modern masters. But the trustees of the museum, many of whom were themselves donors of the glorious Old Masters in the galleries, were old men, as a rule, and opposed to innovation. For years there was a deadlock between the eager, open-minded city and the officials who held back the forces of new life so urgently needed by the public collection.

To meet this problem, a group of forward-looking people, guided largely by two women, formed the Arts Club. It rapidly became the expression of all that was best in Chicago's appreciation of art, bringing to the city not only modern works, but also an exhibition of Greek sculpture, a thing badly lacking in the museum. Before many years, the

Institute offered space to the Arts Club, so that it might give its exhibitions in the place whose magnificent location offered easy access to the population of the city, beside the innumerable visitors from the region centering about Chicago. With the galleries once opened to modern art, and with the accession of the prodigious Seurat and other masterworks of the Birch-Bartlett Collection, the Institute soon veered from its extreme conservatism of the preceding period to its present unequaled position as an exponent of understanding art at the time of its production. This problem, the most difficult in the whole field, is the one which the Museum of Modern Art, in New York, has set itself the task of studying.

Philadelphia's problem was a different one. This city, which had been our cultural capital in the days before the Revolution and for some time after, had developed its collections rather chaotically. Besides the old Academy, which was chiefly a school and an exhibition gallery, a building left by the Centennial housed art works left to the city by certain notable collectors. Perhaps the most remarkable of them, John G. Johnson, had provided in his will that his residence become a museum. But changes in the neighborhood of the old mansion made it hazardous to leave the large group of pictures, many of them priceless, in a place that was not safe from fire. The great need was to bring together the scattered treasures in which Philadelphia was so rich, and this was finally done. A new building, in a commanding location, was erected, though its designers were strangely unmindful of the progress made in museum architecture, since the all-important matter of daylight for painting was sadly slighted. The drawbacks of the building may or may not have lost for the city one of Philadelphia's very great collections, that founded by Peter A. B. Widener and expanded by his son, who finally gave it to the National Gallery.

President Franklin D. Roosevelt welcomed the National Gallery as finally securing for Washington a cultural asset comparable to those which are the pride of European capitals. It is, once more, in its conception, and very largely in its execution, a one-man affair. For if the term "Mellon Gallery" (as it was at first generally called) is gradually being absorbed in its official and proper title, its extraordinary nuclear collection and the vast building it occupies were presented to the nation by Andrew W. Mellon. At the time it was opened, a large group of pictures from the collection of Samuel H. Kress were already included, and he has since added to his gift.

Besides the Widener paintings, and art objects which still further enriched the National Gallery, there are modern works from the Chester

Dale collection, and there is the marvelous assemblage of prints formed by Lessing J. Rosenwald. The magnificent group of works lent to America by the French government just before the World War and later shown in the Gallery, gave it, at the time, a particular attraction. A complete and splendid museum from its beginnings, it is doubtless the culmination of America's unique effort in the field, for it is more than a private collection made public, as was the case of Mrs. Jack Gardner's extraordinary possessions at Fenway Court, in Boston, or the contents of Henry C. Frick's mansion in New York. It is true that the last named of these remarkable assemblages has a fund for purchases, out of which many of the finest works have been added, since the death of Mr. Frick.

Again and again, we are brought to the same conclusion, whether we think of the great collectors just mentioned or, when looking backward, we review most of the public domain in art, what was once the private property of Henry G. Marquand, J. Pierpont Morgan, Benjamin Altman, Mr. and Mrs. H. O. Havemeyer, John D. Rockefeller, Jr. (with his gift of the Cloisters, a museum in itself), Marie Antoinette Evans, Paul J. Sachs, Grenville L. Winthrop, Martin Ryerson, Charles L. Hutchinson, Potter Palmer, Charles L. Freer, Edward D. Libbey, and numbers of others in our various cities. We are constantly reminded that our astonishing art wealth is the result of the imagination and enthusiasm of individuals. Economists tell us that the day of the vast private fortunes is over, and that the buying of such men as we saw in the past half century cannot occur again. If so, and if our museums can be built up only by the few great collections still in the homes that saw them develop, then the urgent need of museums is to achieve an ability to do by collective action what our magnates did for their personal pleasure.

The road ahead is not clear. In Philadelphia and in St. Louis, the purchase of very important works by their museums roused violent criticism on the ground that the considerable sums involved should have been devoted to the material well-being of the community. Such opposition has arisen in other places, and will arise again. A board of trustees, with or without political restraints by public officials, can never have the individual collector's freedom in buying. On the other hand, a museum expert whose entire time is given to studying the needs of his institution and the resources of the world's market for meeting these needs is in a better position to make wise choices than the men of the past (or present), whose best guide was their own preference. If a work of art lay within the field of their previous study, if it aroused their imagination (as the possessions of our great collectors clearly did), they might pay any price for it. But the same men were sometimes appealed to in vain to buy

18. Verrocchio: Lorenzo de' Medici.
Courtesy of the National Gallery of Art, Washington, D. C. (Kress Collection).

things that the foremost authorities declared to be important or even necessary.

To take only two cases: the countless persons who have stood before that supreme masterpiece of Rembrandt, the *David and Saul,* now at The Hague, can hardly credit the fact that it was brought to America for sale at a price far lower than that which one of our very rich men offered for it, too late, when it was in the firm hands of a Dutch collector. Since such a mistake could be made about a master whom our people know well, a similarly flagrant misunderstanding in the less familiar field of Greek antiquities will cause no surprise. Edward Perry Warren used amusedly to tell how he had come to Providence, Rhode Island, to supervise the placing of some sculpture he had sent to the museum. As it lay on the ground, one of the trustees said, "It looks like a lot of junk; but of course you and I know it isn't." Some doubt is permissible as to whether both of the gentlemen were quite sure that it wasn't.

But any multiplication of such anecdotes would take away nothing from the essential truth we have been arriving at in the brief survey we have made of our museum development: it is the record of a most admirable concern for the public welfare shown by a large number of Americans, and their activity has had the most splendid results. When we take up our collections in detail, we shall find them to possess quality as well as quantity such as no one in the world, a hundred years ago, or even far later, would have dared to prophesy.

But great developments are still needed. Men are studying them, and in any number of places. They do not necessarily involve questions of acquisition: indeed, small museums which will probably never have funds for important purchases may evolve ideas for the use of works of art, for the increase of communal participation in art enjoyment, and for ways of inciting and supporting the talent of living artists, above all those of the town or region involved. This achievement, desirable as it is, must not obscure the more general purpose of the museum: to let the artists themselves and the people as a whole know the best that has been done; they can then arrive at values suited to the age in which they live. Before surveying our museums themselves, to see how far they go in meeting this test, let me cite one great scholar's opinion on the subject at hand.

In 1910, Dr. Jean Paul Richter wrote in his introduction to the Mond Catalogue, "Art collections are not the outcome of accident, but of the taste, temperament, and mental equipment of the collector who, in his turn, was moulded by the spirit of the times, and limited by his opportunities . . . The history of culture abounds in examples of the influence of exotic works of art on the civilization of the countries into which they have been transplanted. It also bears eloquent witness to the indestructible power of the masterpieces of great artists of all times; misunderstood or neglected for centuries, their value has always been eventually recognized, and their message accepted as a revelation."

CHAPTER III

THE ACHIEVEMENT

THE WORD "revelation" that Dr. Richter so suggestively employed in the lines concluding the previous chapter is neither too strong nor too Biblical in connotation to characterize the effect achieved by American museum development. I said before that our art lovers revealed a deep concern for the public welfare by founding and supporting museums; the possibilities for creating collections of the highest excellence have been revealed also; above all, there is the revelation of a force that our country, as it was even a couple of generations ago, could scarcely have imagined: art as an effective influence on human affairs. The estimated number of visitors to our museums, some 20,000,000 a year, is proof of this statement, for their experiences, unknown to people of our pre-museum period, cannot be other than an influence on their thinking, and therefore their lives.

To see the truth of this last statement, we need do no more than glance at American conditions. Down to the time when the museums began to have adequate collections, and when they began to enter the general experience of our people, the material and intellectual factors in our civilization were balanced, to a degree, by spiritual forces like religion, literature and music, but not by the graphic and plastic arts. Even music was still far less generally accessible than it is today, when concerts, the phonograph, and the radio have strengthened its effect — and more through making us acquainted with the better composers than merely through the enormous increase of opportunity for hearing music. No one who believes that a people's emotional life is related to its character and conduct can doubt that our new resources for knowing and using the contents of the museum mean a change in America, and for the better.

To doubt this is to fly in the face of centuries of accumulated evidence that mankind expresses in an axiom like "Let me make the songs of a nation, and I care not who makes its laws." Bach and Beethoven outweigh Hitler and Himmler in our thinking about the Germans, even today. The Psalms have outweighed as an influence all the laws against the people who first chanted them, and all the persecutions which that people has endured. The spirituals of the American Negro reduce to silent awe the men who most bitterly oppose the granting of human rights to the black race (and I say this from actual observation in our South). Similarly, the Sphinx and the Pyramids of Egypt, the sculpture of Greece, the architecture and allied arts of medieval France impose upon the world a respect for the three nations represented by those works; and it is such admiring and grateful respect as no material achievement or intellectual prowess could account for. Hugo von Hofmannsthal, in a poem on death, says, "A great god of the soul stands before you" and, better than to death, the words apply to the force we call art.

What we had of art before the period of our museums was of course not to be compared, even distantly, with what we have today. Yet the fact that it was no inconsiderable thing, even then, is essential to remember. A glance at our Colonial painters and craftsmen suffices to prove what I had said on a previous page, that when our people came here from Europe, they were not primitives. For if they were pioneers, and without much material evidence of their descent from the cultured stock of Europe, they brought with them inherited instincts which, at a bound, could produce our great early portraitists, the splendid architects of our Colonial buildings, the silversmiths, the glassworkers, and the rest. But the gap between instinct and knowledge is a very big one. And the decline of artistic genius here, after the Colonial and early republican period, is not to be explained by the increase of material activity any more than it is to be attributed to the Revolution and our cutting off the ties to the mother countries.

No, our history shows that when we were ready to bring forth another line of creative men, like Winslow Homer and Thomas Eakins, their talent, even if inborn — as is proved by their early work — demanded renewed contact with the great arts of Europe. Whistler, Sargent, and Mary Cassatt spent most of their lives abroad. In so doing, they followed the example set by Copley and West, when they went to reside in England at an earlier period. And I am positive that all these artists remained in Europe so as to do better work. Just after the two painters of our Colonial days, Vanderlyn drew the decisive influence on his art from his years in Paris. Connecting him in time with the generation I have mentioned (to which also belonged John La Farge and Homer Martin, men who likewise derived inspiration from the Old World), we have William Morris Hunt, whose position as an artist and as a teacher is unthinkable without his contacts with the galleries of Europe and his personal influences, Couture and Millet.

Today we have a case which apparently reverses the rule just considered. Uniquely among our major artists, John Sloan has never been across the Atlantic. But his friends, Henri, Glackens, and Prendergast, had lived abroad; and it is clear that the ideas and influences which shaped their evolution were at work with Sloan also. His time was already that of the museums, the great exhibitions, and the deluge of art books and reproductions; so that he is not to be thought of as a man working only from inherited instincts such as guided the artless youth of Copley and West. Incidentally, for those who imagine that isolation from Europe — an impossible thing today — is needed for the artist to have an American character in his work, I will affirm that Prendergast, with his many visits to Paris, and with his great technical debt to the modern French school, has a Yankee tang to his painting which makes him as American as Sloan.

So that the fruit of the tree of knowledge need not here be thought of as forbidden fruit, we may join with Leonardo once again in his words, "The greater the knowledge, the greater the love," that is to say, the greater the art. Of course, in recent years the "modern primitives" — men with little or no knowledge — have enjoyed a certain vogue. From most of them people are turning away and increasingly, having found that Henri Rousseau is *sui generis*, and that only the most special form of talent does not need to develop itself through study of the masters. Those last four words sum up Renoir's definition of the training of artists, and he very specifically told where it is to be had: in the museum.

Our excursion into the history of American painters unquestionably proves that they confirm the principle uttered by Renoir: having had less of art in their surroundings than their European contemporaries, they have needed to give stricter attention to the rules (those rendered accessible in museums) than do Frenchmen, for example, who may be directed, almost unconsciously, by the pressure of the artistic atmosphere about them. When we can have the same confidence in our surroundings, and can feel that our traditions are giving us true guidance (and the sense of that sure support is the priceless heritage of the French artist, above all), then we shall develop as spontaneously, as naturally, as the men who, from birth, stand in the classical line.

What thus applies to our artists is no less true for our public in general. The development of a sense of being at home with art, of feeling it as a native, everyday force in our lives, must begin, for most people, with their visits to the museum. As the country progresses in understanding, people will derive this sense, more and more, from the things they have always known in the places where they have lived. Already, there is a responsiveness to art that was not discernible a generation ago. Children who have never set foot in the museum are today ready to see its values in a manner that their elders, at their age, were not. Ask any educator who has considered the matter, even in the parts of the country where opportunities

19. Michelangelo: Study for the Libyan Sibyl (in the Sistine Chapel).
Courtesy of The Metropolitan Museum of Art.

for experience with art are the most limited, and he will confirm the fact of our developing appreciation. The thing is in the air, which is to say that it is in the minds of our people.

The bringing about of such a condition is the real achievement of our museum builders, and their work is not to be measured in terms of so and so many examples of this master's art, so and so many institutions devoted to collecting, exhibiting, or otherwise educating. To speak of these is to discuss the means: the end to be attained resides in the character of the country. And the museum, in its really brief span of activity, has had effects there which defy any estimating today: we see them on every hand, but only with the passing of time shall we be able to point to concrete results.

Agreeing, as I hope, that the intangible achievement of our museums is the essential one, we may proceed to the actual buildings and their contents. I find at least 132 institutions, distributed through seventy-five cities in all parts of the country, worthy of serious study and, as I have said in listing them at the end of this volume, our resources in art works are not exhausted by this group of collections. Leaving aside the vast store of fine things in private hands as being unconnected with our subject at present (though such works will in most cases gravitate to the museums, in time), we omit also the large number of places which have either few objects of value, or have not yet reached the stage of discerning permanent values at all.

Let no one think, though, that such art galleries should be cast into the outer darkness. The histories of some of our greatest collectors record that they began with very poor, even absurd, pictures. Sometimes they covered up all vestiges of them when they came to understand the fine things; but in a few cases at least, they retained examples of their errors of youth as a lesson in humility; with it, one may add, went the pride of overcoming the drawbacks due to lack of opportunity in their early years. What is true of individuals applies also to communities. One hates to say that poor art works are better than none: often they are the worst obstacles to progress, since they impose a false standard, which may cause painful effort when the time comes to break its hold. But we can say that a poor museum is better than none. At least there is a center for the art interest of the community; the person with an idea knows where to turn when he wants to give his fellow citizens the benefit of his trip to Minneapolis, to Washington or New York. Or perhaps he has just been reading, and the magazine or book that fell into his hands had illustrations of works that showed up the poverty of the ones at the public gallery in his town. He convinces a group of friends that they ought to give their collection a fresh start, a modest subscription is raised by the committee he forms, and before you know it, that community is on its way to have a place worthy of the ideals so widely prevalent throughout the country.

As things stand today, many of our institutions are so far from the ideals of the intelligent people who may be found in thousands of places that the lack of connection between the gallery and those who might aid it is deplorable. Everyone interested in the subject knows such cases. Perhaps there is a college professor who sees the weakness of the museum, and is afraid to speak up because he may arouse the opposition of a rich man who has endowed both museum and the college where our professor teaches. Perhaps it is a private collector whose carefully chosen possessions make him shrink from discussion with certain tougher-minded persons who are in power, and who may cause him to be ridiculed as a highbrow or a faddist. Supposing him to be neither, and supposing that college professor to have constructive ideas and not just the intellectual smugness sometimes found among people who have had leisure for study and travel, the two typical individuals I have described are completely wrong if they do not take a hand in bettering conditions.

They may be licked the first time they start something, but the record of America shows that with the necessary ability to face resistance, the necessary faith in a worth-while effort, and the necessary tact and intelligence in presenting ideas in advance of those generally held, their fellows are not so different from themselves but that progress will be made. Sometimes it will come almost overnight: not one of us can realize how many people are privately wishing the same thing as ourselves, and need only one man's example in order to take a stand in support of him. At other times, there has got to be a development of opinion through outside influence. It may even start through one town rivaling another in its commerce or industry, and then in being more fortunate in those who direct its cultural interests. Or the evolution may depend on less easily definable causes.

I can illustrate through telling how this country grew in appreciation of a particular artist, van Gogh. There had been a number of fine showings of his work, any one of which would have been enough to convince people of his greatness — on one condition: their being ready to see his magnificent qualities. But they were not. Finally the tide turned, and the artist was acclaimed wherever a big exhibition of his work was shown. Was it really because the collection was so big? Was it, as many said, because a sensational novel based on the painter's life had just had very extensive sales? But Europe, starting off with incomparably more resistance to van Gogh, had been convinced by his art alone — long before the time of that best-seller. One museum after another, in Holland, Germany, France and other countries, was securing canvases by the master — and with no more urging by publicity than that which goes to any artist from those inconspicuous people, the critics. Was our public swayed by European critics or by the European museum directors? It hardly knew of their existence, and to talk of the immense number of people who enjoyed the exhibition in question as influenced by these factors is as far from the truth as the cynical joke that the one thing needed to make the show a complete success was a glass case containing the ear that van Gogh cut off in a fit of exasperation and despair.

The explanation of people's change of attitude must be sought in workings of the mind far more complex than those indicated by any among the various circumstances just enumerated. As with the swing of public opinion in wartime or in politics, we were witnessing the effect of underground currents or, as they are sometimes called, ground swells; few persons could be aware of them until the general movement of thought had revolved to a point where it burst forth as the conviction of an overwhelming majority. To have told those people, only a few years before, that they would come to such ideas would have seemed like telling them the impossible. And, a hundred years ago, telling people they would have such art possessions as ours would have seemed likewise to talk of the impossible.

If America has museums, it is because, in widely separated places, we have brought forth a succession of men who have sensed in themselves the need of art, and who have had such belief in their communities as made them credit others with thinking as good as their own. Many of them lived to see their judgment confirmed by enthusiastic support from their cities of the museums they founded. It is a pity that artists — especially those who die young — cannot witness the devotion of later periods to their work. With them as individuals, as with museums in the matter of art as a whole, time alone is needed to bring about acceptance, and sometimes far fewer years than were first imagined. The example of what seemed a sudden change of mind about van Gogh may serve to make clear what appears, on the surface, to be a sudden growth of museums in America. We need to see both phenomena as the result of gradual development from within. The statistics on our many hundreds of institutions and the expenditure of a great many millions of dollars that I cited from Mr. Coleman's book in my first chapter, have greater significance, moreover, than the acceptance of a single new artist, even one of van Gogh's immense talent. In his case, I have given my reasons for seeing our evolution as the result of a necessary change of ideas; and in the mat-

20. Raphael: The Alba Madonna.
Courtesy of the National Gallery of Art, Washington, D. C. (Mellon Collection).

ter of museums, it is far and away more certain that only an instinct for art, latent within us during our early days but ready to come to fruition at the right moment, can explain the quite consistent and determined effort which this country has devoted to museums for over a century.

The material results of that effort — the great number of fine works of all kinds to be seen in many of our cities — make one want to go on at once to the objects themselves. But before doing so, I am compelled to pause once more over an element in those small museums omitted from my list. The work of local artists, which friendly fellow townsmen have hung in a public place, may appear pretty dull to some visitor accustomed to looking for masterpieces. For such a person, let me borrow the story, which Van Wyck Brooks retells, of a conversation between Matthew Arnold and Sainte-Beuve. The English critic had said that Lamartine was not an important poet, to which the Frenchman replied, "Ah, but he is important to us." The remark of that great student of literature was not a form of chauvinism. It meant that the poet had certain things to say which — unimportant for a foreign audience — were of deep concern to the people of his own land. A writer of first-rate genius would, it is true, have given to such ideas a universal appeal to which Matthew Arnold would not have failed to respond.

But as a composer often builds his great symphonies on the material furnished him by folk tunes, the naive little songs and dances of country people, so a painter will use the observation of landscape or human beings that he inherits from his predecessors, men who may be of small value in themselves; in the hands of the major artist, these seemingly humble things develop to the point of deep expression. That explains why we now find more of interest in certain works of our Hudson River school than we did, say a generation ago. We were not wrong then in seeing the pictures as rather uninspired performances; we are not wrong now in seeing in them the possibilities of an important art expressing the special look of our country, and profiting by the sincerity (even if a weakly expressed sincerity) evidenced by those earlier men. Similarly, and in the field of things already accomplished, the fine portraits of Copley were prepared for by many an old limner, who, in his day, gave a crabbed but striking record of the faces of New England worthies; and John Vanderlyn produced his superb work partly because there was an earlier artist of his name, Pieter Vanderlyn, if that attribution is correctly given to certain stiff and harsh paintings that have come down to us.

Evidently, the character of these primitives is entirely distinct from that of our provincials of today. Yet the two types are to be approached in the same fashion. We came to enjoy those early men through receptiveness toward painting or sculpture that is unskilled, or inadequately grounded in a study of the masters, or that lacks contact with any creative school. Let an open-minded person approach the present-day men outside the big centers in the same spirit as that which led us to admire our "primitives," and there will result the pleasure to be derived from minor artists of genuine talent; their number may well run, throughout the country, into the thousands.

Raising my eyes from this page, I see on my walls the work of several of such painters. They are so good that only when using the exacting discrimination of the critic would one speak of them as "minor"; they are artists; and, most often, that is enough to say. There is nothing in common between them and certain accomplished but empty producers of work that has at times been accepted as "American," perhaps to disguise the fact that it is in reality no more than bad European. Such censure, both of the artists and the "appreciators," is pretty direct, as I am well aware. But it does not go a bit too far, in view of what is no less than a belittling of the whole country: and that is an accurate phrase for what is done when bad work is held up as "American." The circumstance that it usually deals with American themes is of course quite irrelevant: we are not discussing the landscape or other features of this country, but the pictures — and their painters. "Name them!" was the crisp injunction that an old friend of mine, a lawyer, used to come out with, on occasions like this one. Sometimes one should indeed be specific, but in a book like the present one, I believe it preferable to let any reader who feels so disposed do the naming by himself.

If you grant that inferior works have been received into our galleries on an ill-founded claim that they were "important to us," as Sainte-Beuve put it, you may still ask, "How could we have distinguished them from the genuine things which, even if admittedly less than master work, you were defending a moment ago?" The question really means, "How are we to distinguish a work of art?" For what the bad pictures referred to essentially lack are the constant and permanent qualities of art. Matters as important as those, and alleged to be well decided, ought to be available for reference, like the laws in the statute books. And so they are, these laws of art, only (and again as with our national or state laws) — questions of interpretation arise. In the great majority of art questions, as in most legal questions, a glance at the authorities is enough. But sometimes there come before us problems that were not provided for in our code; or again a case arises in which equally honest contestants claim to see quite opposing results, when the accepted precedents are laid in the balance.

To be more specific, there is the always new question of modern art
— with most of its practitioners destined for rejection, while others will
be added to the roll of the masters; how are we to tell them apart? And in
the second class of cases I have proposed, how are we to tell whether a
newly discovered "Vermeer" is really a sensational addition to the scant
list of the great painter's works, or a shameless (if skillful) forgery? Where
are your vaunted "authorities," your law and your prophets?

The answer is very simple: in the museums (see the supplementary
list at the back of this book, as far as the art resources of the United
States are concerned.) And no statement about those arbiters of
decision, those museums of our country, is more weighty than this one;
that the idea of art deriving from them is no less than identical with the
idea of art afforded by the great ancient museums and monuments of the
Old World. The men who have built up our galleries have given us very
ample material for arriving at a dependable knowledge of art, even if we
could still use many more documents than we have. Since the basic
things in human nature do not change from century to century, and since
the essentials of art change no more than the race, whose deeper instincts
and ideals they express, the one question we need to ask ourselves is not
among those asked just before: in facing an issue of art, ancient or modern, the question is whether we have looked deeply enough into the
classic works. All of truth is there; and it is not I who am laying down the
law; to give but one example: Renoir uttered the words, "There is nothing
outside the classics." But even as he did, immediately after saying that,
we must recall the necessity of being able to recognize the classics, for
they often appear in forms that were previously unknown.

After making so big a claim for the significance of our museums, we
may at last go on to a review of their contents. Exclusion from them
might seem to be the lot of one of the supreme arts of mankind, which is
architecture. (For the moment, I leave aside reproductions, like models
of buildings, casts, and photographs.) But there have been coming into
our museums, especially in recent years, considerable fragments of architecture such as Gothic portals, with columns, sculpture from the actual
buildings, and other significant pieces from the great old cities. And so,
persons of educated and lively imagination can, in their minds, reconstruct ensembles. It must not be forgotten that no work of art is absolutely complete in itself: a painting by Dürer which seems so perfect that
nothing could be added to it was perhaps once part of an altar, which was
part of a chapel; and you did not get the full effect, even of the Dürer,
until you saw that chapel in connection with a larger whole, the buildings
of which it was but a single unit. Or, restricting oneself just to the picture,

21. Bronzino: Vittoria Colonna.
Courtesy of the M. H. de Young Memorial Museum, San Francisco.

we know how the masters borrowed from one another, and it may well be that you cannot appreciate thoroughly the work in question, seemingly so independent of everything else, until you have seen what a certain figure in the composition owes to a sketch that Dürer made from something by Bellini or Raphael.

More important yet, since an artist's whole life is a process of attempting to surpass his former achievement, one needs to know the relation of a given performance to what, in the master's career, went before it and to what came after it. We thought we knew him, after years of loving study; all at once we find him different (usually better) than what we thought, for the sight of a work unknown to us before amplifies our comprehension, and affects every element in it.

With such a conception of our necessary completing of the impressions from art objects of every kind, one may agree that architecture, with all its dependence on size, light, and a thousand other circumstances, may yet create a part of its effect through the fragments that our museums can show. In the Metropolitan Museum in New York, a thrilling example of this is a small bit of marble broken from the egg-and-dart decoration of the Erechtheum. To watch the light move in that translucent material, to see the trace of the stone-cutter's chisel as he worked, now with a long regular plane, as in the "dart," now with sensitive, curving planes, as in the "egg," is to follow the course of the Greek architect at the very height of his country's glory; for he himself worked in masses of moving light and shadow, dividing them up and reuniting them as in that small fragment, by firm, clear lines and by subtle, unseizable transitions which no later men (not even those of the time just after his own) could use again. Emerson said that the universe globes itself in a drop of dew. Evidently that is the truth only for the person whose mind can grasp such a relationship; and the ability to rebuild as a mental image the wonderful thing that was the Erechtheum in the fifth century B.C. is not to be achieved at a blow; but the effort to reach it (if "effort" is the right word for so joyous an experience) is well rewarded.

To see again the close relationship of sculpture and architecture, glance now at the throne (or altar) in the Boston Museum, an object of such importance that with it we equaled the achievement of the Museo delle Terme in Rome when it acquired the famous Ludovisi throne. The design of the work as a whole is the work of an architect; the carving of the figures on the sides is sculpture. And if we grasp the fact that the two arts are inseparable here, we have made a step, at least, toward understanding the closeness to architecture of the Italian frescoes which we possess, for they were a necessary part of their buildings. In many cases, the buildings were indeed conceived from the start as being illuminated by the painter's work on walls which, without such aid, would have had their severe spaces diversified by architectural ornament. Mention of that minor craft, if it may be so designated, brings us back to our idea that all forms of art have the same source. The beauty of architectural ornament during the Renaissance causes us to remember that men turned from vast frescoes to paintings of a miniature fineness or to the work of the gold-smith. Once again we have proof of the truth in those Roman words affirming that art is one thing. If I am dividing it up by means of the several techniques it employs, I do so to bring a semblance of order into this survey of material covering the entire world.

To attempt a description of the collections of classical art in our two chief museums would be to expose oneself to overmuch of temptation in a book of this compass. Two general observations must be made. One is that precisely the institutions which have had the longest experience of their problem, and the greatest opportunity to deal with it, are the ones which exhibit with incomparably the greatest fullness the arts of Greece and Rome. For centuries looked on as the foundation and chief support of European (including American) thought, it is significant that, as our museums reach maturity, the classic works should again receive such attention. The other point may be summed up in the observation made by a Viennese student, on first seeing our collections: "In Europe, we have huge quantities of objects that have been deposited in the museums from time to time, when great private collections have entered our galleries, or when the results of excavations have been acquired there. Of course there are tremendously important things amid this mass of material; but here I see careful selection, to bring out by appropriate examples the various developments among these arts, with regard also for types of execution and of subject matter. There is little repetition, and an astonishingly wide field is covered."

Applying also to the policy of American curators in assembling collec-tions of paintings, prints, and other art works, the remarks of our visitor were especially true of the classical objects referred to at the moment. The words quoted describe, to a great extent, the advantage of a sys-tematic building up of a museum, in contrast to the chance purchasing (even when most happy in its result) characteristic of individual collec-tions. And the desire to make our possessions in the classical field illustra-tive of historical and aesthetic evolution has not prevented our obtaining things which, seen in isolation, are of surpassing importance. Among these, mention may be made of the seventh-century statue of a youth, in the Metropolitan's hall of the earlier Greek arts; it is to be classed with the chief examples of its type anywhere in the world. Now consider the Cesnola collection of Cypriote antiquities in the same museum. It is unequaled for works of such provenance, and recalls the results in European galleries, of excavations like that which General di Cesnola conducted when he was the American consul in Cyprus. To pass on from even the limited part of the collection now shown, and to stand before the great archaic figure referred to just before, is to realize the aptness of that Viennese observer's noting of the difference between possessing quantity (a most valuable thing in its allowing a subject to be viewed from many sides) and possessing single, carefully selected objects of outstanding merit.

At the same museum, once more, there is no lack of other pieces of a very high order, some of them among the small archaic works, others of large dimension and riper development. Such a one is the fifth-century male torso, which, though a mere fragment, is yet charged with the liberating power that permits a competent student to complete it in his mind. Seeing it by this means as it was twenty-four centuries ago, one great authority insists that it is from the hand of Phidias himself. Certainly we have something very near to what we know of the work of Scopas in the head of a youth in warmly colored marble. A fragment from a grave stele shows us sculpture in the round as Greece knew it at the highest point of her development; another work, the head of a young goddess, gives us again the strong wine that only the originals of Hellas can offer, while important marbles of Roman workmanship allow us at least to glimpse certain lost works of the older school, especially those of Polyclitus. An entire court, suggested by such places in ancient buildings, reviews the sculpture of purely Roman conception; the examples of the Republican period, when portraiture was at its finest, are particularly fortunate.

We turn again to Boston, and see fourth-century works like the lovely *Maiden of Chios*, and another girl's head of the highest quality that Greece knew at the time of Praxiteles. Enthralling as they are, they still do not attain the impressiveness of a sculpture representing a woman's head, perhaps that of a goddess, and doubtless but little later than the Elgin marbles; it has that same unapproachable beauty which distinguishes the masterpieces from the Parthenon. At the dawn of the art which was to reach that culmination stands one of the great rarities among Boston's treasures: a small figure from Crete, one of the few originals of importance to leave the island.

Something comparable to its primitive fecundity is seen again in New York when we reach the three Etruscan works representing warriors, and the chariot entirely covered with reliefs in bronze, where similar figures

22. Caravaggio: Portrait of a Lady.
Courtesy of the Museum of Fine Arts, San Diego.

appear. The discovery of the giant sculptures in the round was one of the outstanding events in recent archeology; no other museum, save one in Rome, can show such pieces. And again a unique exhibit from Italian soil is the series of frescoes found at a villa near Herculaneum. Save at neighboring Pompeii and Naples, no such works are to be seen anywhere in the world; so that many a European artist, coming to our country without having visited southern Italy, has been struck by the opportunity offered by New York for knowing what the art of painting was among the Greeks. Of its earlier periods, everything has vanished; and it is only through the incredible preservation of the two towns at the foot of Vesuvius that we have the source of inspiration these works afford. For, more impressive than their rarity or the miracle of their very existence, is their value as art. We return to them when we have studied the greatest achievements of European painting from its renascence, a thousand and more years after Pompeii, through its development in the centuries that followed, and until today: the perfection with which the Greeks mastered the art seems only the more astounding. Their vision continues in the related, if less free forms of ancient mosaics, such as are to be seen in splendid examples from Antioch, in the collections of the Worcester Museum and the Baltimore Museum.

With these works, we are reaching out to sources of art beyond the limits of our chief ancestral countries, those of Europe. Still intimately related to them is Egypt, which exercised a power of fascination for Americans during a considerable part of our history. That led them, as we have seen it do also in Cyprus, to original work in exploring and preserving the heritage of the past. Results of this are to be seen in the Metropolitan's fine collections from the ancient land of the Nile. A tomb of massive stone blocks, transported to our shores and set up again as it was in Egypt, bears witness to the static genius of the mighty civilization; it is again an example in our museums of important specimens of architecture. Entire walls, with incised and painted decoration, magnificent sculpture in the round or in relief, statuettes of a perfection that only Egypt knew (seen also in the master models of her sculptors), ceramics, jewelry, and other art forms round out the story of the race whose span of existence exceeds all others.

As is so often the case in the arts, supreme examples of Egyptian culture are found at a very early stage in its evolution. Of these greatest marvels, as most authorities regard them, the museum of Boston displays a large group. It aroused the especial enthusiasm of Julius Meier-Graefe, when that distinguished critic visited this country, soon after a sojourn in Egypt which led him to consider its art as the summit of all human effort.

These Mycerinus sculptures, of the first historic period of the great land, usher in a succession of grand works, and we follow their course from millennium to millennium until, with the invasion of Alexander, Greek influences merge with the older ones to produce an art uniting the two continents. The incredibly living portraits of this last Egypt are to be seen at their best in a group belonging to the Metropolitan. Again it is our two chief museums which afford by far the widest opportunity in America to enjoy Egyptian art.

If a patriotic Egyptian of today were to oppose a mention of those portraits from the Fayum region as marking the final subsiding of his country, the reply would be that Christianity inaugurates an era so completely creative that the beautiful art of the Copts, even though produced in the ancient land, owes most to the new impulses in human life. With all the rare quality it draws from the age-old traditions of Egypt, it is still only a provincial expression of the genius which centered at Byzantium and there produced the first masterpieces of the new era. They are largely in the form of great mosaics, which must perforce remain on the walls at Istanbul and the other places for which they were created. That precludes our having them in our museums; yet we may claim credit for their being restored to the world, since Americans were active in persuading the Turkish government to allow the removal of the whitewash applied when Islam decreed the covering up of the great images. We added to the museum record we had made abroad when our scholars and workmen helped to give the stupendous mosaics back to the world. (Not to return to the question too often, let a few others among our achievements in conservation be mentioned here. They include such widely separated sites as those of the Agora in Athens, Rheims and Versailles in France, and the ancient cities of the Mayas in Yucatan.)

Admirable copies of the Santa Sophia mosaics in Istanbul were exhibited at the Metropolitan, and had as one of their results an increase of our realization that the enamels in the Morgan collection at the same museum, and also of a Byzantine school, were possessions of simply inestimable importance. Small in size and in number, the changeless glow of their material carries on across the centuries the wonder that occurred when the spirituality of the early Christians united with the Orient's love of color. Other, and magnificent examples of Byzantine art are to be seen at Dumbarton Oaks in Washington, where Harvard University conducts courses for advanced students.

We see this quality in ceramics, rugs, Persian illumination, textiles, and other expressions of the "abstract" genius of peoples who care more for the aesthetic properties, color and design, than for a full representing of appearances. Rich stores of their work appear in a number of our museums. Among them mention may be made of the Iranian Institute in New York, and the Philadelphia Museum, with its ensembles of Near Eastern art.

Such matters bring us to quite modern times; but now our geographic progression takes us back to an age as remote as the oldest Egypt. The Mesopotamian lands, which saw the mighty civilization of the Sumerians or Chaldeans, have yet to give back to the world their most important production. The Louvre, until now the incomparable repository for such art, still points to work more impressive than any that we know today. The University of Pennsylvania, at the University Museum, in Philadelphia, has a good number of remarkable minor works of this art, obtained through its own researches; Boston has a head of the finest type like those in Paris; but on the whole, our institutions are poor in Babylonian material. The same must be said, however, of the British and German museums.

The Assyrians, who followed the Chaldeans at a later time, can be better studied in our collections. Their grandiose production may be appreciated in an important group of sculptures at the Metropolitan, and I have shown (p. 44) the wide distribution of such material at our old centers of theological study; they display objects from the same vast palace that sent to the British Museum and the Louvre their wonderful examples of Assyrian art.

Going farther into Asia, we are beginning to get a conception of India's artistic genius through the expert research and collecting of the Boston Museum, and through work being done by the galleries of New York, Chicago, Kansas City, and other places. If the viewing of life, religion, and art thereby revealed seems distant, and alien to our own, the creative role of the museum is rendered only the clearer for that reason. Should we indeed allow ourselves to make decisions as to a superiority on the part of one culture or the other (and the result of art study tends to destroy the notion that differences mean either superiority or the reverse), at least we should be judging on the first-hand evidence of work that leaps over the barriers of language, time, and space.

These barriers are formidable when we approach that world-in-itself which China may easily appear to be. Yet it is with notable success that our institutions have faced the immense span of centuries, and the vast spaces covered by this faraway art. To be sure, commercial importation had for hundreds of years familiarized us with certain of the later production of the country, and at Dresden, at Delft, in England, in France, and in Mexico, ceramics were produced under the influence of the Chinese.

23. Giovanni Bellini: The Feast of the Gods.
Courtesy of the National Gallery of Art, Washington, D. C. (Widener Collection).

Meticulousness was denoted in French by a special use of the word chinois, while in a different allusion to the race, chinoiseries were decorative works, usually with an element of the grotesque, based on the design and material of Chinese lacquer and porcelain; they were also produced by English craftsmen. Of all such work, European as well as Oriental, there is a very wide representation in our museums, often those of old seaports that once traded with the East.

But knowledge of what were, in reality, decadent arts of China rendered all the more astonishing the contact, reserved for the nineteenth and twentieth centuries, with the great classical schools which now determine our thought of the ancient people. Its expression in masterpieces, traced back to ever more remote periods, is accessible to students in the galleries of a goodly number of our cities. Observation of their visitors will furnish very ample testimony to the fact that we have long since passed the stage represented by Horatio Greenough when he spoke of Oriental art as the ideal of ugliness (thereby merely sharing the opinion of innumerable Europeans, including some in high places). "The greater the knowledge, the greater the love" is the true phrase returning to one's lips still another time when we see the crowds that enjoy the rooms displaying China's grand sculpture, her majestically proportioned bronze vessels, and her endlessly varied ceramics.

For our progress along these lines, or certainly for the pioneer work in it, we have to look again to Boston's great collections. Other cities are forging ahead, however, under the spur of our eager enthusiasm for Chinese art — a field so wide that we do not need to pause over claims for pre-eminence made for one museum or another, according as it has developed its holdings among the periods covered by this school. In Boston, again, the early prominence of Japanese experts, among those who developed the collections there, explains the emphasis on the art of the island empire. Yet, if the latter's monumental sculpture and classical painting do not equal the Chinese models for such work, they have certain qualities of their own, and the humbler art of the Japanese print was a real creation. It has been widely appreciated in our country, and the color prints are to be found in important groups throughout our cities. Often, indeed, Japanese collectors have bought back, at American auctions, examples of their art which had been sought for here during the time when native connoisseurship had been at fault, and had allowed too important specimens to depart to the West.

That phenomenon occurred when Japan, having been opened up to Occidental ideas after long centuries of isolation, came to attach to European art such value as made the country tend to become oblivious to the beauty of the things which had sprung from its own soil. If there is excuse for such a mistake, it *is* one, nevertheless. We can see this very plainly about a distant people, but we do not so easily see it about a people nearer home — in fact, the Americans.

This term, which usually denotes the inhabitants of the United States, has however been universally employed in a wider sense by Spain and her former colonies, and for centuries. It is their very correct word for all the peoples of America — which is indeed a far bigger and older place than the United States. The great monumental arts of the older America were produced in the lands to the south of our border; but some of the most poignant expressions of the American soil are those which saw the light in our own part of the continent. I shall have more to say of this question on later pages. Our present concern is with museums, and so I must register a fact which, to many of us, means only one thing: that we have very seriously underestimated our resources. The fact is, then, that in most cases our museums of art are not the ones where we have been keeping magnificent native works which look back to the long past of the land before the white man saw it. For the art of our ancient peoples, one must usually go to the museums of natural history, which the original Americans enter for reasons of anthropology, a somewhat superior branch of zoology.

Because of this placing I have included institutions of science in the supplementary list. Fortunately, there are certain museums devoted wholly to art which devote space to the works containing our pre-Columbian heritage. Some of it is very much alive today, as with the Indians of our Southwest. They have indeed been bringing forth painting and pottery of renewed and creative vitality, thanks in part to help which they have had from museums like that of Santa Fe, New Mexico, and to officials of the Department of the Interior at Washington. Thus, in the strictest interpretation of the institution we are considering, the art of the Indians comes within its purview; for if there is one point where museums are important, it is in their influence on living art. Even when we come to peoples now dispersed or killed off, we are still dealing with art of such quality that it stands comparison with the finest of the Old World. I regret that Meier-Graefe, when in this country, did not visit the Ohio State Museum, at Columbus. Having been in Egypt only a short time before, he was still under the spell of its greatness, as was noted previously; he would none the less (or perhaps, all the more) have felt the kinship of genius between the men who fashioned the old Egyptian hawks, dogs, and other beasts, and the old Ohio men who carved the same animals for their delight — and ours.

As for the mighty things of the Aztecs, the Toltecs, the Mayas, and the other great peoples of the lands to the south of us, we need no art critic to tell us that they are on the plane reached by Chaldea and Assyria and the China of the classic arts. Lately, a painter, seeing the photograph of an Aztec head at Harvard's Fogg Museum, exclaimed, "Why, it's just like the archaic Greek!" And similar thoughts come even to laymen who visit the collections of the Museum of Natural History and the Museum of the American Indian in New York, the Brooklyn Museum, the University Museum in Philadelphia, the Detroit Institute of Arts, the Chicago Museum of Natural History, the Minneapolis Institute of Arts, the Museum of Tulane University in New Orleans or indeed any of our collections where the ancient art of America is adequately displayed.

Also to be seen mainly in museums of natural science are the arts of the African Negroes and of the South Sea islanders. Yet the work of the first-named group exercised an important influence on modern art, and that of the second is being discovered as a thing of enormous expressiveness; the same is true of certain creations of the Eskimo, a race which, of course, connects America with Asia and Europe.

Mention of the latter continent, to which most of our people trace their descent, leads to the statement of a belief increasingly held by students, even among those who have looked with intelligence at the wonderful things of the exotic races. No breach of modesty occurs if we affirm that it is in Europe, after all, that art attains its highest development. I say this without opposing an idea once expressed in admirable words by Egisto Fabbri, who was as important for his thinking on art as for his own production in painting and architecture. He said that very frequently the most impressive art is the one which comes earliest in the history of a people, with the so-called primitives. He illustrated this idea by the particular grandeur of the oldest books of the Bible and the awe-inspiring quality in the oldest arts of Egypt. The observation holds again when we come to the first great expressions of Italy and France. And so Mr. Fabbri had a firm basis for his differentiation of science and art: the former piles its attainment always higher through cumulative effort, while the latter may soar to its loftiest flight at its beginnings, which no successors to the founders of the school can equal. Therefore I did not speak of the art we now approach in our museums as the grandest, but as the one which has been brought to the highest development.

European painting, as rather few men have noticed, partakes of both the mental activities described by the Italo-American artist I have just recalled: it has a scientific character as well as an aesthetic one. Perhaps that double virtue, shared by no other school to any similar degree, gives

24. Titian: The Rape of Europa.
Courtesy of the Isabella Stewart Gardner Museum, Boston.

to our art its peculiar vitality and its mysterious richness. Therefore our museums have a strong argument for studying the historical evolution of European painting. Since we are speaking of art museums, the criterion of first importance is, of course, the art in painting. It is this which has primarily occuped the minds of our officials, as we must recognize even when we think of their judgment as faulty. I am under no illusion about there being any finality in my own judgment, but at least I have attempted to consider our collections from the standpoint of their artistic soundness.

A splendidly high level has been attained in them, as should be affirmed from the outset. The condition did not come about all at once: no one who can recall the look of our galleries as they were, say forty years ago, will fail to agree that their progress in quantity of possessions, extraordinary as it is, nowhere nearly equals their rise in the scale of quality. One need not go back even half of these forty years to remember on our walls pictures that would not be tolerated for a week, if they were hung again today. Protests would come spontaneously from artists and laymen, collectors and critics. The museums, incomparably more than any other agency, have been building up in our public a sense of what is valid — and to a degree that no one would have ventured to prophesy. As this section of the present book is entitled "The Achievement," it seems clear that the state of affairs I have just described is to be written large into the record. And this is of course worlds away from any thought that the process has gone far enough.

But it is high time to pass on to at least the most salient of our possessions among the paintings themselves. Far more than sculpture, they are that expression of art which has chiefly fascinated American buyers. Even so, and with the outlay of prodigious sums of money, by far the larger part of the master work in painting still remains across the Atlantic, and also the best of it. The galleries of Europe had a long start over ours, and were from the beginning enormously closer to the sources of great works, not to mention frescoes and other decorations which must always remain in the places where they were painted. Coming, however, to nineteenth- and twentieth-century painting, in collecting which we began on equal terms with the Europeans, it is possible to see certain phases of the great modern development that may be studied in America as well if not better than abroad. Once again, comparisons are odious; besides, Frenchmen might say that when they let their modern works depart, it was after extracting from them what was essential, and that as the possessors of a living art, their real concern was to assimilate its qualities, and not simply to own certain rectangles of framed canvas.

Our very success in collecting modern art brings up, however, buying

problems that may as well be faced here. The argument of French collectors in defending themselves for letting masterpieces leave their country
is not to be divorced from the money side of the matter — from, in short,
the buying problems just mentioned. This observation may seem to
accord with the sneering of a certain type of persons — in Europe, Latin-
America, and elsewhere — who have dubbed our country "the land of the
dollar." But the money we have been sending abroad for art works, this
last hundred years or so, is not the significant part of the matter.

Barye remained poor, and so you may, if you like, interpret his words
of gratitude to William Walters on a material basis, though, to an artist
of his grand character, the American collector's insight into the beauty of
his work was probably what counted most. Millet, also in need of money
as he usually was, could not have been indifferent to the financial support
given him by William Morris Hunt; but what is even more certain to
anyone able to appreciate that "man out of the Bible" (Théophile Sil-
vestre's description of Millet) is that the painter cared most of all for the
encouragement that a talented colleague gave him at a time when but
few realized his greatness. We have heard the words of Courbet when the
Boston artists and collectors raised their subscription to buy The Quarry:
they tell far more about his triumph over hostile criticism and the stupid-
ity of the Salon than about the money he got. Corot, Manet, and
Cézanne, to name three others who had early and important aid from
America, were men of means; so that what was essential to them was
certainly the moral support with which to face the attacks constantly
leveled at their art.

All of this adds up to a conviction that what we really did, as regards
these artists, was to offer an example of creative connoisseurship not
unworthy of the best traditions of Europe. When a special pride of its
princes was their ability to obtain the finest art works of their time, they
did so less by money than by a species of judgment that testifies to a
patron's affinity with the artists, and to his being worthy to have their
work within his walls. Moreover, during the period of the Old Masters,
things were simpler for a painter. All he had to do was excel in his work.
Raphael and Titian had rivals, as we know, but it was among great men —
who had nothing in common with the false artists so generally accepted
throughout the nineteenth century. Their hold on the juries of exhibitions, on commissions for official portraits or decorations, and on the
museums, was almost absolute. It remains so in too many quarters even
today, but when Renoir and Degas, Pissarro and Sisley appeared, they had
to struggle amid a mass of spurious productions such as we find in no
time throughout the period of the Old Masters.

Samuel P. Avery, our commissioner to the Paris Exposition of 1867, had done yeoman service in educating our public to appreciate the great Frenchmen of the romantic period. He had helped in obtaining master-pieces for the Walters and Vanderbilt collections, and had presented to the New York Public Library his own collection of prints, numbering well over 17,000 items. But it was only when Durand-Ruel launched the work of the great Impressionists in America that the turning point in their fight for recognition was reached. Before that, however, two of our artists, William M. Chase and J. Alden Weir, had gone to Manet's studio and bought from him the *Girl with a Parrot* and the *Boy with a Sword*. They had been commissioned to get pictures for a New York lawyer, Erwin Davis, who soon afterward presented the two magnificent works to the Metropolitan — at a time when every other museum in the world still shut its doors against the great painter.

The story continued, with ever more emphasis on the appreciation of contemporary work in this country. And so in 1913, American collectors were simply following along their own road when they bought all four of the pictures that Marcel Duchamp exhibited at the Armory Show. The painter did not have the immense European reputation which rendered easier our acceptance of Barye, Courbet, and Manet. It was on its merits that Duchamp's work was acquired; the buyers wanted it for their study and enjoyment, as I know personally, having been in charge of sales at the exhibition. In one case, the purchase was made by a man of modest means, for whom the money meant a sacrifice. The fact belongs in the record of our museums, since all four of the Duchamp pictures are now in public collections. And if the most striking examples of the American attitude toward buying are those concerned with modern art, where reli-ance on one's own judgment is more necessary than with works which have stood the test of time, the characterization here given still holds when we observe many of our collectors of the older arts.

Yet, the most remarkable performance of all was not with the ancients, but with the moderns, for they were the always more compelling interest of that farsighted student of politics and finance, literature and art, John Quinn. A successful lawyer, he had every reason to believe that his large earnings would continue; but the point is that he put every cent of them into his collection, and, at his death, it was necessary to take drastic measures with the twenty-two hundred works he owned for his estate to amount to anything at all. Thanks to the general level of appre-ciation in this country, the paintings and sculpture were sold for what seemed a considerable sum, which would today seem a very small sum for Quinn's superb treasury of the great moderns.

25. El Greco: Christ at Gethsemane.
Courtesy of The Toledo Museum of Art, Toledo.

It is not for the sake of our patriotic pride that I recount such facts, but for their relation to museum policy. If it were proper for our galleries to speculate on the winners in the grand handicap race for high prices, we might garnish our records with sensational rises in the market. That is, however, one aspect of the matter that does not concern the museum — rightly understood — or the good private collector either. Both buy from conviction, irrespective of the passing whims of fashion or commerce. It is when we approach master work (about which conviction must be strongest) that we come to very important factors in a program for acquisitions.

A museum's purchasing policy may set itself the goal of stimulating the public or that of developing broadly representative collections. The small museum, which cannot hope to have a sufficient number of works to cover the whole field of art, may well decide to use its resources for acquiring a relatively few paintings, pieces of sculpture, etc., but such as will most effectively stir the visitors' admiration. Indeed, even in a large collection, like that formed by Andrew W. Mellon, it is clear that he concentrated on masterpieces. A too easy observation made by visitors to the National Gallery is that the Kress contributions do not equal the Mellon in quality. But Mr. Kress was not competing for sensational possessions. Although many of his pictures are of the highest importance, the ideal of collecting they represent is a rounded vision of the various periods under study.

This distinction — masterpieces only or a rounded vision — is to be noted in the purchasing done by a number of our best museums. It should not be confused with the thing that a stamp collector does when he tries to cover all the blank spaces in his album. We do have buying of that mechanical type, just as we have men whose purchases arise from snobbery, prestige hunting, a desire to make their names live on after their deaths, the mere competitive instinct, and other causes of no interest here — or anywhere else, save for the individuals concerned. But if American — as well as foreign — museums have in the long run reaped profit from even quite unpleasant traits among their benefactors, our concern at present is with the way we have developed collections of general and not merely personal interest.

The buying of a work far below the masterpiece class may be of great importance for the understanding of a historical evolution. With what a thrill does one discover, at the museum of Brussels, the relatively insignificant pictures by the teachers of Rubens, whose rise to dazzling heights becomes far more explicable when one sees how much was done to prepare his flight. I return also to the idea of European art as a thing having some of the elements of a science. The constant preoccupation of the Chinese with pure beauty is accompanied by a willingness to resume the course of his ancestors — if an Occidental, speaking under correction, may so express the idea. It would explain what for so many of us is a lack of live evolution in their art, a "monotonous grandeur," as even an Oriental, Okakura Kakuzo, the brilliant Japanese critic, expressed the matter.

If to the sense of beauty and to the study of the classics is added research into aspects of nature and vision that have not previously appeared in art, we have that attitude of the scientist which is so characteristic among European artists, and which has restored movement to their schools at moments when perfect attainment seemed about to cause stagnation. Often it takes time before we can appreciate the aesthetic value of a man who at first seemed merely to advance scientific knowledge. Thus, the old Italian writers dwell on the discovery of perspective by Paolo Uccello who, to modern art lovers, is simply one of the very great men of painting, and that because of the beauty of his work. People tend to underestimate Claude Monet because he gave such intense study to the phenomena of light; but his wide production contains a large majority of pictures possessing indubitable aesthetic value.

Among American artists represented in our museums, three may be mentioned in this connection; significantly enough, all of them were great teachers. Only in recent times have people realized that S. F. B. Morse was an admirable painter, and not just the man who gave us telegraphy. Then there is Dr. William Rimmer, who was long thought of only for his knowledge of anatomy. His own drawings and sculptures are eloquent of this absorbing interest. But certain figures he produced are of a largeness, almost a grandeur of conception, that goes beyond the statement of scientific facts; and there are paintings by him that show his feeling for a very real, even moving, though sober beauty.

There is a more general understanding today of Thomas Eakins, the third of these artists. He delighted in the society of scientific men, and shared the curiosity for new discovery that was so strong in his period of great inventors and speculators on natural phenomena. There are works by Eakins where the position of the oar, propelling a racing scull, is figured out in mathematical diagrams that the painter preserved, with obvious satisfaction in his accuracy. Again, we know how tireless he was in his attendance at hospitals where he could work in the dissecting rooms, and form his mind on the structural secrets of men and animals, separating muscles and bones quite as a surgeon does. Photography was one of the developing studies, during the lifetime of Eakins, and he was of those who made new researches with it, at one moment standing on the verge of giving us the motion picture camera as it was later evolved. Later on, Bryson Burroughs, probably the real discoverer of Eakins' importance, used to remark on the absolutely photographic look of the little waves in the painting of *The Swimming Hole*, now in the museum of Fort Worth, Texas. For most of the earlier commentators on Eakins, all such matters as I have just reviewed were evidence that his work relied on the rendering of facts to do duty for inspiration. Today nearly everybody sees a nobility in his art that mere accumulation of facts could never explain. The spring of line connecting each detail with all the others in *The Swimming Hole* is of the great tradition of painting as it was developed by the Florentines; and the interplay of solid and void in his work, apparently as impersonal as the mathematical equations that Eakins enjoyed solving, is felt by later students to be of the very stuff which makes up the art of composition.

It may now be clearer that great numbers of seemingly unrelated or even hostile elements work together to give us the complex art of Occidental painting. Its mystery (which seems no mystery to the superficial) needs the presence of a diverse and rich series of pictures if we are to profit by it in any adequate way. The achievement of our museums in meeting this need is so considerable that we can think of it only with gratitude, for the moment dismissing from our minds any thought of opportunities we have missed in the past, and of the sore need for more understanding in the future. Such insight is bound to come; we feel confident of that when seeing the work of which we shall now attempt a summary.

This summary can begin where the history of painting begins as a purely European achievement, with Cimabue. The still debated question as to what he actually produced can be left aside, for the picture called by his name at the National Gallery is of the same quality as the works credited to him in Europe. When someone said that in painting there is no master to represent what Bach does in music, Matisse said: "Yes, there is Cimabue." The art of painting at the time of Cimabue was at a stage where high religious expression was vented through newly created form; very much the same thing occurs in the art of music, through the vast and impersonal production of Bach. It is no wonder that there are difficulties of attribution, of saying whether Cimabue did this picture or that. And at the National Gallery another great work of the time, the full length figure of St. Paul, has to be fathered on a vague anonymity.

Of the same august, elemental character is Giotto's *St. Francis*, at the Fogg Museum. Again, questions of attribution may arise if we apply to this picture the criterion of personal work that the Germans call *Eigenhändigkeit*. An idea evolved in later periods, it is out of place here: even

26.   Velasquez: Man with a Wine Glass.
Courtesy of The Toledo Museum of Art, Toledo.

though the grand figure kneeling to receive the stigmata occurs in other places, and therefore causes us to recall that assistant painters executed many of a master's designs at this time, the great fresco at Cambridge is sufficiently near to Giotto for this country to have the means of knowing at first-hand one of the supreme masters. Ravaged by the centuries or, more exactly, by the hands of barbarous men, it has been restored, according to the sound technical principles that the school at Harvard is following and constantly developing. Much attention is given in the collection there to pictures which may be in part retrieved from ruin, and at times, here as at other places, one has to ask oneself (or the catalogue) how much of what one sees is original, how much replaced by skillful hands, even if traces of the process are purposely left visible to prevent any idea of imposture.

Such considerations vanish when we come to a masterpiece in the same gallery, *The Crucifixion*, by Simone Martini. The religious purity of medieval Siena channels the emotional intensity of the work into spaces so grand that the little panel seems big; but aside from the spiritual content here, the actual substance of the paint emphasizes anew the irreplaceable advantage of an original over a reproduction, or over a work that has been tampered with.

That becomes important when we ask ourselves why the next great man we come to, in this reduced sequence of art history, fails to stir us as he did when we stood before his works in Florence. Or if those frescoes by Masaccio at the Carmine are not of the right scale for comparison with the panel at the National Gallery, we can think back to the easel picture at Naples. It moves us through the same unique power that is in the masterpiece of the Carmine frescoes, *The Expulsion of Adam and Eve*. And if the Madonna picture in Washington has hints of the largeness of that Masaccio who influenced the later masters of Florence, its voice is muted to a whisper by the layers of restoration which try to bring back to the work the impressiveness it probably had in the past. For the general public, which is necessarily unskilled in such questions, a warning on the label of a picture like this, or on one that is debatable as to its attribution, might well be useful. These considerations apply to a great many pictures in our galleries, and also to a vast number in the museums of Europe. In the case of Masaccio or other ultimately important masters, it seems hardly fair to a visitor to let him come to an idea that he lacks the capacity to appreciate such art when the fault really lies with the opportunity afforded him.

How different one feels about the National Gallery's *Saint John in the Desert*, by Domenico Veneziano. It is no less than the fourth of the small pictures by this most rare master to be added to the great collection in Washington, and its beauty and power go far to explain the preparation he could give to his extraordinary pupil, Piero della Francesca. That master's work being of the utmost scarcity outside Italy, we are fortunate to have even a few works by him. At the Gardner Collection in Boston, the fresco of *Hercules* is of a stark severity that gives no hint of the beauty in the *Resurrection* which Piero painted at about the same time, after returning to his native city. But it has the unique grandeur of his later life, and to see it in America is to echo the wonder expressed by John B. Potter, for so long the keeper of the paintings at the Boston Museum: "I used to stand before it in Piero's own house, where he painted it on the wall — and now to think of its being over here!"

No less extraordinary is America's good fortune in owning another work by the same transcending genius. Piero's panel of *A Saint*, representing almost if not quite the highest point of the Frick Collection in New York, came to light only a few years ago, and doubtless required the great financial resources of such an institution for its purchase. Certainly (to forsake the chronological order we are following), Ingres' *Mme. d'Haussonville* at the same gallery was considered most desirable for the Metropolitan — which let it go because of its "unreasonable" price. That could be paid by a private collection, the Frick still being that at the time, just as Mr. Widener could buy the Bellini *Feast of the Gods*, which the museum in New York greatly coveted, as it did various other works it has lost.

When they are turned over to the public, in one or another of our cities, only local pride suffers if the collection of a given place has failed to secure the masterpieces. But sometimes they are lost forever. It seems unlikely that Holland will let the Rembrandt I mentioned before, his *David and Saul*, leave the country again; the Kaiser Friedrich Museum in Berlin bought that incomparable Georges de La Tour, the *St. Sebastian*, from right under our noses when it was publicly sold in New York — as part of an American collection; and only less vexing was the case of the superlatively fine *Mme. Moitessier*, by Ingres. A greater work, as I believe, than the master's portrait of the same lady recently added by Mr. Kress to his splendid gifts to Washington, the picture in question was announced in the newspapers as being brought to this country by a dealer, about 1938, when the National Gallery of London stepped in and bought the great painting. It is true that the English museum needed such a work; but then few would blame America if it had reversed the magnanimous words of Sir Philip Sidney, "Thy necessity is greater than mine," and secured the masterpiece for itself.

Concern for the welfare of even friendly rivals plays no larger a part among institutions than among individuals; and our losses of splendid works have too often been due to hesitation or timidity about cutting into resources (there are times when capital itself can be wisely spent). Other opportunities will arise in the future, and as we grow more mature, we shall attach more importance to them; we shall learn, also, how to select and trust the men to do our buying. I return to my belief that we have done remarkably well so far, and the point we have reached in the review of our Italian paintings is a good one to support such an idea, especially as our museums have another beautiful work by Piero della Francesca, the St. Apollonia in the National Gallery.

Any picture by Michelangelo is doubtless permanently beyond the lines of the possible for us, and it may be that the same is true about Leonardo, unless the predella at Worcester, Massachusetts, is accepted as entirely by the master. But among works by very great pupils of his, the delightful Portrait of a Girl at the Metropolitan, now convincingly ascribed to Ambrogio de Predis, was for a long time thought to be a painting by Leonardo himself. And at the National Gallery we have an amazing representation of the chief members of his school. These works include the noble Venus by Bernardino Luini, and his entire series of nine exquisite frescoes covering the story of Cephalus and Procris.

With the Bellini mentioned just before, which Mr. Widener included in his gift to the National Gallery, America could stand comparison with any country, as regards the finest work of the great Venetian. To confirm our position in the matter, there is the remarkable St. Francis at the Frick Collection; and numbers of our galleries can show smaller Bellinis of the most beautiful character. Of a very nearly unparalleled quality is his Christ Bearing the Cross at the museum of Toledo, Ohio. Its acquisition was peculiarly important for this country, since it throws light on the master-and-pupil relationship of Bellini and Giorgione. The masterpiece at Toledo is unquestioned in its attribution, whereas an astonishingly similar picture at the Gardner Collection, called a Giorgione, is of those paintings which render enigmatic any listing of works by the greatest painter of his school. Though the Gypsy Madonna in Venice has an almost unshakable pedigree, the history of even this final refuge of Giorgione scholarship has been questioned. And so we are in the position, at once perilous and stimulating, of making our own decisions about works attributed to Giorgione in our possession. While among them, I will profit by the situation to interpolate a personal preference for the Portrait of a Gentleman at the Metropolitan.

No doubt as to our unsurpassable good fortune is possible when we

27. Goya: Don Ignacio Omulryan y Rourera.
Courtesy of the William Rockhill Nelson Gallery of Art, Kansas City.

come to a work by Giorgione's fellow pupil under Bellini. Titian's *Rape of Europa*, in the Gardner collection, is none other than the canvas which Rubens gazed on and which caused him to state — with the double authority of his genius and of his experience in making glorious copies of Titian — that the picture now in Boston is the greatest painting in the world! Since he had shoulders like Atlas, we will not trouble about his bearing the weight of this affirmation.

Within a few feet of the Titian hangs Raphael's *Tommaso Inghirami*, which Mr. Berenson, with his deep judgment, tells us is finer than the corresponding work in the Pitti Palace at Florence. Still in that great Boston collection is another painting by the Umbrian; it is of special interest as we go from one of our galleries to another, for this predella piece once formed part of the ensemble of five accompanying the Raphael *Madonna of the Colonna Family*, at the Metropolitan; that museum has, in recent years, acquired another of the predelle to accompany its masterpiece, which is further supplemented by a famous portrait from the same hand, the *Giuliano de' Medici*.

The group of works by the "Prince of Painters" at the National Gallery would in itself justify the title of this section of the present book. It is achievement indeed when we can go from that jewel of Raphael's youth, the *St. Michael*, to three madonnas of great importance (one, formerly of the House of Alba, being a veritable revelation in its beauty, especially for people who had never been able to make the journey to Leningrad, where it hung for centuries); and finally there is a great portrait of the master's late manner.

It is tempting to go on with our rich store of later Italian works, those by Bronzino (including a grand one at the De Young Museum in San Francisco and a perfect one at the Metropolitan), Tintoretto, Veronese, Tiepolo, Canaletto, and Guardi, for fine pictures by each of them are to be found in various cities. The magnificent baroque pictures at Chicago give a vivid idea of the power of that school, as does the superb Caravaggio at Detroit, and the impressive portrait by the same master at San Diego; Hartford amazes one also with the extent and fineness of its collections along these lines.

But already I have dwelt for very long on our Italian pictures alone, and even so without mention of more than the one Titian. Yet the Venus at the Metropolitan is a work to be enjoyed more deeply the more one learns about painting, a portrait at Baltimore is a most noble thing, Detroit has two important works by the master, Boston has one, Kansas City has one — and still we are not at the end of our Titians.

We have not said a word about such great masters as Duccio and

Castagno at the Frick Collection, nor about glorious early and late works by the Italians at the Boston Museum. Not many connoisseurs have left such a record of energy and intelligence as did John G. Johnson, whose Italian pictures, a lesser part of his collection at the Philadelphia Museum, contain most inspiring material. We have not glanced at a whole ensemble of Italian frescoes at Worcester, nor the famous Pollaiuolo and other treasures of Italian art at Yale, nor the remarkable Holden Collection in the Cleveland Museum. Bryson Burroughs used to say that no other work of all those under his care at the Metropolitan gave him quite the intimate and personal pleasure that he got from the *Paradise* by Giovanni di Paolo, a master to be seen at Chicago and in other American collections. Of course, says somebody, Mr. Burroughs could not have said that if Sassetta's *Journey of the Magi*, from the Maitland F. Griggs Collection, had been part of the museum while he was the curator. And so one person after another, in one city after another, can go on with well-founded demands for additions to the works I have mentioned.

Yet our purpose is attained if we let the partial survey just made stand as a token of American achievement in the sovereign field of Italian painting. The record of our museums here offers more than a fair test of what we have done as regards the art in all the other countries. For collecting great Italian pictures is a problem of special difficulty. With the Northern schools, our possessions of high importance are sometimes more numerous and more completely representative; yet we did a bigger job when obtaining for our museums their treasures of Italian art. The reason is that, during centuries, this school was the one of chief interest to great monarchs like Philip II of Spain, Louis XIV of France, Charles I of England, August the Strong of Saxony, and Catherine the Great of Russia, with large numbers of lesser nobles, prelates, and rich commoners eagerly buying what was generally to go, later on, to the museums of their countries. Meanwhile, or usually before the rest, the Medici and other great Italian collectors were securing for their land its rightful lion's share of the heritage.

Therefore, we may regard it as well established that scarcely three generations of Americans, beginning at a very late time in the history of collecting, have provided their country with material that bespeaks intelligence and courage in splendid measure. To go on with the account, through lists of our paintings among the great number of masters of all the schools not yet mentioned, would be an almost interminable business. Moreover, it would be unprofitable. At times, one can gain something from art discussion that throws light on the evolution of schools or individuals, that shows the relation of their work to the religious, scientific, or economic activity of their day, and that otherwise furnishes understanding of technical or spiritual phenomena. But even the absurdly insufficient review of our Italian paintings has had to reduce itself practically to enumeration, and it were dull indeed to go on with more of that.

Therefore we shall proceed categorically, taking the other painters almost by whole schools. If we must, for all time, look to Madrid, with the Prado, as the incomparable repository of Spanish art, particularly for the large compositions of Velasquez, our holdings in the splendid field that goes from the primitives of Spain to her late masters are very considerable. The appreciation of El Greco having been delayed till the nineteenth century, alert action by our collectors gave us such works as the prodigious *Assumption* at Chicago, one of the greatest masterpieces of portraiture, the *Fray Hortensio Palavicino* at Boston, and a whole series of noble works, including the unique *Toledo* at the Metropolitan. Similarly Goya, as a distinctly modern genius, was accessible to us — with the result that a tour of our public collections (or of just a few among them) will reveal the salient qualities of the man's art — and in examples of the highest quality.

The dark and rich problem of early German painting is dealt with by our museums in only an insufficient manner. Not to mention Grünewald, since no example of his supreme art is to be seen in Rome, Paris, or London (indeed, only a very few cities can show a Grünewald), we lack material to give an idea of the extent and variety of the school. (To offer at least one exception to this rule, there is the delightful picture by an unknown master, the *Lovers*, at the Cleveland Museum.) On the other hand, we do have Holbein in a good number of impressive works, one can know Cranach, and so grand a Dürer as the one in the Altman Collection at the Metropolitan is enough to reveal much of his stature, though we have few other paintings by him.

Moving on to the Low Countries, we find ourselves far better placed. The two van Eycks that the Metropolitan secured from the Hermitage are works of capital importance; and at that museum also, fine connoisseurship has recently identified another beautiful picture as coming from the hand of the same epoch-making painter or by someone very close to him. His art is to be seen again at the John G. Johnson Collection in Philadelphia, at the National Gallery, and at Detroit. Other great artists of the early Flemish School, van der Weyden, Bouts, Memling, and Gerard David are widely distributed through our cities. Bosch is increasingly sought after (an important example having gone to San Diego in

1504

28. Dürer: Adam and Eve (study for the engraving).
Courtesy of the Pierpont Morgan Library, New York.

recent years), and we have a few pictures by that most creative painter, Pieter Bruegel the Elder. The one at the Metropolitan is such a masterpiece that we are forced to stop for a mention of it.

The New York museum, once more, compels acknowledgment of its great service in revealing the genius of Rubens, the *Venus and Adonis* being a picture on which any gallery in the world would look with pride; there are other canvases of large size and most admirable quality; and then sketches, which give the never failing surprise that is reserved when — the intervening centuries being abolished — we have the privilege of being present at the very dawn of his painting; a monochrome foundation is suffused with growing light as washes of sky-blue, rose, and other colors repeat before our eyes that miracle of nature, daybreak. No less than seven of these wonderful studies are in the museum of Philadelphia and, with Detroit again doing excellent work in its showing of Rubens, other collections in various parts of the country continue the account, though one hopes that they will still add to it in large measure. The school of the Northern colossus is well represented, particularly by Van Dyck.

When we come to Dutch painting, the record of American collecting becomes particularly admirable. Rembrandt and Hals appear in extraordinary quantity and quality, the old Marquand Collection in New York still offering especially fine examples: one would like to pause over the Rembrandts in Detroit, Cleveland, and Toledo; Chicago has a particularly appealing work by him. Boston has splendid ones, while at the Frick Collection, with the *Admiral de Ruyter*, as it has at times been called, perhaps the masterpiece among all single figures by Hals, the *Polish Rider* is unique among Rembrandts. Even so, and with every desire to press on in our survey, we must note that the Frick's other two examples of the great Dutchman stand up most grandly beside the famous equestrian picture; for many people, they even exceed it in effect. Later on, we shall come to problems of gallery instruction; but the present moment is so appropriate that I will note here a sentence which the Kansas City Museum has in the little handbook that visitors may consult in the gallery of the Dutch pictures. It quotes Max Liebermann: "When I see a work by Hals, I feel like painting; when I see a work by Rembrandt, I feel like giving up painting." That impulse in him must have been almost dangerous if he ever saw the work by the master at Kansas City: even for experienced students of Rembrandt, this *Youth with a Black Cap* still reserves surprise as to what the last years of the glorious lifetime were yet to reveal. Here the final evolution is one attaining tranquil perfection, whereas in the *Lucretia* at Minneapolis, the stormy drama of the technique matches that of the subject.

Jan Steen, whom Dr. Bredius places so high, is less well seen in our collections, which is a pity. Vermeer, on the contrary, is astonishingly represented, and we have fine works by Terburg and others of the so-called Little Masters. Dutch landscape art, with van Goyen, Ruisdael, and Hobbema, may be thoroughly appreciated in a number of our museums.

The English school is shown from Maine to California, quite literally. In the latter state, indeed, the Huntington Collection, at San Marino, consists very largely of a group of pictures by famous English painters. We have been slow about recognizing the superiority of Hogarth, and only a very few of our people have collected the marvelous works of Blake. We cannot adequately show the greatness of Constable, though Chicago's splendid landscape by the master exhibits him at a high level. Turner's impressiveness is seen in a number of fine works, again of wide distribution.

The genius of France is one that for over a hundred years has had a particular attraction for our country. At the Worcester Museum an unusually fine example of the Fontainebleau school may open our discussion of French painting in America; the effect of the picture is significantly reinforced at the same gallery by a statue of the period, a work very plausibly attributed to that great master, Jean Goujon. At Toledo, an important Clouet continues the story of this art, which rises to great heights with our showing of its seventeenth-century masters. In New York, the old Historical Society has one of Philippe de Champaigne's noble portraits, and Detroit represents him by a pure and severe *Last Supper*. At the same museum is Poussin's *Diana and Endymion*, a work which by itself can reveal how completely the heritage of Greece and Rome was introduced to northern Europe by French artists. Yet, to feel this in an example of culminating power and beauty, one must see the great Poussin's *Neptune and Amphitrite*, at the Philadelphia Museum. The importance of the supreme classicist being so pivotal, we may list the other museums which have his works: Hartford, Boston, Smith College, New York, Washington, Cleveland, Chicago, Minneapolis, and Kansas City, beside the Fogg at Harvard, where one finds two glorious pictures by him. Add to these our considerable store of paintings by his contemporary, Claude, and you have proof, as with our Italian collections, of the solidity with which our galleries have built for the future. The impression strengthens when we think of our fine, if not too extensive representation of the other phase of the *grand siècle,* in the work of the brothers Le Nain, Hartford again showing a marvelous painting (as it does with its tremendous *Crucifixion,* by Poussin).

Since the eighteenth century is so particularly French, it seems strange that our public galleries do not represent it more adequately. The Metropolitan has two admirable Watteau canvases, but the first was acquired only a few years ago, and the second came later, almost fortuitously, when the Bache Collection was added to the museum. Other works by this amazing master are to be seen at the National Gallery, at Boston, and at Cleveland, but Americans are still too prone to confuse his painting with that of his followers, remarkable as the latter often are. Our Chardins are also less numerous and, as a rule, less fine than one would wish; and though the Fogg Museum now has the marvelous portraits by Perronneau that the Winthrop Collection gave it, and though there is a fine one at the California Palace of the Legion of Honor, his accomplished and — one would think — easily appreciated contemporaries still appear to be underestimated. As against this impression, we may recall two excellent works by Largillière, two beautiful Nattiers, Fragonard's famous *Billet-doux*, his even finer *Lady with a Dog*, and two characteristic works by Boucher at the Metropolitan. By the last-named master also, the small picture of a nymph, at Chicago, is so exceptionally charming as to deserve affectionate mention, while Boston has large and important compositions by him.

Supplementary gifts to the National Gallery by Mr. Kress bring that museum's collection of French eighteenth-century paintings to a high level; they include, beside the two by Watteau, three pictures by Fragonard, three by Boucher, one by Largillière, and that masterpiece by François Hubert Drouais, the very large *Family Group* which so stirred public admiration when shown at the New York World's Fair. It is, however, to the Frick Collection that we must turn for what is doubtless our most extraordinary showing of this period. Boucher is represented once more with an exquisite portrait and with decorations for an interior. These are, however, eclipsed when, in a neighboring room, we come on a unique ensemble by Fragonard. The large panels which that master painted for Mme. Du Barry are installed as they were planned to be, their beauty and completeness placing them among the most astonishing documents on their exquisite century. The Frick, again, shows us a Chardin which, this time, is a masterpiece. Another lovely canvas by the master, at the Phillips Memorial Gallery in Washington, illustrates the type of work which affords a firm foundation for modern art — the chief concern of that collection.

It is when we approach our own time that we realize one of the really splendid achievements of American art appreciation. For if people deserve credit for a fine response to painting when they fathom even a part of the mysterious depths in the older arts, the question always arises,

29. Holbein: Lady Guldeford.
Courtesy of the City Art Museum, St. Louis.

are they really doing so, or are they merely accepting the judgment of the past? How much of what they say is mere lip service to authority? To give no more than that is to react in pretty weak fashion to the creative power of art. Since America, in the nineteenth and twentieth centuries, was itself giving an example of creative power, it logically responded to the men who so defined the period that we recognize ourselves in their description.

At the time of our beginnings as a nation, our wars with the mother country still left us so English in mentality that comparatively few people found themselves in complete sympathy with the French Revolution and with Napoleon.[1] For that reason, doubtless, painters of the British tradition continued to be preferred among us, and men like David, Gros, Ingres, Géricault, and Delacroix — the heroes of France in her rise to new mastery — could not be accepted until later. It is only in recent times that their immense value is being appreciated. Delacroix, it is true, frequently appears in collections dating back fifty or seventy-five years, but almost invariably in the company of the commercial favorites of the time, his work having been sold to our people on the strength of its European reputation, and not simply because they wanted it. Therefore, until recently at least, when such collections were auctioned off here, American bidding would be so weak that the Delacroix pictures were almost always bought by French dealers. The low prices they paid allowed them to send the works back to Paris, where they found ready sale.

Since I have thus arraigned American appreciation, I may be permitted to support my remarks by two personal recollections: one is when I tried in vain to persuade Mr. Charles Taft, the Cincinnati collector, to preserve for us a magnificent Delacroix in the big Yerkes sale of 1910; the other memory is of our loss of the uniquely beautiful canvas, Le Réveil, one of Senator Clark's pictures which were not placed in the Corcoran Gallery. Auctioned off in New York at a low price, it soon found its way to the finest private collection in France, that of M. David-Weill.

Even now, our acceptance of the first group of the great French moderns appears to owe more to able museum directors than to a general appeal of these masters. Thus the two superb works by David and Ingres in the Frick Collection were acquired since the death of the founder. One of our prominent museum officials has stated that the splendid Ingres in the Taft Collection is popular mainly because it represents a beautiful woman; similarly, the success of David's magnificent Mlle. du

---

[1] Writing for the Virginia Quarterly Review (Autumn, 1945), Professor Samuel Flagg Bemis, of Yale, says, "The American people had less love for Napoleon than for England, the enemy." And this was during the war of 1812.

Val d'Ognes, at the Metropolitan, is very certainly to be attributed, in large measure, to the charm of the girl. She is, indeed, so pretty as to lend support to doubts which have been expressed about the authorship of the picture. One theory, not to be lightly dismissed, would give the canvas to David's brilliant pupil, Gérard. To credit it to the older master would be to assign to him a painting characterized by an appeal of femininity found nowhere else in his massive production, but which, in Gérard, is quite typical. Turning to an indubitable David at the Metropolitan, we learn that the *Death of Socrates* entered the gallery partly through the prestige of Sir Joshua Reynolds' still resounding affirmation that David, in this canvas, had attained the greatest height in the art of painting since Michelangelo and Raphael, a claim that certainly does credit to the English master's capacity for enthusiasm about a grand picture.

Though two of the Metropolitan's beautiful canvases by Ingres also had in their favor the admiration of a great artist (that of Degas, from whose collection they were sold, after his death), their acquisition was strongly opposed, and they reached our walls as one of the rare concessions granted to the desires of the curator. Such great museums as those of Boston and Chicago still lack a David or an Ingres. The Walters Gallery, in Baltimore, represents both masters, as does Cleveland; but Gros is to be seen in only one American museum, that of Smith College (with, however, a superb canvas at Detroit probably attributable to the great painter). The immense position in modern art of Delacroix must be considered the explanation of his presence in many of our galleries; it can scarcely derive from our idea of his value as an artist or the pleasure he can give, to speak with painful frankness. Such an opinion is forced upon one by the still scant popular appeal of the man whom Renoir and others have called the greatest painter of the French school. Genius such as his often takes long to be esteemed at full value, yet some signs do point to increased appreciation.

It is with the next group of masters, headed by Corot, Millet, and Théodore Rousseau, that American admiration for a new movement in France manifested itself particularly; our possessions in this field are most notable. They are also so well distributed throughout the country that no single institution need be mentioned.

Works by Courbet including masterpieces — the *Woman with a Parrot*, for example, give to the Metropolitan a representation of the famous realist that is equaled by no museum in the world, save the Louvre. After that statement I should perhaps add that a private collection in Berlin is said to have more than we. I regret not having seen it, but believe, even so, that it has nothing more important than the great

Bride picture at Smith College, to mention that interesting museum again. The master's work is to be enjoyed in various of our public galleries, and so one sees cause for the warm acceptance of Manet which I have dwelt on in previous pages. His work and that of the Impressionists, who followed his initiative, are represented in so many American cities that no further affirmation is needed of our response to that vital school.

The one which follows — the generation which, for the moment, represents modern art — is that, however, which furnishes the best evidence of this country's ability to recognize the essential expression of its day without waiting for later acclaim to make it acceptable. Even so, we must admit that, for very long, the poorer things of the time held sway here. Chicago took the first decisive step in correcting this condition. With the Museum of Modern Art, New York reaffirmed its character as our chief center of appreciation. Some years later, Philadelphia, by welcoming the collections of Albert Eugene Gallatin, Alfred Stieglitz, and others, added strongly to our standing as appreciators of modern art; Columbus, Ohio, had had for years an important showing of it, especially of the Americans in the movement, and there is evidence on every hand that an understanding of the modern trends is rapidly developing throughout the country.

Very special problems are presented by modern art to the persons who guide museum policy, and we shall return to this matter on a later page. But having at last gone through the annals of European painting, as revealed by our galleries, we may now round out our account of America's achievement in collecting, the next step, logically, taking us to the field of drawings and prints.

For some idea of the places which house our great wealth of such material, I must again refer the reader to the supplementary list. It cannot suggest the names of even the greatest among the artists represented. But mentioning a few of those by whom we own original drawings — and they include masters like Leonardo, Michelangelo, Raphael, Dürer, Holbein, and Rembrandt — will suggest how such works amplify the enjoyment and learning to be derived from paintings. The lover of drawings and prints will, indeed, almost resent considering those arts as subsidiary, for they contain much of what is most profound, most immediate, and most intimate in the work of the great men. Odilon Redon, an artist with a very special interest in black-and-white, called it "the art of the North," in contrast to the things having the play of color beloved in the lands of the sun. And, what may appropriately be recalled here, drawings and prints reach out to all the other visual arts.

They are, of course, immediately associated with the craft of the book

30. Bruegel: The Harvesters.
Courtesy of *The Metropolitan Museum of Art.*

in its aesthetic aspect, and also in its incalculably important role of multiplying without limit the number of persons to be benefited by art. Obviously, there is a close connection between this element and the survival of the work, for time deals rigorously with things of which there is but one example.

Almost more suggestive of the value of the collections we are observing is the way they orient us in the thought of architects, sculptors, painters, and (sometimes the same individuals) the masters who furnish designs for the multitude of the applied arts, the grand forms of the armorer, the enchanting field of tapestry, the infinitely varied patterns of textile designers and lacemakers, of ceramists, of wood carvers (for the paneling of rooms, e.g. — or for furniture, with its architectural forms), of the jewelers and goldsmiths, of the workers in iron, leather, lacquer, enamel, ivory, and glass.

Of all these and other forms of the applied arts, our public collections have, in their ensemble, a magnificent representation. It is not confined to collections like those of Cooper Union, in New York, which specialize in them, nor to the big museums, which do have fine and constantly increasing displays of the material; it may be found in institutions which are yet too far from importance as repositories of art in general to claim much attention in our supplementary list — which may indeed have omitted them outright (to my regret).

A mere mention of armor, just above, demands some amplification, even as we hasten on in our survey. To take the most notable collection in America, the one at the Metropolitan, as typifying our possessions of arms and armor in various cities, it is important to put a true valuation on the interest displayed by the crowd usually found in that noble hall. The full-panoplied equestrian pieces, the sinister or heroic or elegant figures of men on foot, the shape of helmets (now of elemental simplicity, now engraved with the most complex patterns), the gesture of swords, the splendid expanses of shields reinforced with design to emphasize their use or merely to express the pride in them of their makers or the knights who bore them, the infinite ingenuity expended on the anatomy of a gauntlet and on the design and decoration of small arms and firearms, — all these things may appear, superficially, to impress the public mostly for reasons alien to art (thoughts of killing, romantic fancies connected with old novels, or questions of economics in a feudal and military world).

Yet, if the severest of aestheticians will analyze the appeal that he himself finds in arms and armor, he must realize that many a man who would fail to see the beauty of painting and sculpture may receive sure and profound effects from the art elements in these objects, utilitarian as they are in their first origin. Indeed, I think that armor room at the Metropolitan is now admirably placed in the museum for purposes of art propaganda. Formerly in a distant wing, where many people might miss it, the collection has been installed in a most central location, so that visitors are certain to see it — and from two floors.[2] Whether they come to it with wide aesthetic experience, or with the simple and human interests referred to above, their thoughts are, to a great extent, running parallel.

The unsophisticated observer may say that he is interested only in those various things outside of art, and that, as a matter of fact, he knows nothing about the subject. Perhaps that was true when he came into the gallery: it is so no longer, if he has given real attention to the objects surrounding him there. He will, if he persists a bit, find himself far along the road that the museum wants to open to him. And his course, just because it is devoid of conscious purpose, and because it is unaffected by the jargon of the professionals, has that natural and healthy character which is desirable above all others.

Perhaps, later on, he becomes aware of the architectural quality in the design unifying the elements of a suit of armor; perhaps he sees the identity of genius in the man who planned the curves of a helmet and the man who carved similar curves when executing a portrait, whether in ancient Sumer, five thousand years ago, in Mexico, one thousand years ago, or in our own time, as with Brancusi's *Mlle. Pogany* at the Philadelphia Museum. When art, rather than a given school or period, is what occupies his mind, he can utter the old words *ars una* as a spontaneous discovery of his own. If so, well and good. But if he never does, and just enjoys art objects, without comparing their qualities and analyzing their nature: well and good, too. The theorist has, however, a right to look at museum possessions, and not only our sublimated man in the street.

With the mention just made of certain works of sculpture, we return to the major arts. And with all the relationship we have noted between their essential psychology and that of the great craftsmen, we may as well remind ourselves that logic has been used by the world during all the time when it has made a distinction between the fine arts (*belle arti* or *beaux*

---

[2] A story told by one of the devoted men who served the Metropolitan Museum as president has significance here. It was doubtless that "first citizen of New York," Robert W. De Forest himself, who was the interlocutor referred to, an old gentleman who, on a visit to the galleries, had been noticing with pleasure the way two small children, unaccompanied by any grown person, were enjoying the exhibits. Hearing the little girl say to her brother, "Now shall be go and see the armor?" the observer could no longer refrain from speaking to them, and offered to be their guide. Whereupon the girl, drawing herself up to her full height, replied, "Thank you, sir, but don't you think I know my way about my own museum?"

arts, as they are called in other languages) and the applied arts. The question is one of having clear ideas, rather than of establishing a hierarchy based on importance or merit.

We may agree that a Greek vase (one, let us say, that has on it no pictorial design) can be so fine in proportion, in the sweep and yet discretion of its contours, and in the power of its red and black, that it is immeasurably preferable to a mediocre painting, of one period or another. Similarly, a Turkish rug may be so noble in pattern, so suggestive of nature's drama, of the light and color in the garden of an oasis, that this impersonal work of splendid craftsmen tells more of the character of man as the artist than does an inferior sculpture. Such confrontations, however, befog the issue, one which must recognize the fact that the applied arts impose limitations, through matters like utility, treatment of materials, etc. These obstacles to the free play of the mind prevent the fullest expression of idea and aspiration, which are prerogatives only of the major arts, as they may perhaps best be designated.

That much said, we can enter a field as yet untouched in our vast review. The words "mind" and "aspiration," used just now in defining the fine arts (to call them that, once more), were chosen for the way they prepare an approach to the work of the Middle Ages. We have previously mentioned the Copts as an example of a Christian people who produced things of great beauty but who did not free themselves from their debt to preceding civilizations. We have glanced at the mighty arts of the Byzantine world, already plunged to the full in the current of an era which stands in strongest contrast to that of the glorious world we call pagan. Yet, even with the spread of Byzantine culture to the north of Europe, so many Oriental elements persist in it that the race to which most Americans belong does not feel that it has spoken its most characteristic thought until France, Spain, England, and Germany have greatly modified the arts brought to them from the East.

When that occurs, we have the Romanesque and the Gothic schools — whose hold on our loyalty and imagination is explained by their position as fundamentals in the expression which concerns us most directly. Therefore, also, one can understand why, despite the difficulty of collecting material generally fixed in place — as parts of buildings, Americans have done such extraordinary work in transporting overseas the great architectural ensembles that are necessary for any insight into the grandeur and completeness of the period they represent.

Once more referring the reader to our supplementary list for a detailed statement of the institutions possessing the material in question, we may again concentrate on the largest and finest showing of it — at the Clois-

31. Rubens: Isabella Brant.
Courtesy of The Cleveland Museum of Art, Cleveland.

ters, that branch museum of the Metropolitan, in New York. Philadelphia's effort is, however, so considerable, and has yielded such admirable
results, that mention must be made of it, even here. Again, certain
objects in the important group at Chicago are so very fine as to deserve
attention also, although one more attempt is being made to keep our
statement within some bounds of brevity.

The Cloisters, while containing individual objects, or groups of
objects, no less than superlative in quality, enters a larger category of
ideas, as the most considerable attempt yet made in our country to
re-create the whole effect of arts of the past. Coming down to a part of
that time very near our own, the restoration of an entire town, Williams-
burg, Virginia, while spread over a wider area, offered no such difficulty
as the assembling of elements which succeed, to an amazing degree, in
recapturing the impressiveness of the Romanesque and Gothic eras.
Leaping over the centuries again, another example of such imagination
by an American (the same one in all three cases) is the essay in architectural unity that has given us a pioneer success, to many of us a very
important one, in the magnitude of its scope. The reference here is, of
course, to that unique ensemble of buildings, in the heart of New York,
which constitute the collective work called Rockefeller Center.

One needs such a reminder of the city planning which went on in the
great capitals, the provincial towns, and the big monastic communities of
the medieval time. The art of Mont-Saint-Michel would not have been
itself if applied to any spot in the world save that rock in the sea. The
personality of Spain asserts itself as different from that of France in the
way the houses at Toledo are related to the slopes on which they stand,
and in their relation to the cathedral spires of the wonderful city. The
genius of a people expresses itself in the ensemble of a town or in any
detail found in it. Thus, a fragment of Greek marble preserved in a
museum is enough to tell us of the life that circulated through the whole
statue of which it was once a part; and so a person of sufficient experience
and judgment can see recorded in an isolated figure or head the character
of some mighty collective work of the Middle Ages. It is tempting to
let one's mind tarry over certain sublime things of the thirteenth century
and the fourteenth century at the Cloisters, but we must resist, save to
say that there is sculpture there to give an idea of the greatest art that the
Christian era has produced. And of the arts allied with it in medieval
buildings, we have superb examples also. To change our point of observation and see two others of such works, let us note the stained glass window
from Chartres at the museum of Princeton University, and the frescoes
in the Catalan chapel preserved entire at the Boston Museum; then

returning to New York, we take delight once more in the story of the unicorn as told in tapestries which have perhaps not yet failed to enchant even one person of the thousands who have seen them at the towered building overlooking the Hudson.

And still the essential point about the Cloisters, with its courts and gardens, its chapels and treasure chambers, is the one we have touched on before, the re-creation of a distant period. In various of our museums we essay that feat, more or less exactly, through rooms dealing with the later centuries, the eighteenth in France and England for example, or even the earlier nineteenth in America. Always the museum man must remember one thing above all: that he is of the twentieth century, and that his vision is that of his time. His understanding contains elements that the past did not have, and so the expressions of earlier periods have aspects of quaintness, or of nostalgia for the beauty of long ago, that could have no place in the minds of the people who first planned the rooms and lived in them. The warming pan that today is restored to its place on the hearth because of the pleasant gleam of its brass was once a thing that inspired quite different ideas; and the flintlock, which, for us, makes a fine, sturdy note as its dark metal and wood detach against a white wall, to our forebears was a reminder of the deadly threat of the Indians.

And so, even with the things of our own soil and of a time almost within the memory of living man, we cannot create a truly authentic interior of that past age. We are always in danger that something of self-conscious make-believe will enter the job, something of stage setting. In the theater, this is acceptable as a help to following the play of emotions which remain constant in men and women, no matter how much time has passed. But when the properties are examined and turn out to be mere cardboard and paint, their power of illusion vanishes. The classic example is that burlesque of the strong-man act in which a Hercules-actor, with bulging muscles and at the cost of terrific effort, lifts a "500 lb. weight" above his head, and then, a minute or two later, a little dog wanders onto the stage and trots off with the mass of "iron" in his mouth.

Returning to the period rooms of the museum, we may see more clearly now that if on the stage — the true realm of illusion — unreality is fit only to be laughed at, how much more flagrantly is it the contrary of art when we come to the genuine objects which alone have a right to space in our galleries! The stimulating of relationships amongst them that they had only when they were in actual use, the substitution of space relations among them dictated by another period's notion of "aesthetic effect" becomes intolerable when once we perceive that it is a thing of artifice — like the "500 lb. weight" that the little dog picked up so charmingly. And so the wise museum man keeps to his role of giving sympathetic exhibition to his material, and does not confuse a period room with a stage set.

It may appear that I am going to extremes in applying this reasoning to early American interiors, so near to us in time and place, as has been remarked. But to locate them outside the rule we have been trying to make understandable is to put them outside the category of works of art. Here the challenge to "define your terms" crops up with all of its old vitality. For present purposes, I can give a definition, and fortunately in the words of a great man. Renoir said, "Shall I tell you what is needed for a work of art? Two things: it must be indescribable and it must be inimitable." He went on to illustrate with modern buildings, describable to the last detail by measurements, in contrast to the columns of a Gothic cathedral, which he said were "as various and inimitable as the trees in the forest." If the twentieth century — even in America — could imitate the nineteenth century, it would prove that there was no art then; and we must believe that there was, or admit that the life coming down from the long past had suddenly failed to continue. And we do not believe that.

But the Renaissance, says someone, does not its very name declare that the genius of antiquity was reborn at a new time and on new soil? We return to our museum (where all questions are answered — or should be) and enter galleries that we have not yet looked at, those of Renaissance sculpture. They answer the question asked above far better than does the splendid representation of Renaissance painting previously touched upon. For that art does not tell as much about its relation with antiquity, since it had to evolve with but little help from classical examples in its own field. Almost none of these were accessible till Pompeii and Herculaneum began to reappear, in the eighteenth century. It was through sculpture that Italy was fired to emulate the antique, and so it is through sculpture that we shall presently answer the question about the rebirth of Greece and Rome. For a long time the galleries of Renaissance sculpture in our museums lagged far behind those devoted to painting. That art always makes the first appeal; and then there was more difficulty in getting fine specimens, since Europe had most of them in places beyond the reach of the collector — who satisfied himself, for educational purposes, with casts.

But now the situation is changing. For some years, indeed, our older collections, in Boston, New York, Philadelphia, and other cities, have had

32. Hals: Admiral de Ruyter (so called).
Courtesy of The Frick Collection, New York.

splendid works in various media. Masters like Matteo Civitali, Benedetto da Maiano, Francesco Laurana, and members of the Pisano and della Robbia families are represented. A cup by Benvenuto Cellini, with a deftly perfect small figure, is in the Metropolitan, where we follow that Florentine sculptor to France in his inspiring of Jean Goujon; for at the same museum there is a marble relief by the Frenchman who, by the bye, surpasses the art of his preceptor. At Worcester, as was previously noted, there is a large and important statue by the same sixteenth-century genius.

But with the creation of the National Gallery, the public was made heir to pieces of an importance unknown before in American museums. The mighty name of Donatello appears, with the accession of the Widener gift, and it is not with work in stucco, by which his school widened the numbers of his contemporary public, but with marbles of unique importance. With the Mellon and Kress Collections (since added to as the latter benefactor became further aware of the needs of the gallery), we have come into possession of portraits of Lorenzo de' Medici and his brother Giuliano, both by Verrocchio, and the former a prodigious masterpiece. Together with sculptures by such men as Ghiberti, Desiderio da Settignano, Rossellino, Pollaiuolo, Giovanni Amedeo, and Bernini, with Germain Pilon and Coysevox again representing the development in France, we now have a group that our national museum can describe as "one of the most comprehensive in the world, rivaled only by the four leading European collections in Florence, London, Paris, and Berlin."

I intentionally keep this part of the statement as to our achievement in collecting to terms even more general than those used in telling of our work in the galleries of painting. For my purpose, here, is to get back to that question of the word "Renaissance." Benvenuto Cellini boasts in his autobiography that he replaced the missing part of an antique marble in a manner so perfect that no one could tell where the ancient workmanship ended and his own began. As I have related elsewhere, I have seen this claim disproved by quite inexpert observers who, today, clearly perceive the difference between the work of the old Roman who carved the original and the sixteenth-century sculptor who restored it. Perhaps Benvenuto told the truth in saying that his contemporaries saw no difference; but that would be but one more example of the rule that men need time to arrive at full appreciation in art matters (or, very frequently, at any appreciation).

The outstanding idea forced upon us by the Cellini story (and it could be confirmed by innumerable others of the kind) is that the Renaissance is a period with its own character, one so powerfully asserted that it is in no wise to be confused with that of antiquity. Understanding of a truth like that one is doubtless a more precious thing than the enjoyment of even such masterworks as we have mentioned. How high they rank in the history of sculpture is a relative matter, for it depends on the valuation put on them by different individuals or periods, according to the needs of each. What is no relative matter is the significance of the Renaissance as a rebirth, not of the past, but of human genius. After the Dark Ages (which were less dark than we once thought them to be), man brings forth new art on new soil.

The fact demands insistent statement because it applies so intimately to the last section of our museums that we inspect, the last one to arrive in history, and the first one in importance to Americans; for it is the one devoted to the art of their country. On later pages, there will be much to say about the new problems opened up by American art. But, coming to it just after our consideration of the Renaissance, we are led to notice certain differences. The first is that American art, unlike that which began with Cimabue and Niccolo Pisano, does not inaugurate a vastly different period; also, since it does not stem from men who had to create new forms, as those two Italians did, it develops, hand in hand, with the European art of its time; yet as a final characterization, it shows a constant eagerness for some new expression, one suited to a people increasingly more detached from the past, as we indeed are. Two possibilities for such a development seem to exist: one deriving from our architectural or engineering accomplishment, a thing suggesting machine forms, while the other rests on elements in the ancient traditions of America, our heritage from the soil and the earlier peoples who told of it in terms of drama, humor, and beauty.

Both of these developments are still matters for the future, to a very great extent, though some results of each are already to be noticed, and others will doubtless be recognized when more fully evolved works show us the role, as forerunners, of certain earlier things. Such a case has previously been noticed in these pages. It is that of the limners of our Colonial days. The very names of these American primitives have usually been lost, and their pictures, but a few years ago, had a standing hardly above that of curios; yet today it is recognized pretty generally that they already register essential characteristics which were to persist in our art. In the same way, the sturdy simplicity of many an old New England jug, which had been prized merely as an antique, turns out to have a better claim to our interest. For the logic of its forms appears again, after a century or two, in the legible, functional outlines of a silo, and the one thing is as American as the other; the sense of proportion in both is again what makes us admire the best of our great buildings in the cities. Seeing the photograph of an ensemble of such buildings in the skyline of New York, a great sculptor-architect, Duchamp-Villon, said that the pattern of the modern cathedral was there. Another artist, Diego Rivera, was commenting on the frequently noted similarity between the plan of our modern apartment houses and the dwellings that the Indians piled one upon the other in the cliffs of our Southwest; he observed that the same cause produces the same effect. It explains the name of a Chicago club, the Cliff-dwellers, in one of the great buildings facing the lake front.

It needs more than the lifetime our museums have thus far had for them to do their work of clarifying our ideas about American art. Much more remains to be done, especially in the wide fields just glanced at. But our galleries have already done much to bring about the better understanding we have today. A single example, from the field of painting, will be enough to illustrate the point. The Mellon Collection contains one picture by the old-time American artist, John Quidor. Loaned to a great exhibition held at the Metropolitan Museum in 1939, it told numbers of people who had never heard even a mention of his name that here was a genuine and vital figure in our school. Then the Brooklyn Museum made patient and thorough researches into old documents, the records of exhibitions and collections, and there resulted a showing at the institution of a considerable part of Quidor's surviving production. It was not only fine in itself, but threw light on the mentality of his time. A master like Albert P. Ryder thus stood revealed as far less the isolated talent he had formerly seemed; he took his logical, historical place with the newly found painter, who stands between him and Washington Allston; for that splendid dreamer is also in the succession represented by Quidor when we follow, in retrospect, the line to which he belongs.

The work of the museum with American art is not confined to cases like that just described, where an artist is brought back from obscurity, or indeed from oblivion. It is a basic principle of art appreciation that many types of painting and sculpture are to be seen in their true light only when people have had very extended opportunity for contact with them. Thus, New York had had a picture by Thomas Eakins on the walls of its museum from 1881 continuously. A work of small dimensions and without sensational qualities of any kind, it was overlooked by most people. Even those who gave it some attention had to have their impressions amplified by further examples of the painter's art. Bryson Burroughs, whose understanding of Eakins' great talent caused him to add other paintings, when the chance to do so came along (or could be created), built up, at the Metropolitan, a fine group of the artist's work, the first one

33. Rembrandt: Man with a Beard.
Courtesy of The Metropolitan Museum of Art (Marquand Collection).

in this country. Long before it reached its present extent, it had convinced a great dealer as to the significance of Eakins. One-man shows at
an influential gallery were the result, great collectors bought there, and
other museums secured pictures by the artist for their walls. An achievement of the kind especially to be demanded of the public galleries of
America was thus added to those previously cited in this chapter; our
collective Museum of the New World had done immeasurably more
than increase its possessions, for it had given its people a wider and deeper
understanding of their nature.

Unfortunately, the same cannot be said about the handling of all our
important artists. Consider, for example, Maurice B. Prendergast, with
his rare and beautiful qualities; it must regretfully be noted that his
success came almost in spite of museum attitudes. Boston and New York,
the cities where he spent his entire life (save for the trips to Europe),
kept the doors of their great museums closed to him, and with hostility
rather than with indifference, for admirers of the artist repeatedly proposed his work in both places. Neither of them can claim to represent it,
even at present writing, when other public institutions have long since
welcomed it, and the best of our collectors see in it the one American art
of its period that can be set beside that of its important contemporaries
in France.

Before leaving this part of the subject, we may return to its pleasanter
side in recalling the way the Philadelphia Museum made known the work
of that founder of art appreciation in the city, William Rush, the earliest
of American sculptors — a man of delightful talent. The same galleries
house the most extensive collection of works by Eakins, a gift of the
artist's widow.

In the nature of things, as they have been and still are in nearly all
museums, it would be wrong to judge the institution on the too narrow
basis of its successes and failures at recognizing individual talents. Its
mission has been to show as much as it could of the country's art, when
such production has met with general sanction. We hope for increased
leadership, and title to leadership, as our museums gain in mature discernment, and are willing to risk being ahead of the public. Meanwhile,
they have done important service in letting artist and layman see American work on walls that also show the fine things of Europe, both by its old
masters and its moderns. To a long-continued test of this kind, the
country owes most of its conviction that our art is a valid link in the long
chain we have been reviewing.

The historian and the philosopher doubtless take pride in having
established a connection with the past; but, thank goodness! our people

as a whole give but little thought to such matters. They go to their museum for enjoyment, a matter not of the past but of the vivid present; they do not, however, despise their scholars for assurances that the things to be enjoyed in the galleries have their foundation in solid and healthy tradition. And could there be a better tradition than that of the respect for humanity to be seen in the portraits by John Singleton Copley? It is the kind of respect that Americans can understand, for it includes that frankness which made the old painter register the straight-laced primness of the New England lady, shrewd housewife that she was, as well as a sense of humor, and a generosity befitting the helpmate of so opulent and influential a person as her husband. (The two magnificent effigies referred to, those of Seymour Fort and his wife, are at the Hartford Atheneum.)

Copley stands as the best of our Colonial painters because he adds, to the human element just noted, the splendid technical qualities which place him with great painters generally, irrespective of time or country. But as Americans, we have a right to take an especial pleasure in pictures like those of Ralph Earle, which, though lacking much of the drawing and color we have seen in the great masters, still can tell us of local character and life. Young William Carpenter, in his red suit, sitting bolt upright in his chair, as Earle portrayed him in the Worcester Museum picture, looks out at us, after a century and a half, with all the manly and thoughtful reserve of the well-bred boy that we should like for a brother or a son. The satisfaction our people take in a true statement like that is akin to their recognition of a beautiful statement. Such a one was made by Washington Allston in his painting of a moonlight night at the Boston Museum.

What if Allston struggled for years in vain over his big picture of *Belshazzar's Feast*? If his personal talent did not fit him for a work of such scope, if only men like David, Géricault, and Delacroix in his period were equal to the problem of a vast composition, then the wise appreciator of art will turn to Allston for the things he could and did give; they are of a high order and generously offered. With William Morris Hunt and John La Farge, as we have seen, America tried again to reach the stage of evolution that France had attained. In a later generation, Twachtman's picture of *The Hemlock Pool*, in the Phillips Academy gallery at Andover, tells how near our painters stood to the pioneers of Impressionism. Certain canvases by Childe Hassam might well be mistaken for the work of Monet or Sisley, and without casting on our painter any suspicion of his having merely copied the splendid art of the Frenchmen: it contained the most important teaching of its time, but the approach to it, by Twachtman, Hassam, and Alden Weir, was simply that of intelligent men who recognized the problem they had to study. How fine a use they could make of what they learned is shown by Weir's portrait of Albert P. Ryder, in the collection of the National Academy of Design.

Yet immediately, Ryder having been mentioned, we are reminded that the painting we enjoy most in the American sections of our museum is not that which emphasizes the school study which set out to bring us abreast of Europe, but the things which sprang from a native urge to express ideas inherent among ourselves. Thus Ryder's grand picture of the Resurrection, at the Phillips Memorial Gallery, or his Macbeth and the Witches, at the Cleveland Museum, are on themes which have occupied the minds of millions of our countrymen, and the treatment of the themes is one evolved in intense meditation and hard work in a New York slum. Although Ryder had been abroad, and retained till old age the luminous memories of Rembrandt that entered into his own poetic fantasy, his connection with the great school of romanticism was one of feeling its dominance in his formative years, and thus continuing its qualities not by imitation but by instinct.

Those same words apply to Thomas Eakins. The head of that masterpiece, the Signora Gomez d'Arza at the Metropolitan, suggests some noble Spanish portrait, while the tremendous power of observation and rendering to be observed in the veined hand is reminiscent of the scrutiny that the French primitives gave to their subjects. Yet, though Eakins spent years in France and Spain, and profited mightily by their teaching, his vision remained so much the one he had from nature that the real key to his art is to be had from another picture in the same gallery, that of Max Schmitt in his two-oared scull on the Schuylkill River. The observation of those waters (on which the painter himself is seen rowing, in the distance), the rendering of the silhouette of tree stems and foliage against the sky, at an hour of the day accurately registered, everything tells of the "return of the native," and the renewed strength he felt on his own soil — scant as was the welcome that its people accorded him.

Yet, to see the teaching of our museum simply in terms of national qualities is to miss by miles the goal it sets and the use that artists have made of the institution. Having convinced ourselves of the astoundingly local note struck by the Max Schmitt picture, we must also envisage it, in the way that Eakins did, as a problem in perspective. We have studies for it, where a geometrical network of lines tells him, for the final painting, where he is to place each detail. Knowledge like that could not be acquired in full by even a sovereign genius like Paolo Uccello, the founder of the science. It needed the contribution of one student after another to bring the matter to the point we see attained in the Eakins picture. He

34. Vermeer: Young Woman with a Water Jug.
Courtesy of The Metropolitan Museum of Art.

would have been the first to say so, and his own patient work in the museums found its continuation when he, a teacher for many years, regularly brought his pupils from Philadelphia to New York in order to take them through the Metropolitan.

I have already called attention to the purely American side of Prendergast's work. The museum, for him, was largely a matter of his great contemporaries in France. He rarely spoke of the Old Masters, though, at the very end of his life, a volume of reproductions after Giotto was his constant companion, and others of the old mural painters had fired his imagination and led him to try his hand at mosaic. Yet the great aesthetic experience of his life was due to the art of Cézanne — universally sought by museums today, though unknown there in Prendergast's early years. That he could be the first of American painters to recognize the genius of Cézanne and then, with all the excitement of such a discovery, still have so much quality of his own as to remain but slightly or not at all influenced by the great Frenchman, is why his pictures form an essential part of our museum's teaching that there is such a thing as American art.

It would be tempting to follow this thesis, as it continues to be illuminated by the efforts of living men, some of whom are producing work of great beauty or of important intellectual promise. But our subject is the museum, and if I have commented on the tendency or quality of certain of our painters, it has been to indicate the problems of our galleries, and their achievement in dealing with the rich and varied material that the country offers them. Certainly, as to the work of living men, our institutions have never before been as well aware of its importance.

Without lack of appreciation for what other places are doing, it seems imperative to mention here a work as valuable as that of the Whitney Museum of American Art. Here an artist possessed of vast means showed the esteem she gave to her fellow professionals, first by a studio club and exhibitions, and then by endowing the project permanently and providing funds for steady purchasing. Another effort in the same field (and connected, very significantly, with a general scheme of education) is the Addison Gallery of American Art, at Andover.

Two rather special museums that are contributing in a distinguished way to our study of American production are the Phillips Memorial Gallery, in Washington, and the Museum of Modern Art, in New York. The role of the latter is particularly important for its great exhibitions of contemporary material from abroad, while its research in the fields of the Indian and of the applied arts (with special reference to the machine), besides its work with architecture, offers unique opportunities for artist and public to see the relationship of native and foreign art. The fact that our workers stand this test in the admirable way they do gives the best of reasons for a statement made very early in this book: that the explanation of America's great effort with museums is that it wants museums. And now we have proof that it wants them because it breeds men who, quite like those of the long centuries we have just traversed, are themselves carrying on as artists.

CHAPTER IV

1. PROBLEMS AND THEORIES

AFTER READING the pages immediately preceding, someone might well conclude that the millennium was just around the corner. At any place in our fair land a museum is apt to spring up overnight; after a given number of apprentice years, it will have a good director, and money will flow to support his plans for assembling the finest collections obtainable. With the further breakup of Europe (which we have done our best to prevent), many a new source of museum pieces may appear; (perhaps not, however: even in her impoverished state, Europe is apt to cling to her art treasure; France has already passed a law designed to prevent the exploiting of works of art as Greece, Italy, and other countries had done previously). But we generally assume that our museums are to have many new accessions of fine things, giving the true idea of the course of art, its culminations, and its direction.

This is a highly optimistic way of looking at the current health of our museums, but it will stand up under examination. However, at this point, an obvious question is: what does the public, the Americans for whom we have been building these museums get out of them when they go there? How many of them do go, and how often per year, or per lifetime? The magnificent achievement described in the preceding chapters boils down to the work of a few individuals, relatively — as compared to the scores of millions who might have contributed, by their interest at least, and been benefited during our museum period. Whether we think of Mrs. Jack Gardner bringing over her Venetian palace and cramming it with her treasures, or J. Pierpont Morgan making his prodigious collection, or John Quinn doing his extraordinary work with modern art, our history has largely the character of a series of one-man shows.

And that is not, in the long run, the way to solve our problem. We must work for the era of the common man. The museum will have a share in that task. If the technique of the institution is largely democratic, and if its purpose has increasingly been one of making the collections available to the largest number of people, we must face the fact that it does not touch the lives of a vast majority. Efforts are being made, in various cities, to widen the public reached by our collections. The prob-

lem is one of especial moment in America, and the means used in solving
it (such as publicity unknown in Europe) are developing as we realize
the extent of our task.

But perhaps the biggest problem facing our museums is to be seen in
the contrast between the individuals, rich or poor, who, through innate
or acquired art appreciation, have built up the instruments of culture
here, and the masses who have remained ignorant of the feast before
them, even to the point of denying, by their indifference, that it *is* a feast.

The older social philosophy was to consider the masses as an inferior
human breed, acceptable as tillers of the soil, churchgoers, soldiers, and
so on, but not to be given too much education. Our period rejects this
concept, which still, however, has many belated adherents; and they
could make out a pretty good case for themselves by pointing to the
"popular" expressions of art. This *ersatz* is composed of many things, all
of the same kind. The most conspicuous are the advertising pictures,
along our country roads and in public conveyances. They are planned to
catch the eye for a moment, and through their success in doing so, they
have become a big factor in modern business. Even bigger is their failure
to hold the mind for more than that moment they aim at, or it would be a
failure if there were any intention on the part of their producers to have
them taken seriously.

Admitting that most large-scale advertising is bad, an "art director"
said he thought the pictures in the magazines showed much improvement. It is true that the cruder illustrations of a generation or two ago
have gone out of style, but instead, we have work more photographically
dull than that which afflicted us in illustrations by the older men. Doubtless, the newer type of schooling must be blamed. The flippant brush
strokes which are supposed to "jazz things up" and to denote "technique"
are a poor substitute for the skill and knowledge possessed by such old-
timers as A. B. Frost, Charles Dana Gibson, and Frederic Remington.

The illustrator may be a true artist or a mere commercialist. When
we reach the work of Winslow Homer (not to mention the great men of
the past), we see that telling a story or representing a scene, a person, or a
mere object (which is illustration, after all) has been the point of departure for much of the best art of all time. What has given illustration a
bad name is that many of its practitioners have never gone beyond the
point of departure. To disguise the fact, resort is often made to a coating
of sugar or — as in the case of cartooning — of salt. But we do not reach
the plane of art when sentimentality, comic ideas, political ideas, and the
like are added to an imitation of something in nature. That was indeed
the formula for success of most nineteenth-century work, and it still serves

·many men today. It carried into our galleries no end of things that we have since thrown out, and so people are on their guard against "popular" painters, as they so wrongly style the producers of our advertisements and magazine covers.

It is not men like these, however, who are favored by the more sophisticated Americans, those who have been to college and/or to Europe. They have sat at too many dinner tables where exhibitions were discussed not to know that certain artists are well thought of and that others are not. Even when the talk turns to those who draw forth admiration, the sentiment does not convert itself into a desire to have a picture and live with it: the very words suggest certain highly improper feelings that men have for women. I vouch for the fact that, in one cultured home, I heard it stated: "The place for art is in the museum." But if the dinner-table speakers remain pure in this respect, they all appear convinced that nothing is better form than to have an opinion on painting: in many circles, it appears that to be articulate about art is a social talent ranking higher than an ability to discuss the theater, music, or books. These, after all, are apt to be the concern of nearly anyone, while pictures and sculpture are more mysterious; yes, the museum is the place for them.

We do not yet encounter an intelligent perception of art values when we enter many houses where works by the great masters are to be seen. Lest I be thought to regard certain characteristics of buyers as peculiarly American, let me recall the question put to William M. Chase by Whistler, after the latter had lived abroad for some thirty years. "Tell me," he said, "is it the same in the States as here in London? You go to some rich man's house, and everything is wonderful: paintings, porcelains, tapestries, until — there on the mantelpiece, or in a corner, you see some rotten little thing that gives the whole show away." The "rotten little thing" was just the one the owner had bought on the strength of his own taste; the other stuff had been sold to him by dealers who had the cleverness not to expose him to criticism as having anything second-rate.

We must go a step further in recognizing how slightly most people's lives are affected by art. In collections which are not only devoid of the little telltales that Whistler laughed at, but which show actual scholarship on the part of those who assembled them, one can see evidence that no real feeling entered into the matter — unless it was such a one as competitiveness, the desire to have the rare and important examples that outshine all rivals. In such cases, Tennyson's old words, "faultily faultless," give us a clue to our lack of enthusiasm: one has only to note the omission of material which would give a new vitality to the ensemble. But for

35. Hogarth: The Lady's Last Stake.
Courtesy of the Albright Art Gallery, Buffalo.

connoisseurs of the type under discussion, it would disturb the "harmony."

How different was the case of old Henri Rouart, in Paris! One could well feel that he had his Cézannes as a result of living for many years with his Greco, the first one to influence the artists of Paris. "I don't see how you, a modernist, can get excited over old stuff like Delacroix or Gros." The answer would be that those men have never ceased to be modern — alive: and then one would understand that the bewilderment of the questioner arose from his seeing only the school to which the recent pictures belonged.

Such a man is of that miseducated type which is further from art than the people who never bother about it at all. As the latter include so large a proportion of our citizens, and as the numbers of visitors who enter the museum are, to an extent, the measure of its success, and also an argument to be used when grants of money are sought, much thought has been devoted to the question of increasing attendance at the galleries.

To achieve this result, tests of various kinds were applied, and the discovery was made of an unhappy phenomenon called "museum fatigue." There is really nothing strange about the thing: there might be "library fatigue" if people, through centuries of reading, had not learned that the way to enjoy books is to read them one at a time, for an hour perhaps, instead of trying to cram samples of sixty novelists, poets, and dramatists into the same number of minutes. That is quite the equivalent of what visitors do in rushing from a gallery of the Greeks to one of the Chinese, thence to paintings of the most varied type, with a look at the etchings (since a wedding present is to be bought).

Once more, also, we must remember that the vast public collections we now have are a modern development, one for which people have not been prepared, either by the reading habits mentioned just before, or by (what is still more important) the habit of seeing art in their accustomed surroundings. There again, books usually having a place and proper use, their essentially lovable character has come to be appreciated. How strange that Benjamin Ives Gilman, in that study of his, which contains so much that is admirable, should say that "the solution of the problem of overgrowth in museums is as simple as Columbus's egg. They must not be allowed to become so large." Public libraries are often very large also; but in cutting things out of either the library or the museum, you will destroy its balance and, for somebody, its greatest utility; perhaps it loses interest for the very persons we most desire to aid. William M. Ivins, Jr., writing for the *Bulletin of the Metropolitan Museum* (September, 1934) has stated, "In a certain way it may be said that the great museum and the great library constitute the two halves of the community's memory of the past"; and he goes on to quote the words of the great Marquess of Halifax, "The best Qualification of a Prophet is to have a good Memory."

Simplifications attempting to equal that of Columbus with the little egg problem are often mere self-deception. Some matters are essentially complicated, and they have to be recognized as such. How much nearer the truth Mr. Gilman was when he wrote, "We must rejoice in proportion as museums are unnecessary; and look upon the conservation of art therein as the Greeks looked upon existence in the underworld, all of whose years were not in their minds worth a single day of warm and breathing life."

The life referred to is the one that the people and the objects lived at times when they dwelt harmoniously together, day after day, and in the quiet evening hours when friends dropped in, and a new feature of the home was enjoyed in common, or an old one was marveled at for the hundredth time. A vase to contain wine or oil would serve its material purpose quite as effectively if there were no red or black figures painted on its flank; so that if the Greek spent money for such decoration, it was because he liked to see it every day. Here was a popular art that shows up the poverty of what we call so today. Yet Keats, two thousand years later, rejoins the ancients in their love of that beautiful thing, and proves that England, — not to speak of the modern world in general — has not deviated from the character of mind coming down to us in that priceless heritage of Greece.

Keats' famous ode is Mr. Gilman's own answer to the critics of museums. It may also comment on the length of time needed till we reach his hypothetical period when museums will be unnecessary. In one sense, that day will never come: certain things will always be too precious to be entrusted to the hazards of individual care, and great numbers of others are of such importance to all men that they must remain accessible to everybody, as only a museum can make them. But the basic idea behind the words of our critic is true gospel, even if it implies the idea that all men need the museum. There are some who do not.

Reverting once more to the question of books, I give heed to the lesson I once had from a great librarian. Though his international success came from a deep love of the things in his keeping, he affirmed that there are broad classes of admirable people who have no need of reading. Similarly, in my thought about the museum, I cheerfully admit that very fine lives may be lived by men utterly untouched by its influence. Shakespeare's "man with no music in him" who would be fit for "treasons, strategems, and spoils" is indeed a type, but it would be the blackest of pessimism — almost misanthropy — to say that all men unresponsive to art are of such a type.

Yet, before anyone can say that art means nothing, either to himself or some other person, it is imperative that there be opportunity to try out the question. Conscientious and even regular visits to public collections are not enough, any more than Sunday churchgoing is enough, if the rest of the week is spent irreligiously. One of the good Paris art dealers, when showing his wares, would often warn a prospective client to be careful in his choice: "Getting a picture is like getting married — you're going to live with that thing, you know." They do know that in Paris, more than anywhere else; which is why taste and knowledge are at their height there.

And to add one more testimony on the subject, I cannot refrain from quoting again some words of Diego Rivera's that I have set down else-where, "I hate museums." On my exclaiming in surprise, he added, "Oh, of course I've had some of the best moments of my life in them. But I hate them for their effect. In the past, men had works of art in their homes, to see at any hour; now they say that one should see them in the museum."

One reason for the powerful development of art that modern Mexico has shown resides in the fact that a vast number of Rivera's compatriots have continued to have art in their homes, if it be no more than some specimens of good earthenware; and in an astonishing number of house-holds — even in the cities — there will be some example of the ancient sculpture that the soil still gives up in such abundance.

And so the problem of the museum goes immeasurably beyond the confines of the building. We ask too much if we say it is the museum's business to change the public's attitude toward art. It can give invaluable aid, suggestion, or even inspiration in that matter, and it will give always more in proportion as its exhibits are kept to the highest standard. But the current between it and the people is clearly reciprocal: each affects the other, and we come back once more to Emerson's idea that we take from a place what we bring to it. The process of improvement must go on out-side of the building as well as inside. And what goes on within the museum will be nullified if the home life of art, its contacts with people, streets, and manners, is at variance with the patterns proposed by the masters. William Sloane Coffin, a very wise president of the Metropoli-tan, used to say that this great museum had less influence on the public than city shop-windows. John Cotton Dana had already made such an observation.

All this has a direct bearing on that question of "museum fatigue" which we glanced at. I pointed out that the feeling would not occur if

36. Constable: Stoke-by-Nayland.
Courtesy of The Art Institute of Chicago.

people had any real understanding of the way to use the institution. It goes without saying that everything possible should be done by architects, lighting experts, and the persons concerned with the placing of benches, with ventilation, and with all other matters of creature comforts. The museum should have every material attraction it can, and should keep the visitor's mind free from any unfortunate memory that can be avoided; it should leave an impression of time happily as well as profitably spent. Such things seem almost too elementary to say here. But now that the obvious *has* been said, and assuming that these matters are disposed of, the director and his staff may feel free to devote themselves to their one pre-eminent study, the quality of their exhibits. If the public has no taste for such things, all the scientific presentation in the world will offer no help whatever.

When it is agreed that compromise with ideals, in order to get paintings and other art objects of easy attractiveness, is not the right way to make gains in attendance, and that, for such a purpose, we do not need to concern ourselves excessively about wearying the public, the museum is still not absolved from efforts to reach the largest possible number of people. I have said, above, that no problem is more urgent than getting the understanding and support of everyone capable of responding to art, and though the present book does not pretend to be a manual for museum personnel, a few ideas may be offered to advance the necessarily gradual work to be done.

I take back no bit of my severity (if it was that) toward certain of our people when I say that they are, in the mass, magnificently worth striving for. In the first place, they are of identically the same stock as the men who have given us our great museum development. Everybody's experience will furnish examples of families that remain commonplace even while one of their members rises to splendid heights of character or achievement. We see those two latter elements in the records of the exceptional persons who have made our museums what they are. We admire the qualities of these men too much to permit ourselves an illusion that any action of ours will produce more such people; but at least we may observe similar potentialities among their neighbors, today as well as yesterday. Everybody will recall, again, how often a single contact — with a person, a book, or a picture — has marked a turning point in the inner evolution of some man or woman. Only after many years, perhaps, will its effects be recognizable; but at times they may be traced directly and wholly to the occurrence.

That was the philosophy once offered by an old professor to a young one, who had been resenting the lack of response from his classes. He was told that the result of his work — extremely earnest and well-prepared work — might appear at some completely unexpected time and place, even in a far future, when some mind, which had been slowly assimilating his words, would burst forth with ideas, and so act in a way to compensate, a hundred times over, for that part of the professor's effort which did indeed remain fruitless.

The return of old graduates to a university, their testimony as to benefits received from him, or the very record of their lives doubtless permits a professor to appraise his influence on his students. He is in a much more advantageous position than the museum worker, who far less frequently knows which ones, among the innumerable visitors to the gallery, profit from his exhibits. Yet, his conviction of the public's deep pleasure and benefit is none the less a sure one. He has only to observe how people react to the paintings, sculpture, ceramics, and other exhibits. Some will be listless, hostile, frivolous, or otherwise unresponsive. But (and the the reader can verify this for himself) no round of the galleries, at any hour on any day, will fail to discover many — the majority of visitors, I believe — whose manifest quality of attention and warmth of glance offer the best evidence that the collections are meeting at least a sufficient response. Of course, only by speaking with them can we estimate to what extent they are moved by the sight of masterpieces.

Here we are dealing, most often, with residents of the city where the museum is located. But what does a visit mean to people from the small places where no art works are to be seen? One of the attractions of New York in the summer is observing the pilgrims from all over the country, who come in larger numbers during the vacation season than during the rest of the year. These people have an absolute hunger for something to bring a bit of color into their lives.

I remember one such person — from a Midwestern town that stays in my memory as the most unattractive I have ever seen anywhere. My host for the day, a worker in a lithography plant, showed me the few things which might have some slight interest. They were few indeed, and of a deadly commonplaceness. Finally, as if he had had an inspiration, he said, "Oh perhaps you'd like to see our art and book shop." Not quite believing he could make good on his offer, I gladly assented. He took me to a business building on a side street, up to the top floor, and along an ill-lit corridor. Sure enough, on a door at the far end of it, were the words *Art and Book Shop*. We entered a cubbyhole of a place, where a schoolgirl sat at a table, doing her homework. No one was there but this guardian of the treasure — which I did not need very long to inspect: a dozen or two lithographs and woodcuts on the walls, a few modest shelves of books. I will say, though, that the various things shown were on a consistently good level of quality.

I looked around to my host — who was beaming.

"Pretty nice, don't you think?" he asked me.

"Yes, indeed, there are certainly things here that I like very much, and some of the books are ones that I've been meaning to read for a long while. But how do you get customers to come here, so far from the center of things? I should think you'd need a place with a shopwindow on the street level."

"It might be better, of course. But I just couldn't afford it. I make a hundred a month where I work, but when I've paid expenses at home, and for my wife, and for my daughter here, there isn't more than enough left for this room — and the cost of bringing books and prints from New York."

"But," I pursued, not understanding, "how can you do any business here?"

"Why, I don't do much, to tell the truth. But the only places in the whole city where you can buy books are the drugstores, and what they have doesn't amount to much. And what pictures you can see are not even as good. So I thought it would be such a nice thing if our town had a real art and book shop, and I just made up my mind we would, too. I'm so glad you like it."

After twenty years, I still see that little man as a symbol. That art and book store in the bleak town to which I have never returned is a token of America's love for beautiful things, of its dream of owning them and making them. And if a person is ever tempted to despair over museum conditions, let him think what a fight is being put up, all over the country, to have the barest tithe of what our big cities offer in abundance.

Perhaps it is clearer now why I said that trying to help our public is so splendidly worth while. We are impatient about limitations — and forget how quickly they may change for the better. We are rancorous about the way a stupid trustee, representing a still more stupid group in the community, has blocked the road to progress that we had at heart. But in his small town, before that trustee had made his fortune in the big town, there was no one like that art and book man to set him on the right track, when his mind was still open. And — come to think of it — there's a lot of hope for the son of that trustee. There's a lot of hope for no end of people and things in America, if you stop to consider how much we've done thus far.

There is also a lot of discouragement, so we've got to do more. The main obstacle in the way of progress is popular apathy, which is chiefly

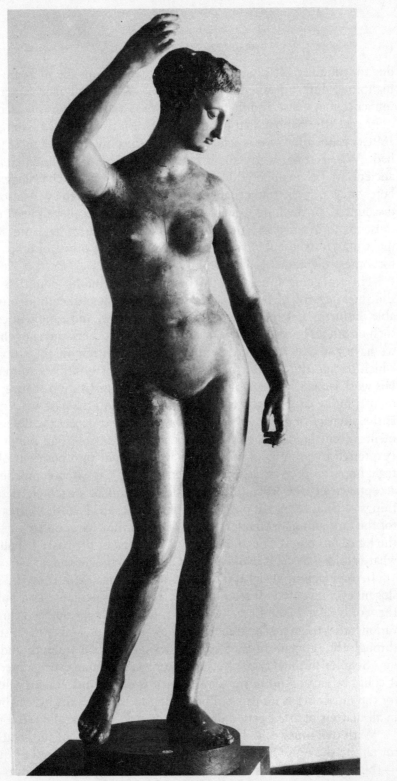

37. Jean Goujon: Diane de Poitiers.
Courtesy of the Worcester Art Museum.

due to ignorance. It expresses itself in remarks about the museum being highbrow, dull, un-American, and so on. A form of hamstringing its influence may cause a smile today, but it was a very serious menace until quite recently: Sabbatarian prejudice. The Metropolitan Museum, until 1891, was not allowed to open on Sundays, the only free time most people had. We need not worry about hatred of modern art or indifference to ancient art (as a supposed form of conservatism, as "archaeology," as a bore, or even as the fraud that certain persons claim it to be). Also to be discounted, in the long view of our problems, is the alleged need of the museum to avoid class antagonism, which, on the other hand, would make it an instrument of social snobbery, or, on the other, of propaganda for some proletarian utopia.

The foregoing hindrances to better understanding doubtless exist. But their negative character makes dealing with them directly an unprofitable business. Let the museum survive and grow, and time will correct such errors; any one of them may, however, be bothersome enough until we have got past it. The only valid way of fighting all the stupidities which darken the sky for the museum director is positive achievement. His work is part of the fight for democracy, his institution sharing enormously in the effort to give to all the people what in the past was regarded as the privilege of the few. In such a course he must expect the discouragements, even the dangers, incident to popular control. Bad public taste (expressed by prominent men who have been put into positions of strategic importance as regards the museum staff) has often compelled the acceptance of unworthy things or the rejection of extremely desirable things — even very great ones. Both of these results furnish a bitter drink for the museum man who loves his work, and they have, unhappily, been the lot of our officials on all too many occasions in the past. I shall offer what I think is a way to avoid them or at least to reduce them.

In approaching it, let me sound a warning against one of the worst slogans ever invented. It is so bad, in fact, that it is perhaps never put into the words "Art Made Easy," which do, however, sum up the claims, in various advertisements by teachers, critics, publishers, and even museums, through the program of their gallery arrangement, instructors, and buying. Schiller affirmed that art is joyous; only a charlatan ever claimed that it could be easy. And so my plan (which is that of many men who care for the museum) is no panacea promising to bring results overnight. As in all matters of art, a period of normal growth must be allowed for.

With that much said, I go ahead to my conviction that the great lever for raising the museum to its proper place and its proper level of quality — the highest level — is a body of art lovers throughout the community.

That is no very sensational discovery, someone will say, especially if he disregards what was said just a bit before about the things to be done by the museum itself, the positive achievement which offsets negative elements.

Returning once more to Renoir's pregnant words, that the place where the young painter learns his art is the museum, one can see that institution, quite obviously, as the place where other persons susceptible of enjoying art catch fire from it, and go on to the acquisition of works of art to live with. When there are enough such persons, and their daily experience with pictures, sculpture, and kindred objects in their homes has made them see, always more clearly, the difference between good and bad, and even, as the French say, that the good is the enemy of the best, then the museum will be kept automatically to that level of the best which will not tolerate the merely good as a substitute.

Over twenty-five years ago, when I told a college class that my ideal of success with them would be realized only if each of them became an art collector, I added that, to many, it would seem as if the goal proposed were that each should become a millionaire. Few people need encouragement on that point, especially if the price they have to pay is not too high. But neither that price nor the prices paid by rich men for works of art were in my mind. Nor were such things in the mind of a certain museum worker when, lecturing in a very "art-conscious" city, he told his audience he would believe in their seriousness when he saw a really good dealer's gallery in the town, one that proved the people's desire to own fine works: merely a Platonic interest was expressed by occasionally going to a museum of Old Masters, to a modern exhibition, or to a lecture — even his own.

By a coincidence, it was in the same city that I had tried out my scheme for making the museum a creator of amateurs, as art buyers are called in France, and usually with accuracy (the word primarily means art lovers; it is true, of course, that many Frenchmen buy for investment, or even for speculation). My first move was to break down sales resistance. So deeply rooted is the idea of art collecting as a millionaire's game that you have to present concrete evidence of your claim that people of modest means can own fine, original works. But there are such; etchings and lithographs by the greatest masters, provided you take those which appeared in large editions, and there are Indian, Mexican, and simon-pure American things. Getting them may mean many a hunt, though that is no hardship: it even adds to the memories that the works evoke later. The auction houses frequently yield some fine piece from an old residence, while for people who have reached the stage of judging contemporary production, there is the greatest privilege of all: that of becoming the virtual collaborator of a young artist of talent (or of genius, who knows?), one still at a place where even five dollars for a picture is a godsend.

Suppose our collector has not reached the stage of sure judgment; suppose the five-dollar, one-dollar, ten-dollar, or fifty-cent purchases do not turn out to be the masterpieces that have, indeed, been bought for such sums, or even less. An object of some interest has entered a household. It has sent not only the purchaser but other people in the family to the museum (or perhaps just the library) to check up on the acquisition, to see whether it is really a treasure — or just "junk." I repeat that I am not offering a short cut to art appreciation; time is needed, but it is time well spent, and enjoyably spent. And it takes us along the one road that experts have followed in arriving at their knowledge: the road of experience. Imagine what it would mean to a museum to know that its public includes a substantial group of people with the background such experience affords. Standards would be kept up, or rather lifted up, by visitors who demanded an always better showing at the place which had the resources — of men and of money — to get the best.

Everyone who knows the museum field will testify that I am not building castles in the air, but am describing conditions as they exist. The man with one Greek vase will want the public gallery to show where his possession fits in — at least chronologically; and in quality too (for that last point, he will get insufficient help from the books, splendid as some of them are). The woman with a jug she bought for flowers will want to know about the Virginia or Carolina hill people of today who made it, and how it compares with the things produced in Colonial times. The same applies to the possessor of a chest painted with fine frankness of color and design by some old Pennsylvania German. Or if one of his descendants has painted a picture today, why isn't it as good as something that sells for thousands of dollars? The latter work originally sold for less than what the recent one cost, because the artist needed the money in order to eat. That was the time to buy from him, and you can give either one of two good reasons for saying so: because you think he deserved to eat, or because it is always agreeable to pay a price that has not yet been jacked up by half a dozen speculators' profits.

So that if a museum trains up a breed of buyers, it is helping itself, the artists, and, above all, the community. Some members of it, to be sure, are so overwhelmingly impressed by the reputation of famous painters or great ceramists or sculptors, that they will accept nothing that has not been sanctioned by the vast majority, above all nothing but what

38. Poussin: The Triumph of Neptune and Amphitrite.
Courtesy of the Philadelphia Museum of Art, Philadelphia.

is vouched for in books. They lack understanding of good objects that are as yet unacclaimed and, not being able to pay the prices that the spotlighted things command in the galleries of the big dealers (to which most fine works gravitate), these collectors give their imagination free play in the auction room or in the shops of the less scrupulous dealers — and come home with fakes. These may be either the kind willfully produced as such, or the works of genuine but minor artists that have been sold under great names. That is just too bad, if the buyer sincerely wanted fine things, and was not merely a bargain hunter.

At times counterfeits are discovered in museum collections, and then someone is sure to say, "What difference does that make? If the painting or sculpture was so beautiful that it withstood detection for a long time, why should it not continue to give people pleasure?" The answer to the two questions is that they both rest on a false premise: the object is not beautiful, any more than is the wax dummy which for a moment may have imposed on someone who thought it was a living woman. And, in the museum, that work did not give pleasure: it was accepted with the respect that the name attached to it had every right to command. Visitors who could well appreciate the master's real work may have noticed that they rarely looked at the object in question, telling themselves that their lack of response came from the heavy varnish which they thought must conceal its quality; or had it not been dulled by "restoration," or was it not just one of those inferior productions which even great men turn out occasionally?

None of these explanations was correct. Even the last one, the "subjective" one, would not satisfy a person really sensitive to the master's true note. It was probably this very person who finally plucked up courage to tell the museum that it had gone wrong. Then the bandages fell from the eyes of everyone else, and what seemed strange was that the mystification had endured as long as it did. But while it lasted, much harm was done. The public to be reached by art — office workers, schoolteachers, housewives, doctors, and the rest — were led to think that they had better not bother any more about things beyond their comprehension. To be sure, if the museum was a good one, there would be genuine works by great artists — and it is always surprising how surely these things produce their effect, and on even quite simple people. As the latter gain in appreciation, and discern ten qualities where at first only one was recognized, they naturally get more from the masterpiece. Indeed, the great test of its claim to that splendid title is that it constantly grows on acquaintance. And the forgery, as Ouida tells of it so incomparably in *The Nuremberg Stove*, is dead.

Though the book has enjoyed immense popularity, especially among children, my experience is that few people remember an exquisite bit of insight it affords. Even if you have read the story, let me briefly refer to it once more, for some one who has missed it. The scene is in an antique shop, where a little boy has fallen asleep among all the magical things he has seen for the first time. They come to life in his dream, and enchant him with their grace, their strength, their wit, their beauty. Only two of them take no part in the festivity which is in progress, and he asks his neighbor why that is. "But child, don't you see?" is the surprised reply; "they can't. Those are forgeries — they have no life." Sometimes it seems as if the lady who wrote those words left nothing at all for art critics and the rest of us to do — save apply her test. To be sure, there is sometimes dissension as to whether a given work has life; but that state of affairs does not endure. Murder will out, and life will out.

Since I have mentioned one of my favorite pieces of writing on art, I will go on to another which bears out the first one. For Cousin Pons, the hero of Balzac's great story of that name, is the man who responds to the life in paintings, in sculpture — or in a fan, if it be like the one he bought, a fitting evocation of the lovely Eighteenth Century lady who wielded it. And of course Cousin Pons is the perfect example of the man who can himself have a happy life amid art works — on an income of nothing a year.

Those last words belong to Thackeray, another writer who loved painting and drawing. But I want to insist once more on that Balzac book. Suppose it were disseminated widely by our museums. They would gain the gratitude of countless persons, who would be stirred by that masterpiece of story telling (which is principally about other things than art). You can't tell — we might have a larger number of people who would get the joy of existence that made up to Cousin Pons for the thousand slights he had to endure from his rich relatives. Certainly, collecting in Paris has increased many times over since the great novelist published that tale. I doubt our having there an example of cause and effect; more likely, Balzac had that sixth sense by which artists respond first to the direction of their time.

Post hoc or propter hoc, let us imagine the book, or some other book, increasing the number of our collectors until an American city could sustain 35,000 art dealers, as does Paris (with about half the population of New York. Of course, the buyers come from everywhere; but then New York, also, draws on our whole continent.) Juggle the figures to suit yourself: all I ask is a multiplication of art lovers. Then, I say, you have decreased the museum's problems in the same proportion, or even in a greater one.

Take the question, for example, of the staggering confiscatory taxes on great fortunes. We are told that their possessors — or former possessors — can no longer pay for the museum as, very largely, they have done until now. But if we had, throughout the community, men with such an enjoyment of art as that of Cousin Pons, and in numbers such as we very easily could have, the support of the museum would be a light burden for them, indeed one that each of them would be delighted to share. He would thereby have a voice in the direction of the museum, which, in its turn, would benefit.

If the ideal collector is a very rare bird, there are, even so, numbers of real *amateurs* throughout the country, and admirable ones. Compare their possessions with the old collections at the New-York Historical Society, for example, though, even there, most of the bad things are kept out of sight. The fullest proof is obtained when one can see intact groups of the things people used to buy before the rise of our museums. The advance in understanding is enormous. Even when we look again at the Jarves picture at Yale, the choice of the best American connoisseur of his day, we are once more brought to the conclusion that if indeed there is no such thing as progress in art, there is progress in art appreciation. James Jackson Jarves may have had a stronger, more original mind than any present-day collector. To have attained his level meant immensely more, in that far-off time than at the present day, with our facilities of travel, the increase of exact reproductions (our constant basis for comparisons), and then the piling up of detailed analyses by scholars — permitting immediate decisions on all but the most difficult questions of attribution. With such aids to knowledge, a very minor student may (and should) know more than a genius did, a century ago.

To be sure, the opportunities for acquiring fine Old Masters were incomparably greater at that time. But what did it matter if a dozen Vermeers were then to be bought, when the very name of the artist was not yet discovered? No, our period has innumerable advantages for the connoisseur, and Americans have, on the whole, made excellent use of them. No one can estimate what the country contains in the way of small collections, or of households with just one or two good pictures. It is on such places that we must draw when the great assemblages of art works are no longer available. Perhaps there are yet to be more of them; it is not easy to be a prophet, about finance or anything else. But one can look to the past and say that, for not less than thousands of years, men

39. Claude Lorrain: Cattle at a Ford.
Courtesy of the California Palace of the Legion of Honor, San Francisco.

have found fascination in collecting. We need to go further in linking up their instinct with the museum — not that it may absorb all their possessions, for that would be a catastrophe. On the contrary, we need a thousand homes with art in them for every one so constituted today. But if certain great things now in private hands ought to be in the museum, that institution should reciprocate by increasing the measure in which it is the public's guide.

2. THE PROBLEM OF THE AMERICAN ARTIST

UNDOUBTEDLY, many persons will look on my last idea — that the museum be our mentor — as turning attention away from modern art and from American art. Such a notion can derive only from a wrong understanding of the whole matter. Every competently directed gallery in our country today refutes the superstition that museums exist for the sake of what is past and what is foreign. Even a collection of ancient art, if it is the true art which is always true, can be studied by a modern American with the utmost profit, for it is a means of knowing whether we are on the right track at a given moment. If there was any excuse in 1810 for those Pennsylvania artists who spoke of the Academy as a museum "and consequently not likely to become of much importance, either in the improvement of artists or in correcting the public taste," there is no excuse for such ideas today.

As to the things we call specifically modern, I shall speak a little later, separating the subject in general from that subdivision of it which comes under the heading of American art. All of the latter is modern, since all of it was produced in the modern period (save, of course, that great body of American art which we owe to our Indian predecessors on this continent). The place where it is fathered gives to an art its national character; and the time when it was produced leads it to be properly called modern when, as with our art, it dates from the modern time. The term is one which denotes a period and not a school: the "reactionary" is as much a part of the modern world as the "progressive." Whether we prefer one direction to another is a separate issue.

And so we get to the question of American art in the museum. Two overlapping theories about it are heard, one placing emphasis on the function of the museum as the judge and guardian of art, the other stressing the American artist's need of public support.

To sustain the latter point of view, a hundred arguments come readily to mind. Historically, the artist has had a difficult time here. From the start, our people have been busy with practical affairs, as was natural in a country where everything relating to daily life had to be built up from scratch; later on, the chances for material success being enormous, attention tended to center on that rather than cultural matters. Even so, as we have seen, our record in art is, all things considered, amazingly good. The government, however, did not sponsor an art program; and rich tourists, who have often been important buyers in countries like Italy and France, simply did not visit our shores — at least, not as connoisseurs. Since the invention of photography, portrait painting, the steady source of a livelihood for many artists of the past, has dwindled more and more, while most of the handicrafts, another way of earning a living in earlier centuries, have been killed off by the machine. That is true of Europe also; yet most European countries have managed somehow to make life more possible for the artist; he has too often found our country, for all its wealth, a particularly adverse environment.

What more natural, then, than for the artist to see the museum as a patron, like the princes of the past? It has not merely money to spend, but walls on which to display pictures: in fact, that is why those walls were built. Besides, it can provide a magnificent avenue for reaching and developing private buyers, who could support all the real artists we might bring forth. Then too, the public showing of their work, the opportunity to see it together, as well as in comparison with the classics and the modern schools of Europe, would do for our workers what no amount of effort by individual supporters could possibly accomplish.

William Cullen Bryant, in his profoundly considered and eloquent plea for the founding of the Metropolitan Museum, emphasized the importance it could have in offering big exhibition spaces to our artists who, as he said, were usually held down to the production of small "cabinet pieces." That had been one of the disappointments of John Vanderlyn on his return to America. Trained in a school that admired and wished to emulate the sweep of David's vast records of the Napoleonic epic, Vanderlyn thought our young, heroic commonwealth should have the same inspiration. Out of his own pocket, as we have seen, he paid for a building in which to display such work. Its financial lot was disaster; and when S. F. B. Morse painted his large and splendid picture of the old House of Congress, he fared no better with the work, which is today one of the proud possessions of the Corcoran Gallery. To be sure, when, at a later time, the opportunity to deal with big walls arrived, most of our painters who were employed on them proved inadequate — and the word is modest when applied to men like Kenyon Cox and E. H. Blashfield. A later muralist, Gardner Hale, is similarly reserved in his book on fresco painting. In speaking of such men, he merely remarks, "The less said of them, the better."

Even for men who painted things of moderate size, suited to private residences, the road was difficult enough. And nothing is more regrettable than the judgment forced on us when we note that the late work of many American artists is inferior to their early production. Some of them, in their youth, had quiet years of study in Europe and then, returning here, deteriorated chiefly because of excessively difficult material conditions. The same is true of others who never went abroad, but who, starting with clear minds and high ideals, met defeat also. The great (and generous) public could not effectively be reached. As one foreign observer stated the case, "In Europe, the artists live badly, but they live; here they starve" — which is to say that they are forced to find a side line to make ends meet. Leaving aside the men who sacrifice all artistic principles, few people can keep up their best effort with the drain on their time and energy involved by a potboiler such as commercial decoration. That was what John Quidor worked at, and it probably explains the fact that, in his eighty years in New York, he could paint so few pictures. One cannot guess what the country has lost through such conditions; one cannot estimate the number of unknown men who have striven for art and who could echo Victor Hugo's words, "The terrible thing is not to die; the terrible thing is not to live."

When strong emotions color a question, it is difficult to consider it in the light of reason. Yet we must try to do so. The man most sympathetic toward artists must admit that not all of them have had talent enough to make their work valuable to the world; many an imaginative youth has confused a liking for art with the ability to produce it. In the recorded words of Ingres there is a passage in which he strongly urges a pupil to return to his native place and continue the honorable business career of his father. Such words, though hard for a youngster to swallow, might have been salutary for many a one here — where, moreover, there was not such magnificent training as that to be had in Ingres's atelier. We have to recognize from the start that the professions of painting and sculpture are to be undertaken only by very exceptional men.

But then, granting freely how natural it is for the artist to think of the museum as a patron, we must, I believe, firmly decide that that is not its role. Benjamin Ives Gilman, following a splendid tradition, has argued that the museum's work is to preserve and show the things which have been proved by humanity at large to have enduring value. Only institutions like the societies of "Independents," with their principle of

40. Chardin: Lady with a Bird Organ.
Courtesy of The Frick Collection, New York.

"no jury," can offer a complete alternative. For if the collective judgment demanded by Mr. Gilman is not to prevail, then every claimant to a place on museum walls may possibly be right in his opinion of his work. Some would indeed be too well balanced for such pretensions; but seeing the bad things in galleries, many a man is willing to desert modesty as he thinks (perhaps correctly), "My work is better than that." And so the thing extends itself quite literally *ad infinitum, ad nauseam* — and both the muses and the public are done the worst disservice.

No, there must be a firm check on access to museum space — for the sake of the artists no less than for that of the public. This does not mean that the museum should fall back on the past; only a little latitude is needed to make Mr. Gilman's arbiter — humanity at large — mean the contemporary public, and the ideal state of affairs would be a public able to recognize important production at once. Meanwhile our curators and purchasing committees can look ahead and secure, besides what is already of value, what will be recognized with the passing of time. That is, of course, the hardest of jobs, but we must continue to build up competence for it. Perhaps, we are today ready to judge nothing nearer than the work of fifty years ago; that is no disgrace — indeed, it is not doing badly at all, if our philosophy of making acquisitions for a permanent museum is really valid. But let us, in the next generation, cut down that fifty years by ten, or by twenty, if we can.

Let us have the freedom of choice which comes with treating contemporary works as nonpermanent acquisitions. If changes of judgment on the Old Masters are known to occur (not frequently, but still at times), how much more likely is it that modern work will turn out to have merely a "historical interest"! Yet that quality, which accounts for the influence of certain artists on great numbers of men in their profession, as well as on amateurs, is a quite sufficient reason for including in a museum particular works which do, in fact, have a merely historical importance.

To speak personally for a moment: I regard Picasso as an artist who will endure because of certain pictures that seem to me masterpieces. Not everything in his enormous production can merit that word, clearly; and some of his paintings look to me like failures, save as testimony to his researches. But precisely such tentative work may explain the purpose of another man who took up the idea that Picasso conveyed to those near him before passing on to something else. And so, to show the evolution of numerous modern artists in true perspective, the thing of genuinely historical importance should be accessible to students and the public.

Though we are here dealing with modern art in the broader sense of the word, the idea just developed applies particularly to our own painters and sculptors. Just because they are ours, because we have so very special a warmth of interest in them, we need also a special freedom both in accepting their works and in sending them to the attic if we find, in the long run, that time does not bear out our first hopeful opinion of them.

A plea for generosity to our artists is not even the most distant cousin to the "America First" philosophy which would tolerate inferior things done here, simply because of their nationality. The so-called "friends of American art" who have made this mistake may yet come to be recognized as the enemies of American art. For when one visits certain galleries and sees room after room of bad stuff (almost always the work of men who did not know it was bad), one can hardly repress the idea that something is wrong with this country, or that artistic talent is feeble in this country. For our artists, it would be an unhappy day indeed when such a feeling became general. To make matters worse, the chances are that in such a museum there are no other rooms for the really fine American things: they are more likely to be interspersed among poor things.

Nobody doubts that love of one's country is a wholly admirable thing; and most of us can enjoy the enthusiasm of people who have a special flair for appreciating the excellence of local products. But they must not ride their hobbies too hard, though it is such as they who have created in Europe certain very instructive and sympathetic museums that bear frank witness to a belief in groups of regional artists. The latter, if taken singly, are perhaps of slender importance; yet taken together, they may combine to utter an eloquent statement about their nation, and testify to the most intimate feelings of its people. To recognize the appeal of this sort of museum is not, needless to say, to fall into the nationalist fallacy in art appreciation.

Art appreciation demands the constant exercise of what P. G. Hamerton called "nonpartisanship." The very time we live in is already spreading snares for our freedom of judgment; when we visit outmoded collections, and when every additional glance makes us more certain than the last about the poverty of the work, our one explanation as to why it was ever bought will doubtless be that the collector merely followed the dictates of his time. Now, let the far stronger element of love of country enter in, and you will see how it can mislead. If you don't see that in terms of our country, go to German, English, or Spanish museums of the nineteenth century, and try to find any reason but nationalism for the presence of most of the paintings they exhibit.

It is in the newer museums of the United States that one particularly regrets the presence of bad works by Americans. Sometimes they are the only things there; and then it is easy to understand why the cultivated people of the town keep away from the gallery, and decline to support it. Their attitude is only natural, for they think of the museum as a commercial sample room, something that gives the artist a chance to make a sale. If visitors are, on the contrary, convinced that a picture is in the museum solely because of its artistic merits, they will see the whole place more favorably.

In cities where collections of fine old pictures or those by the great French moderns accompany the showing of inferior things by our men, a no less unfortunate effect is produced. For the thoughtful observer may easily work out a piece of logic like this: "Americans, with their intelligence, their respect for the classics, their energy and power as organizers, have shown on any number of occasions that they can build up a fine museum of works by the masters. That is to say, we are a people of collectors, like our cousins the English, for the British Museum and the National Gallery contain perhaps the finest assemblage of art works in existence. But to the British school, in its own paintings and sculptures, such praise cannot be given. Down to the present, and noting some exceptional cases, England will take rank in history as the greatest conserver of the art of the past, far more than as a great creator of art. Judging by what America shows in the gallery I am studying, and in others I have seen, our record is going to be a similar one."

If our observer is, for example, a man about to make his will, he may decide (and perhaps, on such premises as we have just heard, should decide) to give his resources to activities in which his countrymen have proved their creative ability. If a soil is unfitted for one type of crop, wise farmers will plant the thing that does flourish there, even if they care far more for the product that would fail. The final indictment, then, of the museum-as-patron theory is that, in taking the welfare or the livelihood of American artists as its great objective, it is almost sure to lead to a seeing of American art as the crop doomed to failure. This is anything but the truth, and the museum that contributes to the forming of such a wrong idea is doing a bad job.

Our painting, as we have seen, has its roots in the healthy innocence of a people with a single-minded desire to register the truth about the world or — more modestly — that part of it which, in their Colonial isolation, they knew so well. With a few helpers from abroad, and a few models in the shape of imported pictures and casts of sculpture, they went on rapidly: it is already more than two hundred years since the birth of Copley. He grows in our esteem, not because of any matter of patriotic pride, but because his work has such astounding vitality, and so

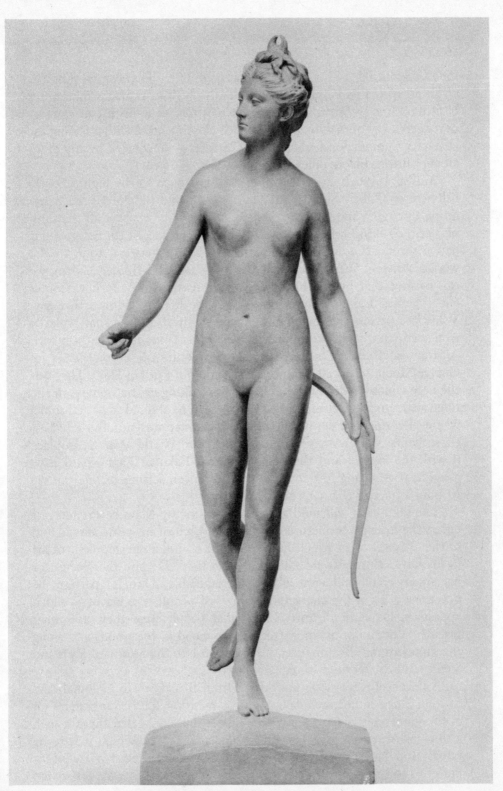

41. Houdon: Diana the Huntress (terra cotta).
Courtesy of The Frick Collection, New York.

much, specifically, of the painter's quality of form. That central problem of his art is met by Copley when he creates his broad planes by the use of firm outline. Sometimes naively, delightfully hard, his use of contour never gets away from a live reality, and is closely united with a feeling for character — prodigiously distinctive character — unequaled by any other artist of British blood, unless it be Hogarth.

And so, through an early school which goes on to the high accomplishment of Gilbert Stuart, and very soon touches the great French tradition through Vanderlyn, we come to landscapists who, for all the thinness of their beginnings, fix our attention on the special character of our native scene. If romantic temperaments give a personal tone to the work of Allston, Whistler, and Ryder, of Inness and Homer Martin, we can balance that by the uncompromising realism of Winslow Homer and Thomas Eakins. Even the long later life in Europe that saw Whistler's personal development did not diminish in him that typically American sense of nocturnal beauty which made me mention him with Allston and Ryder. So also, the famous picture of his mother is, as George Moore observed, the portrayal of an old Puritan lady. That was the note which made it look so foreign as it hung at the Louvre, in the room with Ingres, Delacroix, and Courbet. One wanted it placed somewhere else, and not simply because our painter was not the equal of those giants. The Louvre planned, just before World War II, to place it with the Homer and the newly acquired Eakins. That would have given its true setting to the work — an American setting, as one can say without a trace of chauvinism.

The same idea will hold good if a painting by Maurice Prendergast enters the Louvre. A picture by him would tell of his years abroad and of the closeness with which he studied the essential development of art in his time. But it would tell more than that. Despite the interest of his superb color, and with all his unpredictable charm of pattern, he never lost a jot of the characterization — of people and places — which appears in his earliest efforts. And what people were they, and what places? Why, those he knew from his boyhood in the woods and along the shores around Boston, even if his response to the beauty of Paris and Venice came, later on, with equal felicity.

A dozen others among our artists, from Blackburn in Colonial days to John Sloan in our own day, might be mentioned as irrefutable proof of the statement we have seen made by our museums: that there is such a thing as American art. The future alone can say how high it is to be rated. But that is not the point — which is that we need not concern ourselves to the slightest degree with any question as to whether we are creative in art or merely the conservers of it who build museums. The question has long since been answered by definitive and authentically American achievement. Our only questions are as to how it shall go on. They will be answered — at least in part — by the Museum of the New World, of which I shall have more to say later on. It is already helping to direct our artists, and they in turn will help to give to that museum its distinctive character — a character no museum of the Old World can have.

3. THE PROBLEM OF MODERN ART

IN SPEAKING OF the role of the museum, we saw, just now, that it was giving to the artists a part of their direction, and there is, certainly, most ample authority for stating that, at all periods, artists have learned from the work of their predecessors, work such as museums now exhibit. On the other hand, what counts most in a masterwork is something that the influence of other works of art cannot account for. Our greatest thrill comes from contact with things never before done, even if we find, on knowing them better, that they continue the unbroken line of the classics.

The museum can give invaluable help to the artist; it can never lay claim to creating him. The men who do derive entirely from its possessions are the *Epigonen*, as the Germans call the poor race of imitators of the past. Compare them, even when they are honest, with a man like Ingres. Haunting the masters for eighty years — from his very first drawing to his very last — and helping himself to museum treasure with full hands, he yet remains an archetype of the creator. For if he gave passionate study to the vases of the Greeks and to the madonnas of Raphael, the essential guidance of his hand came from life — from the men and women he depicted or from the subtler essence we call the life of his time.

Therefore, if Ingres, great lover of the past that he was, still ranks as the modern (or, to use his own word, the "revolutionary") of his day, how easy it is to see why a forward-looking period like ours should have an immense interest in its own image as projected by modern art. The term applies to all the products of the modern period, good and bad. (To be sure, when they are very bad, we simply do not classify them as art, just as we do not think of mentally or morally defective persons as "Americans," although, by nationality, they are that.) The type of modern art which has chiefly engaged public attention in recent years is based very largely on a conscious, intentional departure from naturalism. At first a mere puzzle to the majority of people, it has come to be recognized as including most of the expressions of genius in our time, and so has also come to monopolize the term "modern." This explains the remark — made in all seriousness — that Picasso was modern in 1912 (at the height of his first cubistic period), but was no longer modern in 1922 (when he was producing his neoclassical pictures). In other words, Picasso's modernity — his response to the need of his time — could be measured, according to the speaker, by the extent of his departure from natural appearances. But the question of what constitutes modernity is not as simple as that. The college instructor, in marking examination papers, is right in what he does, for the answers demanded of the boys and girls are fixed in advance by the contents of the textbooks. But the problems set by modern art do not have answers in advance: new solutions are demanded. The neoclassical Picassos of 1922 were new solutions to problems set for him by new experiences; and if the painter needed at that time to respond to the great statues he had just seen in Rome, he no more ceased to be modern than did Delacroix when, at the end of his life, he took from Raphael figures of the angels in his *Heliodorus*; and it was of the essence of Cézanne's creatively modern art that he followed Signorelli and Greco in so much of his masterwork.

Is all of Cézanne to be called masterwork? Yes, it is — unless you deny him the title of master. If you recognize the essential quality of his mind, you see it not only in the color he was able to handle in his maturity, but also in the heavy, Courbetesque troweling of his youth when, as he himself said in reviewing his work later on, he had not yet understood the difference between sculpture and painting. But the man's the man for all that. Or as the Spanish proverb has it: "*Genio y figura hasta la sepultura*" (we have but one "genius" — that is, one essential character — from the cradle to the grave). Therefore the young Cézanne, expressing his vision through painting with a black-and-white basis for the form, or the older Cézanne "modulating" the color, as he described the process, was always the same man.

And Picasso, in his early naturalism, in the geometrical research of his cubism, and in all the uncanny logic and intensity of his later developments, is still the *Malagueño* he was at birth, the man haunted by the fateful spirit that we hear in Andalusian singing. No wonder that he separates from Braque, with whom he worked so closely for a long time! The Frenchman, after his years of bold experiment, settles down to the magnificent style by which he constantly deepens and enriches his art. It is the Spaniard who continues to invent and perfect new forms. Some pages back, I spoke of works by him that may be looked on as failures. But only Picasso could have made them. The failures of a man so extraor-

42. Ingres: Madame d'Haussonville.
Courtesy of *The Frick Collection*, New York.

dinary are still important things; those in question take away nothing from the quality of that unresting mind which, more than any other, doubtless, has dramatized for our period of rapid change its conception of modernity.

If we use that word in its only reasonable definition, nothing could be more grotesque than remarks like the one I quoted about Picasso's varying phases. Although it was based on a fundamental and widespread error, we need not let that fact deprive us of a necessary part of our vocabulary. "Modern" is by no means identical with "abstract" (another approximation of ideas, and likewise to be handled with some precaution). To clarify by an example. no collection formed to cover modern art completely, or even its essentials, could omit Derain. Yet a purely nonrealistic work by him probably does not exist. The artist who has influenced the central current of his time most frequently, he suggested necessary developments followed up by the Cubists; yet he cannot himself be included in their school.

Since we have seen that the problem of the modern masters is beset by complexity and even controversy, how can we propose to admit them to a place whose task is to set our standards of truth? Actually, however, we cannot ask the museum to give us truth: at best it offers only what most men have agreed upon. Modern art, simply because it is of today, does indeed stand at the farthest remove from what Mr. Gilman called for: work that has been lived with and — by that surest of tests — deemed worthy to preserve in public galleries. Nevertheless, we look forward to reducing the period of probation, at times to the vanishing point. The process has already begun, and we are nearer to an ability to judge contemporary work than we were, say, thirty years ago. Sometimes we seem to go too fast in this matter: people who grew up with the point of view of the earlier time are not without disquietude when they see the work of youngsters in their twenties hanging on museum walls. But though mistakes are occurring, the mere age of these artists is no conclusive argument against them: Masaccio did his incomparable frescoes while still in his twenties — he died, in fact, at twenty-seven. In attaining mastery while still so young, he was not different from most of his peers — it is the exception among them who has not done important things in his twenties, or before that. But to appreciate such production at the time of its appearance calls for an almost prophetic eye, and few can claim that.

Another difficulty about evaluating contemporary art: we need the authority of time in order to feel safe about the conflicting statements made about it. Sometimes both sides are right: remember the bitter words exchanged among the artists of Renaissance Italy — with their partisans (quite as in our day) making things worse than the great men themselves. But even if we recall Michelangelo's terrible description of Raphael as showing more study than talent, and explain his severity by his resentment against attacks on himself, we must not overlook the fact that these fierce controversies were based on principles also. And Ingres, even when he so misunderstood Delacroix as to call him "the apostle of ugliness," did so on what he regarded as the loftiest premises. The example of very great men is therefore a confirmation of our claim that time is our nearest approach to the touchstone which decides values.

But are there no standards, no principles? Forty years ago, Matisse answered that when he said that there might well be laws for art — and then challenged his opponent to show him the book in which they were written down. There is no such book, and since we cannot always wait for the judgment of time, our best guide is the man whose interest in modern art is combined with a rich knowledge of the art of the past. The chances are that he will succeed better than will a committee: the latter offers too many alibis. The success or the failure being collective, we do not know who is responsible for it. Let one man in the museum be the director and be given power; we can see, after a while, whether he uses it well or ill, and may then continue him in office or replace him.

That may be rather cold comfort when a lot of money has been mis-spent, and the public has been rendered hostile. People may well ask whether museums should not rule out entirely the acquisition of modern art. That is not the true solution. Even if we can reach no decisions that cannot be appealed, we are not released from effort to reach such deci-sions. What is the "final" opinion on Rembrandt? A little research into the opinion of the past will suffice to show that he did not always hold the pre-eminent position accorded him today, and it is easy to find men of various admirations — for the early Italians, for the Orientals, for many of the moderns — who will strongly maintain that Rembrandt is to be rated lower than he was a hundred years ago. Do we therefore hesitate about giving space on museum walls to the master?

The famous Dutchman has on his side, of course, three hundred years of admiring testimony, while the men of today are vouched for only by their contemporaries — and rarely by more than a small minority among those. "Do you approve of modern art?" people constantly ask its adherents. It is tempting to reply, "Do you approve of modern life?" (for it is the only one we can live). "Modern art is the only kind we can produce," is more to the point. We may happen to think that our art today is less great than that of some older school, just as we may recognize that another man's children are bigger and better than our own. But it is our own that we are duty-bound to bring up, and certainly those of ancient Egypt and Greece are beyond any bringing up. It follows that the first requisite for dealing with modern art is to like it. In the days when I was troubled about most of Mallarmé's writing, I asked a French poet if he could understand it. His answer was, "By dint of loving it, I have understood it." Many will say that this was wantonly reversing the logical order of things — that one must understand first and love afterward. But art has a logic of its own, as has been said in various ways by various men — William Blake, for example.

The very anger against the "perversity" of modern art, still to be found today, sometimes affords a proof of its authenticity. For the very syllogisms intended to beat it to earth only demonstrate a quality it has in common with ever so many accepted schools. Intuitiveness, the characteristic most general throughout the art of our time, is to be distinguished — unmistakably and pivotally — in the greatest arts of the past. We spoke of Poussin, shortly before, as a type of the classic. His paintings give an impression of calm, unemotional reasonableness; and therefore some youngsters — and some writers who were not youngsters — have called him cold. You can convince them of the contrary in five minutes: by showing them the master's drawings. "But those are so modern!" (I am not inventing but quoting this example of what may seem to be a fantastic use of the word.) What is here meant is fiery, spontaneous, intuitive. The qualities are there; and they are in the paintings, as you see when you come to like them. And when you come to like modern art, you will see again that the anger against it also arises from its building on intuition — and its using logic only at a later time.

Modern art, then, is of immense value as a means of understanding better a thousand things we thought we knew before. Naturally, no real admirer of great modern works would consent to having them used merely as instruments, no matter what the gains so obtained. Among these are certain very significant ones, and everybody remembers that our better understanding, today, of arts like those of the South Seas, of Negro Africa, and of ancient America is a direct result of preoccupation with such things on the part of Gauguin, Matisse, Picasso, and others of their type. Knowing but few references to these "exotic" arts in the writings of travelers and others, I cannot affirm that no one beside Dürer spoke of these things as real art. But certainly they were generally regarded as curiosities, to be described as "barbarous" or "savage," in short, as belonging to the infancy of the race. But in the light afforded by an understanding of modern art, we can see that the nature peoples (one of our

43. Delacroix: The Lion Hunt.
Courtesy of The Art Institute of Chicago (Potter Palmer Collection).

friendliest terms for them) are no infants at all. Some of mankind's wisdom, religious sense, and sense of beauty must be sought among them.

They do not have systems of writing comparable to ours, and of
course no method, like the printing press, of multiplying copies of writing. What do they have instead? Tradition: the handing down from
father to son of laws, science, moral precepts, and the principles of art;
and memory: the retaining of past lessons by living minds instead of by
written pages. But then — since tradition and memory will sometimes be
at fault — another faculty will have to be used to get at a hidden truth
and a living beauty. This faculty is intuitiveness. One sees it in the cos-
mic grandeur of ancient Mexican art, as the movements of the sun, the
stars, the waters, the animals, and man himself are accounted for — at
times with an accuracy surpassing any that Europeans have attained.

I hope it is agreed that intuitiveness is one of the elements of art that
recent painters and sculptors have revealed to us particularly; therefore,
if some of us have failed to discover logic in modern art, perhaps they may
yet recognize it there by means of more acquaintance with the "primitives." Ingres smarted under that last word as it was applied to him in
his early days, when the primitives of Europe were unappreciated. Those
of the other races (beside some of the more ancient ones of Europe)
should help to clarify our minds when we see the successors of Ingres, the
"revolutionaries" of our own day.

But once more, we must avoid "using" art, even to prove a quite
valuable point. The great figures of Easter Island do not need the
sculpture of modern Paris to bolster the idea that they are impressive.
And the great moderns do not need the things of Crete or Byzantium or
Palenque as buttresses for their support. And if we leave open a decision
as to which of its phases represents modern art at its best, perhaps there
yet may be agreement that it does have a rightful place in the museum.

And it pays for that place in terms of the attendance record. We
have observed previously the effort of museums to reach the largest group
of people they can and, considering the way that modern art has gripped
the imagination of America, exhibiting the work of today is one of the
best means of arousing public interest and support. We have more to
consider on this matter — and from other points of view.

At present, let us glance at a segment of the public not always thought
of as such: the artists. Numerically unimportant, they have a strong
influence on opinion; they are known by the critics and collectors, so
that their words, reported even at second or third hand, may have much
to do with the success or failure of museum showings and acquisitions.
If their attitude toward the public gallery has at times been marred by

selfishness, only a moderate appeal to their disinterested judgment need be made for them to respond in a way that confirms one's confidence in their fundamental love of their work. More than any other class, they are the beneficiaries of the museum and, from the time of its founders, this fact has been well understood in America.

4. CASTS AND OTHER REPRODUCTIONS

IN READING, just now, of the place of modern art in the museum, many a person may have been tempted to say, "Old stuff. What he says applies to the conditions twenty years ago. But New York's Museum of Modern Art has had more than fifteen years of existence, and it's an enormous success. The rest of the big places in the country are headed just the same way, and perhaps some places — in California, for instance — are a lot more modern than New York."

Perhaps they are, in one sense of the word. And perhaps it is not the best one. Very strong suspicion attaches to men or places that go all out for modern art without balancing their enthusiasm with an understanding of the older things. The artists who have produced the best art of the modern age — from the French Revolution on — were profoundly prepared for their work by their knowledge of the classics. No more addicted to self-analysis than artists usually are, they could, nevertheless, give chapter and verse for every principle they used in their work. It had no ambition to be an encyclopedia of bygone schools and traditions; but neither was it rootless. Nor did it build only on the school just before it. Now, rootlessness — or at least the failure to get more than a superficial toehold on immediately preceding modern work — has today become the vice of a lot of people.

Their world began in the twentieth century; and as the great men of that period draw their strength from all manner of early sources, the professional modernists cannot understand the very painters and sculptors they imagine themselves to be following. The man who has no insight into the history of art will fail to distinguish between an open road and a blind alley, unless he has a pretty strong instinct. That is about the best thing an artist can have, but in that case he will assert his own ideas from the start, as was done by profoundly original men, such as Géricault, Courbet, Cézanne, Redon, and Seurat, all of whom, be it observed, built on knowledge of the classics. Merely going along with whatever school is modern at a given time does not prove that a young man will himself do anything worth while.

For Renoir in his youth, Impressionist theories and techniques offered what I have called "the open road." When his generation had exhausted its possibilities, it became a blind alley for the great numbers of men who went on with the formula, and thought themselves modern because they did so. How different was the course of a master like Cézanne! Exactly contemporary with Renoir, he was, like the latter, for years a contributor to the development of Impressionism. We have already noticed the tenacious individuality that was to make of his art, from first to last, a single thing. Taste, which he called the best judge, made him ally himself with the other true artists of his generation. But far from giving exclusive control to the brilliant ideas, of Monet, for example, he constantly returned to the Louvre, drawing from the antique and from Michelangelo, and above all studying that great transmitter of classical values, Poussin. And so, because he reoriented art in the classical direction it was losing, his true place is at the opening of a new period, instead of at the close of an old one. Therein, with all his external unlikeness to David, he still resembles him. Both men refused to be the decadent followers of even such splendid schools as those which preceded them.

In the case of David, everyone knows the means employed to free himself from the too graceful and facile painting in which his teachers instructed him in his youth. The clarity and force of the Greco-Roman art in which he saw salvation bursts the delicate network of line, and the mother-of-pearl shimmer — still put to charming use by certain masters — really spelled the decay of the type of genius which reached its apogee in Watteau. A firm sense of form, based upon David's study of ancient marbles, takes the place of the exquisite fragilities of the declining eighteenth century; and a whole torrent of new energy — that of the Revolutionist himself and that of the men he sired — was set free on the course it would take for a hundred years. Far longer had classical sculpture exerted its influence on the artists of the Renaissance, who made it their special study.

With all the misuse that weaklings have made of the classics, Greece and Rome still have the fecundating power they evidenced when a Michelangelo, a David, or a Cézanne addressed himself to them. And the best reason, after all, why modern art should not be separated from the older schools is the need of public and artists alike to compare the different periods with one another. Dull people will use a Greek figure in order to ridicule a modern one, just as their artistic forebears did, centuries before, when they used classical art to show up the "barbarity" of the Gothic. That very word Gothic, as is well known, was invented to express condemnation of the men who were supposed not alone to have departed from classical perfection, but to have acted as its destroyers.

44. Courbet: La Toilette de la Mariée.
Courtesy of Smith College Museum of Art, Northampton.

Today we see the harmony between even the two periods, and we are coming to recognize those moderns who are able once more to utilize the high qualities of the ancients and of the Gothic artists.

Cézanne's gift to art — a renewed sense of structure and organization — is in some ways comparable to the quality that gave David his power to reform the school of his period. Yet, the opalescent haze of the later nineteenth century makes it seem a very different time from the cultured and witty *dix-huitième*, while the last of medieval art, against which Michelangelo reacted, was of course still more different in outward appearance. Inwardly, however, the three periods have in common their *fin-de-siècle* character, something that menaces art with exhaustion if new strength is not forthcoming. The contribution of the men who in each crisis gave a fresh breath of life to their periods is essentially the same: all three appealed to the basic authority of the classics.

Perhaps we are today ready to understand more fully Cézanne's phrase, which was a bit puzzling to the men who first heard it, "I remain the primitive of the way I have discovered." Like other primitives, his scope had to be extended in many directions. The same was true of David. Unfortunately, we see immediate followers of both who — carrying to perfection what the founder of the school had brought forth — yet lead to sterility if other forces are not added to their own. Ingres, the great pupil of David, can show no vital artist among the many men in his studio; indeed, it is the weaklings of academic art who seize upon his authority. Picasso, who follows a part of Cézanne's teaching, is also a source of error for those who do no more than attempt to repeat his performance. It is all too easy to see the outer aspect of pictures: today there are men who imitate the appearance of Picasso's painting with such skill that they deceive both themselves and the public, quite as the academics, a hundred years ago, did as echoers of Ingres. The true value of that master reappears, for example, in Renoir. He stems, originally, from the school against which the classicist made his bitter fight; yet, it is men like Renoir (Degas, Seurat, and Matisse come also to mind) who reach, in their so different painting, a mastery of line that affords a new reason for loving the linear quality, even though Ingres himself had seemed to have said the last word about it.

The men who pay the best homage to the masters are often the very ones who are outwardly most different. Miró, who renews the contribution to modern art of Picasso's native Spain, might seem to have little in common with his older compatriot. Yet, without that great liberator, Miró would surely be very different from what he is today. And it is practically certain that other men, recognizing perfectly the immense value of Picasso's art, will turn even more from its formulas. No one, for a long time, will be able to affirm that antinaturalistic painting has said its last word with the generation that originated it: there may yet arise some great talent to advance antinaturalism along its own lines. But the chances seem to point quite the other way, and whatever estimate the future will put on the Surrealists, there is no question but that they base themselves on a resumed acceptance of visible things, and are therefore a part of the reaction against the "abstract" art which preceded their own.

Even if we abstain from judging this or that individual in the Surrealist group, it is clear that the post-Cubist period has approaches to art different from theirs. Among these is the strong work of Rivera and Orozco, and it has had its great success because it offers one of the new solutions possible. But, as I shall attempt to show later, these two Mexicans derive very largely from elements in their native soil which are, for the present, inaccessible to North Americans (as we are called by the Mexicans) and — even more — to Europeans. So that, since the traditions of ancient America (those drawn upon by Rivera and Orozco) are unfamiliar to most artists outside of their country, other sources of inspiration are needed.

And there remain in the museums certain great wellsprings always to be tapped, the ones which have given strength perennially to the revitalizers of art. When mere virtuosity threatened in Italy, after the time of the baroque masters (still not the men prophesied by Michelangelo in his terrible warning, "My style is destined to make great fools"), what do we see? A new land, first with Jean Goujon and then with Poussin, resorting once more to the inspiration that the Italian Renaissance had caused to gush forth like a fountain in old soil. And its waters have not dried up in the centuries since then. When they nourish a new growth, its leaves and flowers will have a very different look from those of other periods.

To make available today the source of strength which has so often served in the past is the museum's very special duty. To speak practically, however, how can American museums offer their public an adequate idea of classical art? The supreme originals of Aegina, Olympia, and Athens can never enter our galleries. Such possessions as we have, almost exclusively in New York and Boston, represent the effort of collectors and curators whose work will be expanded unquestionably (and the effort does go on, as witness the lovely Greek head at Toledo and the superb Roman statue at Minneapolis). But adding to our treasures is limited by Europe's having already gathered up most of humanity's heritage of the surviving sculpture of antiquity.

Robert Henri used to argue against excessive zeal on the part of our museums in making collections to compete with those of Europe. Let us agree that there may be excess and that, along many lines, we shall never be able to compete successfully. But, fine as Henri's teaching was when he called upon our artists to seek a living and even local inspiration, he was quite wrong when he said that Americans could always see the art of the past abroad, and that the airplane would make visits to Europe as easy as the railroad today makes a midwesterner's trip to New York. Shorten the distances as much as you like: only a small minority will be able to benefit fully by the galleries of the Old World. Before World War II they were visited by countless Americans who sailed across the Atlantic — and were always mere visitors abroad. When they came home, it was to occupy themselves with American matters, however fine a glow of memory may have surrounded the treasures of art they had seen in London, Paris or Rome. Airplane travel, however widely available, cannot change this situation.

For one essential fact remains: we live over here, and the place to see art is the place where we live. What gives to music, and even more to literature, their intimate place in our lives is that we can have them at any moment we are in the mood for them. And the recurrence of that mood depends partly on our being able to satisfy it. The attitude to painting and, even more, to sculpture, is too often that these arts are not natively American, and that liking them is an acquired taste. We are told that they should be seen where they naturally grow: in foreign countries. This point of view must be fought by the museums, which, in fact, were founded to wage just this battle. Its successful outcome should prove amply that the classics belong to Americans as much as to the other peoples.

How can our museums prove this fact when Greek sculpture, as we have noted, is so hard to get that only our biggest and richest galleries have any appreciable amount of it, and then nothing like the collections abroad? The answer is — by the use of casts. "What — those dreary things?" you exclaim. And just your choice of words is proof that you have never looked at them aright: they are marvelous things.

In many a glimpse into the studios of the past that the old painters afford us, we see casts doing their work as models for artists and students. You will be well repaid for consulting a book on Jan Steen if you look at no more than the scene where a painter turns from his easel to criticize the work of two pupils, a girl and a boy, who are drawing from casts. The picture is so wonderful, with its deep interior and those two healthy

45. Renoir: Le Bal à Bougival.
Courtesy of the Museum of Fine Arts, Boston.

youngsters, that you catch your breath at its beauty. And Jan Steen is the last person in the world for anyone to think of as academic.

You object that I am transferring the discussion from the museum to the school, or perhaps to the artist's studio, which is not a place for the general public. It is not, to be sure, and yet the man in the street, if he is to enjoy art as part of his birthright, will be well advised to follow the man in the studio in his approach to painting and sculpture, for he is the greatest expert in those fields.

There is doubtless a tendency, even a fast-growing tendency, to think that museums have outgrown the need for collections of casts. This is not because people now own what they formerly went to see at public galleries, though excellent casts are being sold at the museums themselves, and to an increasing number of art lovers. No, one accusation against the plaster works is that they accumulate grime; another is that they take up large amounts of valuable space. The first charge is repeated here only because it has been quite seriously made, despite the ease of answering it. Properly treated, the surface of a cast can be kept as clean as can marble. Before answering the other accusation, let us glance at the matter of casts in general.

In tracing the antecedents of the National Gallery, one of its officials, Mr. John Walker, has dug up some very choice bits of Americana. Prominent among them is a scheme originated by F. W. Smith around 1891; to large numbers of our people, including members of Congress, it was so dazzling that only by great luck were we saved from a monstrosity which was to have covered sixty-two acres near the Washington Monument. A whole city built of Portland cement, and representing the various countries of the world, was to have been filled with "casts and copies of historic art objects. The United States was to be represented by an elaborate Acropolis in true Greek style, with a model of the Parthenon, which, in characteristic American fashion, was to be much larger than the original."

Another passage in Mr. Walker's article (published in Art in America for October 1944) also deserves to be quoted: "One of the principal arguments for Smith's scheme, and an argument greatly encouraged by foreign museum authorities, was that America should be satisfied with reproductions and casts, since it would be impossible to acquire important originals. An eminent professor of architecture was quoted by Smith's supporters as saying that 'he would restrict a National Institution to casts of antiquarian remains, considering the fictitious value of originals in comparison.'" It is highly unlikely that those "foreign museum authorities" encouraged the scheme with the deliberate purpose of forestalling the spoliation of Europe through American purchases of originals. We had not gone far enough at the time to be a menace, and the lack of understanding displayed by that "eminent professor of architecture" was, we must regretfully admit, pretty nearly typical of the country.

The one extreme represented by those sixty-two acres of casts does not justify our going to the other extreme, and abolishing casts altogether. No one who knows originals can doubt that the difference between them and reproductions is a matter of two thoroughly separate orders of existence. For a profound and conclusive discussion of the question, the reader will do well to consult Henri Focillon's book, *The Life of Forms*. To people who have not experienced the different effects on the eye of, say, the etched line due to acid biting into metal and the soft line of lithography, it will at first seem strange that the contrasting characteristics of these graphic techniques are given so much importance by the great French critic. Yet, they are as distinct as the effects on the palate of a raw apple and a baked potato. With the two forms of the graphic arts, however, we are still dealing with originals. When we come to translations — from carved and crystalline marble to dull and molded plaster, for example — the disparity becomes far more marked, especially when the reproduction is made by men unacquainted with the artist who produced the original work, at a different period and in a distant land, very probably. Speaking of this matter, that distinguished sculptor of today, Jacques Lipchitz, said, "There are casts and casts. Plaster may be used with a sense of its beauty: when an artisan like Gonon made plaster casts of Barye's work under the eyes of the great man, I prefer the result, a thousand times over, to the bronzes of later date, for they lose so much of the beauty of those glorious figures."

There are, of course, no casts of the Parthenon marbles made under the eyes of Phidias. And very early in our experience with antique sculpture, we come to feel the difference between Greek work and that of Roman copyists, near as they were in time and place to the masters they followed. A hundred years ago there was far less knowledge of this fact; and it was with intense emotion that David, in his old age, wrote to his pupil Gros, to say that, having seen the Elgin marbles, he was forced to the idea that all work from Roman sculpture, such as he and his school had done, was based on a false foundation.

Therefore, we are making no admission at all if we say that our casts of Greek marbles are not to be mentioned with the originals. Rather, it is underlining further the incompetence of that previously quoted "eminent professor of architecture" who spoke of the value of originals as "fictitious." Not merely admitting but claiming, as we do, that the full quality of the classics cannot be appreciated from casts, we still affirm that place must be made for them in the museum. Without them, we have — as regards the Parthenon sculptures, for example — nothing; with them, we have something evocative enough to let us see, in the mind's eye, much of the splendor of the marbles themselves.

To arrive at this result, our galleries must obtain as much as they can of work that was shaped by the hands of the masters. To exhibit these original pieces along with the plaster casts would be a mistake, for the unlikeness of their effects would lead to confusion in the mind of the beholder. But it would be a mistake, also, to create a museum of casts entirely divorced from a great collection, especially if, as is sometimes proposed, they be separated by a considerable distance. There could, of course, be such a gallery for the education of students taking specialized courses in art history, and for people who have reached a sufficiently advanced point in their enjoyment of classical art. It would also serve as an invaluable reference collection for curators, who may, at any moment, need data on a piece whose purchase is being considered. Their decision to acquire it may well mean the outlay of a vast sum of money, which perhaps cannot be recovered if the acquisition turns out to be a bad one. In thinking of the general public (our chief interest), we must not forget the people who want to go more deeply into things; they have every right to expect the museum to furnish the material for their study. Without such workers, scattered throughout the community, the museum is deprived of the very group that best shows its influence. Moreover, collectors and scholars constantly influence the lay public, which is thus genuinely benefited.

As an instance of the layman's need for casts, let us recall that torso of a man in the Metropolitan Museum which one authority does not hesitate to attribute to Phidias. I said that a competent student, looking at this relatively small piece of fifth-century marble, can mentally reconstruct the figure as a whole. How? Not by studying fragments exclusively but by seeing, as well, the completely preserved pieces of sculpture in the galleries of the great European centers. Shall we add a little note to the label under the Metropolitan torso, directing students to the British Museum, in order that comparisons there may convince them that our object is important? Or shall we try to attain the same result by a series of photographs hung nearby? With a skillfully lighted statue before it, the camera can perform invaluable service in telling about details of carving, the grain of the marble, and related matters. But these are,

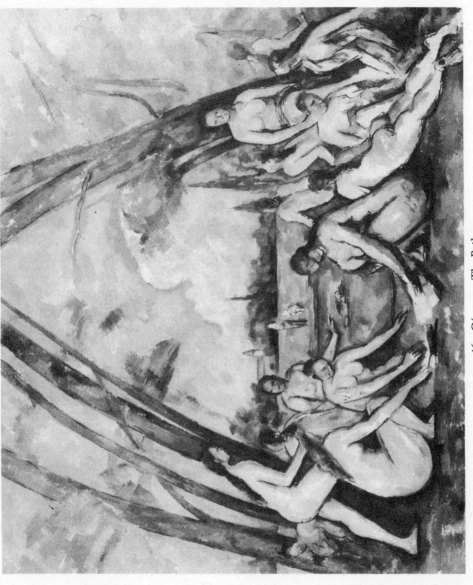

46. Cézanne: The Bathers.
Courtesy of the Philadelphia Museum of Art, Philadelphia.

again, for the practiced eye of the expert; and museum men know how slightly photographs appeal to the layman, though, to the professional, they may offer quite decisive evidence.

The average man needs to see the sculpture in full size and in the round, so that, walking around it, he can get an impression of the work as a whole. The best photograph is still two-dimensional, whereas it is of the essence, with sculpture, to think of it as three-dimensional; no collection of photographs can add the extra dimension. Precisely that idea of the nature of the art is what we want to build up regarding the "Phidian" marble we possess, as well as our other works. Directing even an earnest student to London, to supplement impressions gained in our museum is, of course, out of the question; and, for practical purposes, directing him to a gallery of casts in another part of the city is not much better. He won't go; or, if he does make the effort on his next free day, his memory of the piece he has seen at the other place is dimmed, and the cast collection seems a mere wilderness of lifeless things. In discreet proximity to the living marble, the plaster casts easily kindle into warmth and light; reciprocally also, their greater completeness permits a seeming miracle: the restoration to its original entirety and appearance of what had seemed, five minutes before, a hopelessly mutilated piece of stone, one which retained so little of human semblance, and suggested so little of art that it did not hold the eye for more than a moment.

Thinking over his golden hours at concerts by quartet players and large orchestras, a French poet suddenly exclaimed, "I have just heard the Tenth Symphony of Beethoven!" The composer wrote but nine, as we know; but so powerfully do they stimulate the imagination that by a happy poetic license the enthusiast evoked for himself a new creation of Beethoven's genius. Perhaps such a concession to fantasy is not without an element of danger, for our task is not to write postscripts for the masters, but to appreciate what they have left us; they alone could add to their works. Yet many an intelligent person has tried to form an idea of the great battle pictures by Leonardo and Michelangelo which have been lost to us through the ravages of time. To attempt a reconstruction of those vanished glories is no mere waste of effort, though the documentation for such a task is woefully insufficient.

That is not the case with thousands of fragments of Greek marble. The close relationship between them and larger pieces which have been preserved or — more probably yet — the relationship between them and Roman copies really does permit a valid image, burningly actual before the mind, to be derived from the casts that our galleries are banishing today. Tomorrow, space for casts may well be found by museum directors who lack it now. The reason? It hinges on a rule I once evolved concerning art collectors: there are ten thousand reasons for not buying a picture, there is really only one to make a man buy a picture. He buys it because he likes it, which means that the ten thousand reasons for not buying it are dissipated like smoke in a breeze. When we like the classics well enough, we shall find room for a full showing of them — not in the gruesome terms of those sixty-two acres near the Washington Monument, but amply enough to throw open great vistas of enjoyment.

We have already seen the importance that New England scholarship attached to classical studies, and so we need not be surprised to find a rather modest Connecticut city setting a fine example to the country, over half a century ago. To honor the memory of his father, a generous benefactor of the men set free by the Civil War, William A. Slater conceived the idea of a museum which should show the possibilities of classical study in America by bringing together the best reproductions of art works then available. Edward Robinson, who had returned from Greece a few years before, was asked to assemble a group of casts for the new Slater Memorial Museum at Norwich, Connecticut, and the result was "the finest collection of casts in the country, in the most effective installation ever made." The example followed in the work was that of the great museums in Berlin and Bonn.

At the time, neither Boston nor New York had an original Greek marble (the Cesnola Collection was chiefly of Cypriote material), and the museum at Norwich, not content with representing only the ancient schools, went on to give this country its first casts of Renaissance sculptures. For the inauguration, Mr. Slater sent private cars for his guests from Boston. Daniel Coit Gilman, the president of Johns Hopkins, Robert Porter Keep, the principal of the Norwich Academy, and Charles Eliot Norton of Harvard made the addresses at the opening of the institution. Its influence was soon felt, even New York sending a representative to study the work done by Norwich; and Providence, Springfield, Pittsburgh, Buffalo, and other cities owed their early collections of teaching material to the Slater Memorial Museum. When originals began to enter our galleries and their superiority (reinforced by the prestige of their high cost) became a matter of general knowledge, people went to excess in underestimating the value of casts. We need to restore them to their proper place as invaluable aids to appreciation.

Painting presents a different problem. Its greatest centuries are nearer to our own than are sculpture's, and the multitude of works that have come down to us make the use of reproductions incomparably less necessary. This statement applies, however, only to the larger and wealthier places that can pay the high prices demanded by original canvases of the masters. Where such things are available, photographs or color prints would obviously be absurd on the walls. Every museum has a stock of them in its reference rooms, where they may be freely consulted. And qualified persons may have access to forgeries, which are sometimes bought as aids in judging works offered for sale, and of doubtful authenticity. Sometimes they turn out to be genuine, in which case the museum acquires a treasure, perhaps, and often at small cost. If they are shown to be false, however, the museum not only saves its money but is spared the mortification of having misled the public during the time the work remained on the walls.

We can be positive that that time would have a limit. For one thing, as we have said before, there is a dead quality to a bogus object. The fact that we cannot precisely define the mysterious element does not make an experienced person doubt that it exists. The forgery, whatever its initial success in deception, still contains some telltale sign of its origin; it is derived not from any experience of life or of nature, but from the sight of other works of art. It might seem that the reproductions currently on sale today, things deriving from a scientific instrument, like the camera, would leap over the element of personal experience that we have noted as the basis of a painting or a drawing. But even when photographic accuracy exists, the original drawing or etching and the reproduction of it are not the same thing. Paper like that of the original may perhaps be obtained, or it may be doctored to have a look of greater or less age; printer's ink may be so treated as to avoid its usual fatty sheen; and there are other subterfuges of the counterfeiter which may render expertizing, even by very competent men, a hazardous business. If they fail, on occasion (as a rule through hastiness, fatigue, or overconfidence), the experience of people who know best is still that the genuine thing has a vitality, a timbre or quality of tone, that gives a sensation radically different from that of forgeries or of honest reproductions.

Evidently we have now reached a category of things where the average person throws up his hands and withdraws. Even so, he is not quite right if he expects the commercial prints on his wall, though they do possess elements of beauty, to do for him what originals would do. One day or another, he is going to see something in a museum, or at a dealer's place, that will destroy his pleasure in the reproductions he has. Their shortcomings are doubtless very subtle, like that of music over the radio as compared with what we hear when in the presence of the performers. Speaking of the quality of radio and phonograph music, a composer

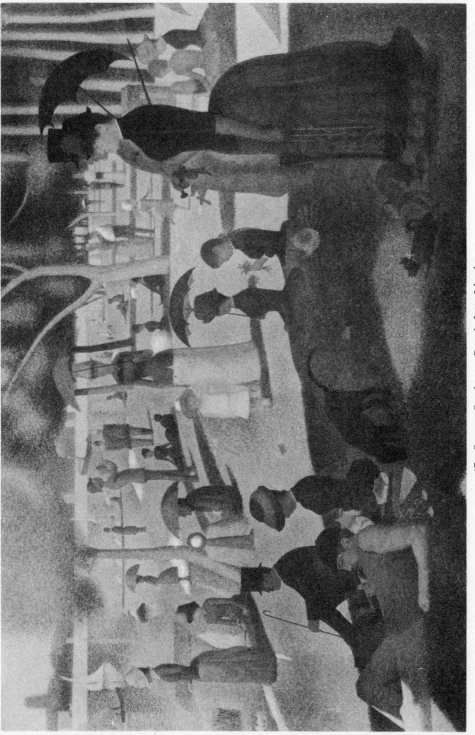

47. Seurat: Sunday on Grande Jatte Island.
Courtesy of The Art Institute of Chicago.

remarked, "Of course it's a wonderful achievement to give us such things at all; but just the same, they are music with the vitamins left out."

The difficulty in following such affirmations, unless one has already become aware of the total inferiority of reproductions, may cause some reader to think that I am talking metaphysics. I am not; and shall now offer a concrete example of the matter in a field where absolutely irreproachable reproductions might seem possible. The field is that of etching, and I am taking the extreme case of an original plate; the trouble was caused solely by the printing, which was done by a later hand. There is a dealer in Paris to whom I shall always be grateful. Seeing my enthusiasm for Claude's etching of *The Dance by the Waterside*, he said, "Wait a moment, I am from Lorraine myself and, for the sake of our great man, I want you to see a really fine proof from that plate. It is expensive; I doubt that you will buy it. But I should be sorry if you had reason to regret buying that print from the late state of the etching." It is still one of the works that I prefer; but I simply could not take home that proof, even though it cost but a small sum, after seeing the picture in its full beauty. (I could not pay the price of the fine print, but I bought something else, and my conscientious friend lost nothing through his frankness.)

So far, we have been discussing the great museums, or at least those which own a few choice things. But there are thousands upon thousands of American institutions which simply cannot have originals. This means not only those of small towns or such as will never have the money for masterworks, but also colleges and schools. There is a joke among French art dealers about a certain painter whom they call "the Corot of the poor." This may cause a healthy laugh, the first time it is heard, but the words are not without a trace of cynicism. Renoir — to cite another relevant tale — once inquired gently about the genuineness of a painting in a country house. "What!" replied his host, "for a country place?" Equate this with the curious idea that inferior books and prints are good enough for poor people, country folk, and children.

But these are not inferior beings. They should not be offered inferior or imitation art products. Nobody should; and it is not of such matters that we are talking when we discuss reproductions. A fine print after a Dürer drawing, seen on the wall of a schoolroom, may have a lifelong effect on any number of children. And wise teachers, using the really marvelous colorplates of ancient and modern paintings, can start their classes on the road to really solid art appreciation. The very things which one rebels at when the claim is made that they possess all the qualities of their originals may be valuable study aids. We must not forget that in the time of the Old Masters, engravings, chiaroscuro prints, and other means of spreading the ideas of the great men were sources of inspiration and real understanding for thousands of artists. And, if these prints were in themselves works of art and therefore had the power to kindle enthusiasm that comes of their contact with human hands, they were incomparably less accurate than are reproductions made by modern processes.

The relatively few people who can own masterworks may feel that the resonance of oil painting, with its various depths of pigment, its transparent glazes, and its sudden gleams of thick impasto cannot be equaled by the thin film of printer's ink on paper, however wonderfully it follows the effects of the richer medium, or tells of the dry elegance of pastel, or the limpidity of water color. But sometimes their connoisseurship stops right there, especially if they are intent on proving to themselves the wisdom of their investment, having paid a thousand or ten thousand times the price of a reproduction. Sometimes they travesty the legitimate satisfaction of the owner of a thing still offering some subtle memory of the master's hand, by refusing to share their possession with the world, on the pretext that it would be "vulgarized."

Such persons are probably the very ones who see no more in a work of art than its uniqueness — a quality that the poorest handmade things have in common with the *Mona Lisa*. Contrast such snobbery with the insight of innumerable men and women who know only reproductions, the sole approach to art possible in towns distant from museum centers. In some places (for example, in California), really important work is being done by organizations which, either through voting by members or through the decisions of a director, are assembling systematic collections of reproductions for study that is both serious and enjoyable. The visitor to such places may well be amazed at the knowledge of art he finds there. Perhaps the students have attempted a general survey of the past, or have concentrated upon one attractive phase — Raphael and his followers for example; or they may have set themselves the fruitful problem of understanding modern art in its relation to what local painters are doing. Whatever the type of study, its results are often so fine that people with far greater resources can be properly humble in the presence of those who have so intelligently used "commercial reproductions."

Often there is a central bureau that arranges for a sort of renting system, by which members can take things home and live with them for a while, until exactly the right work is found for permanent acquisition. This system has had such excellent results that many a museum director with masterworks on his walls might envy the functions of these unsung institutions; for if costly originals, always in danger of damage, cannot be circulated freely in people's homes, those are, after all, the places they are supposed to reach — and that reproductions do reach.

Governor Ellis Arnall of Georgia has written of the South as the "new frontier," showing that the ravages of the Civil War and of Reconstruction really set back this section almost to a pioneering stage. Perhaps, in large parts of the South and West, the remaining frontier conditions mean a permanent lack of the great fortunes which today are needed to create museums like those of Boston, New York, and Washington. It does not follow that these regions lack people of ability and judgment — a crucial factor in the art life of a nation. They form the membership of those institutes, clubs, and study groups just cited for developing intelligent appreciation in their communities. The significance of their role is clear.

To render it even more so, let us think back to the old days when the most intellectually advanced parts of our country were without the treasuries of art which exist there today. It was not museums but the native genius of Americans that gave us masterpieces like the portraits of John Copley and the architecture of Thomas Jefferson. It is true that the latter, before producing the designs for his admirable buildings, had the benefit of a sojourn in Europe and of acquaintance with great French artists. Nevertheless, though Monticello, the Lawn (that nobly porticoed court at the University of Virginia), and other delightful works are based upon a study of older things, indeed classical things, they are so creative that they may well serve to demonstrate the presence among our people of that type of genius we call "primitive"; we might better call it "fundamental."

Turning to another artist who possessed that quality, Pieter Bruegel, we see a man who departs so markedly from the Italianate line of painters around him that (despite his descent from splendid artistic forebears, like Bosch) he is rightly considered a primitive, the founder of a new line. He looked at his world with a new intensity, as did Copley and Jefferson. In the case of the latter, the really extraordinary feature is that his mind could apply itself so felicitously to problems of art, and not merely to those of statecraft — in which field not everybody has caught up with him, even yet.

Jefferson is one of the builders of the Museum of the New World, because of the directions he gave both to our intellectual and our artistic achievement. It is not beyond hope that the intensity of interest in America that we noted as characterizing Thomas Jefferson will again lead to creative works such as he gave us. To cultivate the mind by means of the riches that museums of the past reveal is not enough. What counts

48. Matisse: Studio, Quai St. Michel.
Courtesy of the Phillips Memorial Gallery, Washington, D. C.

is the use we make of the mind so prepared. The test of that is offered by the museum that keeps pace with the living world, and in turn suggests ways of moving ahead. A people as eager as ours for constantly better conditions will not rest content until its museum goes beyond our long memories: we want it to show us the elements which make the future. Such a result must come from the sum of efforts made throughout the country to give us the collections which will tell the meaning of things as we see them here and now.

5. THE MUSEUM AND EDUCATION

BEFORE COMING to that collective institution, the goal of all the effort witnessed in these pages, and therefore dictating the title of this book, we have still certain problems and theories to consider. We may approach them by way of a glance at the message to museum workers that flowed from the active mind of John Cotton Dana, head of the Newark Public Library. The *enfant terrible* of his profession, he published such statements as this, "No other public educational institutions give so little return for the money spent on them as do museums." Yet his was far from being the negative type of mind, for he bristled with constructive ideas. Many a museum man who, at the beginning, had his teeth set on edge by Mr. Dana, found himself, later on, to be following in a course strongly affected by the innovator. It is a pity that his books, which he had to publish at his own expense on the presses of a small New England town, are not in general circulation. At the New York Public Library, for example, they have to be consulted in the carefully guarded cabinet devoted to works too rare for the public reading room.

Developing his museum activities in connection with the work of the Newark Public Library he planned, in the most detailed way, for the institutions he wanted to see throughout the country. Thus, he said that their location should be at the "center of daily movement," and not just at the center of population. He laid down specifications for a building sixteen stories high, with 10,000 square feet to each floor. The entrance and the spaces near it were to contain a "hall of wonders," habitat groups of animals, and "expensive and historical art." (This was, of course, for a town of moderate size where all museum possessions were to be shown in one building.) It should keep everybody "interested and feeling good about the whole thing; in that way they would vote money for upkeep and development — because they would be getting something for their money." Most museums were to him examples of conspicuous waste (no quotation marks surround those last two words, my notes tell me.

He may perhaps have retained them from a reading of Thorstein Veblen, but he was quite capable of originating them — and many others — himself). His training, moreover, was along lines which fitted him for philosophic rather than aesthetic reasoning.

Mr. Dana's own type of museum was to reach out to the life of the community in every way possible: its paintings were to be displayed in the windows of vacant stores, in small halls, and even in private houses — for a week or a month. Explanatory leaflets for the widest free distribution were to accompany them. He remarks, "This is not done because paintings have a very high value as promoters of happiness, etc., but because this is the period of the oil painting." The same policy was to govern the use of bronzes, among which there would be originals and copies; and he proposed to use reproductions of paintings in color "both the expensive and the cheap"; the same would apply again to wood carving, brocades, and so on. Here Mr. Dana had quite drastic things to say about the persons who make a fetish of what is merely antique: "The fashion is very injurious; for being set and followed by the elect of the art world, it is very soon followed by the 'commonalty,' whose powers of observation are thus inhibited." Or again, speaking of old furniture, he says, "The thing that makes the chest worth while is the use of it; and nearly all of this museum use can come as well from a good pictorial presentment of the chest as from the chest itself."

The definition of his words "museum use" was inspiration for designers. He was a pioneer in the movement to bring artists and manufacturers together — evidently a most desirable thing for both. He advocated annual exhibits, to make a city known to itself and outsiders. For example, he tells us that the exhibition of New Jersey textiles at the Newark Museum cost, for all expenses, including materials, labels, arrangement, and labor, less than $800; it brought to the museum many gifts, and was visited by 50,000 people.

The temptation is to transcribe one detail after another, and in a few more cases I shall yield. Thus, in *The American Museum, How It Can Be Made To Flourish*, he wrote in 1929 of Renaissance Italy and of how its nobles wanted to produce effects by art. Ancient and foreign works were insufficient in quantity, and often unsuited in quality. So they ordered Italians to produce — with magnificent results. Now America, as the writer continues, not only does not pay its artists as Italy did, it does not even courteously invite them to produce, and the result is that "there is very little American art." "Art has always flourished where it was asked to flourish, and never elsewhere."

Again we read: "Good taste and keen interest in the pots and pans of daily life do not emerge from the awed contemplation of unfamiliar objects enshrined in the cases of a public institution, as has just been illustrated by the case of the ancient chest"; and in another passage he says, "It is to the products of living men and women, not to those of men and women long since dead, that we must look for the art of our day." His words have all the "kick" that people got out of them when I reviewed his books, years ago, for that finest of our weekly papers, *The Freeman*.

My article was entitled "The Temple of the Muses," the intention being to suggest the rather novel form of worship being offered to the Sacred Nine. And now, with all cordiality to that courageous defender of living artists, we must look a bit more closely into his ideas. To his statement that a "good pictorial presentment" of the old chest was of nearly as much use as the chest itself, I immediately added his explanation of what this use was; for I did not want our previous strictures about reproductions to prejudice the reader against Mr. Dana in his campaign for setting museum possessions to work in the modern world. Even so, one feels that he is skating on thin ice when he refuses to draw a line between originals and imitations. In another passage, on the contents of his ideal museum, he is even more outspoken on this point, saying, "Of paintings there are many, chiefly recent American, but with an abundance of copies of old masterpieces."

If we drop this question as one on which we simply cannot agree, what is to be thought of those words quoted just before, about the products of living men and women? Isn't our author falling into the bombast of the election-time spellbinder when he says that we must look to the people of our day for the art of our day? Of course we can't get it from the "men and women long since dead." His emphatic style and his high aims cause one to overlook the absurdity of what he sometimes says, and one is reminded of a parody of Theodore Roosevelt's address in Paris, some thirty years since. He had admonished his listeners as to certain tendencies among them that he disapproved of, and a French journalist replied with a "free rendering" of the Colonel's speech, in which he was made to say, "I tell you that that nation is the most populous which has the largest number of families containing the largest number of children. I affirm, and I can prove what I say, that if certain men and certain nations are wealthy, the reason is that they have more money than the poor ones."

Quite obviously, it is to living artists that we must look for the art of our day. But is all of it good? We remember the words of Ingres when he asks, "What if my period is bad?" And at a later date, we have the

49. Rouault: Portrait of Verlaine.
Courtesy of the Phillips Memorial Gallery, Washington, D. C.

testimony of Maurice Denis: "Van Gogh never fell into the silly trap of speaking of art as good because it is modern." Do you like French art today? Certainly, when it is good, but considering the immense output in France, we have to admit that most of it is bad. In modern times — and in every country — it is the direction that counts; for the farther a man like Bouguereau goes on his course, the worse he is.

Consider this fine sentence of André Gide's: "It suddenly seemed clear to me that if there were no names in the history of art except those belonging to the creators of new forms, there would be no culture; the very word implied a continuity, and therefore it called for disciples, imitators, and followers to make a living chain: in other words, a tradition." The "art of our day," "modern art," "French art," "recent paintings, chiefly American": those words are all very attractive, but it is André Gide's "living chain," with its provision for the minor talents, that gives us art without adjectives, the thing itself, which is always good.

Tied up with this matter of creators and followers, is Mr. Dana's great interest in the applied arts. Like the rest of us, he was new to the question of their place in the machine age, and he, by himself, could not solve the problem; it is still an open one. Yet, we are coming to see what is needed; it is that instinctive reaction which causes us to decide what we want among countless commercial objects. André Gide's sentence throws light on the question because his culminating word, "tradition," explains why men at certain times and certain places do not require elaborate proof by experts to know that their objects of daily use are well shaped and well decorated: their decision comes spontaneously from within themselves because of that "continuity" of good taste, implied in the word culture, as the French writer observes.

When the continuity is disturbed in a period as revolutionary as our own, a good bit of time may well be needed to restore it. Toward such a result, Mr. Dana asked for a "museum-city," something which he said would be "far richer in every respect than any city museum can ever be." Agreed; but did he ask himself how the "museum-city" comes to exist? There are such, Florence, for example, and we know its history. With its environs, it dates from very ancient times, and the Etruscans, who first built there, learned from the Greeks, who, in turn, were heirs to the tradition of the great peoples before them. It is to the "city museum" that today's builders of the "museum-city" must look for their knowledge of tradition.

And again, in a place like Florence, even after the wanton destruction World War II has wrought there, we can still read much of its secret in the stones that remain. First, there are the great structural masses decreed by the architects, and in those masses appear the subdivisions that vary the units of which each building is made up, while retaining the mathematical proportion underlying the whole. Next, we may note the statues in the niches, inside and outside of the edifice. Here the forms are freer, as they respond to the intense individualism of the Florentine. But as the kings and prophets created in stone by the masters diminish in size under the hands of lesser sculptors, who also produce decorative groups or bands of figures tapering off into mere abstract design, we are made to feel again the harmony of even these works with the architectural ensemble. And when ceramists, textile workers, and a hundred other artisans draw their patterns, it is clear that they have consulted those more creative men who, still feeling the genius of ancient Etruria, went on to match themselves with problems that their ancestors had left unsolved.

Of these problems, the chief one was the finding of a true relationship between elemental forms — the sphere, the cylinder, the cone, and others — and naturalistic forms, especially those of human beings. Their anatomical structure was studied with passionate interest by Renaissance artists. With the earlier men, still following the Gothic line, there are wonderful expressive and aesthetic elements, but not the articulations of the figure that the scientific mind of Florence demanded. Then, when research into the play of muscles and bones had solved their problems, much of the "abstract" quality was lost. Finally, for one great lifetime, the two things work together. Matisse used to say that if a head by Donatello were rolled down a stony hillside, and all the features were knocked off, it would be reduced to a meaningless mass, whereas if the same accident befell a head by Michelangelo, a grand form would still remain.

Italy did her great work by understanding the difference, noted by André Gide, between the creative mind and that of the followers, to whom he assigns the important role of carrying on culture. Even the coming of the machine does not abolish that relationship. What stands behind Mr. Dana's remark that "this is the period of the oil painting" is the fact that, with the applied arts so confused by new conditions, it is painters and sculptors who have continued the tradition of creative art. A former mayor of New York is said to have invented for such men the epithet of "art-artists." If he did, he would class himself, at the other end of the educational ladder, with Nicholas Murray Butler. The famous Columbia University president, asked about the changes in art during his long tenure of office, replied, "I know nothing of art." As a private individual, he had a right to be content with that state of mind; but men heedful of the prestige of Columbia felt a certain regret over his disregarding the words we have heard from William Morris Hunt when he said that one is not obliged to advertise his ignorance.

If Mr. Dana saw no very high value in oil paintings as "promoters of happiness," and if our Tammany man really spoke of "art-artists" in the scornful sense usually understood from his words, the world in general has little doubt that, in the modern period, the great tradition guarded by museums has been preserved chiefly by painters and sculptors.

That does not mean that the museum is to be used as an art school. In the earlier times, some of the institutions were indeed given that job, and today an art school is often connected with them. A conspicuous example is the very large and complete school of the Chicago Art Institute: but that is a different matter. To define "museum use" as Mr. Dana did, in terms of inspiration to industrial designers, is again to narrow down the function of the galleries to that of the trade school. We are not retreating into the ivory tower but seeing the museum in relation to a wider public, if we assert that neither the art school nor the trade school is the goal of effort, though it is imperative for them both to base their teachings on the masters. Colleges and universities must also look to the museum as a chief authority on the subjects they deal with, but it is not to be thought of as a department of those great treasuries of knowledge. A sentence of Benjamin Ives Gilman's may well be recalled. Speaking of the book we have mentioned before, he says, "It is here argued that a museum of art is primarily an institution of culture and only secondarily a seat of learning."

The key word he uses there has often been understood in too narrow a way, and so, "culture" may bring up visions of blue-stockinged pedants of both sexes, the overprecious, highbrow coteries, and other sterilities which, for the plain man, seem to have monopolized the term. But see it in its combinations — physical culture, ethical culture, musical culture, and political culture. All of these were ideals that the Greeks had, not for any separate group of persons but for the community as a whole. Thus you will see that Mr. Gilman is right in his argument that culture — his objective for the museum — is a term more inclusive and important even than learning.

Glancing back at those subdivisions of the subject mentioned just before, we should object if, for example, the enthusiast for physical culture or for ethical culture tried to dominate in the museum. He is mistaking a part for the whole. The testimony of art through the centuries includes more ideas about life and the world than does even his study, necessary as it is for health or conduct. No specialist may use the museum

50. Duchamp-Villon: The Lovers.
Courtesy of the Museum of Modern Art, New York.

for his own ends; religion itself, a wider field than ethics, does not spread a circle inclusive enough to contain the manifold collections of a great museum.

This dictum may seem akin to the arrogance which sometimes mars the claims for a subject. But consider the facts: a disinterested search into the past and present of all races brings together a mass of material and, afterwards, the best available judgment decides what represents mankind as expressed through art. How all this is to be used will depend on the appeal it makes to each individual among the endlessly varied multitudes who visit the collections. The job of the museum worker is not to impose upon these people any particular theory about what they see. Information, whether in lectures or publications, may and should help them to understand relationships, ideals, history, techniques, and the other details that assist in making clear the enigma which art objects often present at the beginning.

Too often the approach of lecturers, docents (museum instructors), and writers is along lines that completely fail to lead to the essentials of the matter. These are not to be sought in the history of a school or an artist; even less can they be understood from anecdotes about the subject of the work or the nation which produced it. While such little stories offer an easy stock in trade for causeries about museum possessions, they are aside from the point. Yet, if they carry with them a bit of humor or sentiment, they may have a momentary success with the reader or listener. All sorts of other information — about prices, names of owners, vicissitudes of loss and rediscovery, religious associations, and curious customs in which the objects were used — appear very instructive, and so the person receiving guidance imagines he has learned something of value. But a hundred times as much, if of the same nature, would leave him as far from understanding as he was at the start. With such information, he can make a certain effect at a dinner table — and still be without the faintest notion of the significance of the works to be seen in the museum.

That significance is in every case a question of the beauty created by art. Confused by many people with nature, art occupies a totally different sphere. A man eats, fights, and dies; his portrait does none of these things. If it is a work of art, it is, like a landscape, a vase, a building, or a rug (when these are works of art) to be considered under the heading of aesthetics; and as the derivation of the word shows, that is a matter of feeling. Intellectual elements enter in, both for the production and the appreciation of art: there are mysterious correspondences between certain mathematical quantities and our physiology and nerves, and the rightness or wrongness of these quantities will produce sensations of harmony or discord. In music, these proportions are measured by the number of vibrations per second of a violin string, for example; in the visual arts, they are matters of wave lengths, for color, and of relationships of line and space, for form. We have never been able to reduce them to a science, though from the time of the Egyptians and Pythagoras, many men have tried to discover the laws of proportion. In ancient Mexico, they had to do with astronomy, the guiding principle of the country's religion. In medieval and Renaissance Europe, the golden section, derived from antiquity, was often used as the true canon, and it has been useful, in certain cases, to artists and those who study their work.

But we fall into danger if we try to impose as universal any measurements ever discovered or, doubtless, still to be revealed by analysis. They may be right for a supreme work like the Parthenon. But try to build another such edifice. You will soon realize that subtle deviations from your carefully measured lengths and widths gave the whole life to the original, and that your "repetition" of it is a dead thing. The Acropolis, which serves as the pedestal for the temple, affected every line of the building, as did the sunlight of Greece and, above all, the mind of Greece. Sooner or later, that mind would have varied the proportions, the decoration, and every quiet space or emphasis. We have the earlier and later works to prove this. And so it becomes clear that the classical, impersonal qualities of a work of art have to be vivified by something connected with the experience of a people or an individual, in a world that does not stand still, but that offers us constantly new horizons.

That something, which we define as the romantic element, does not mean anarchy in the matter of art interpretation. What it does mean is the need of a special competence on the part of instructors — a special and freely adaptable understanding of the varying periods, schools, and temperaments. Without that, the earnest or even casual museum visitor will be offered the sterilities of meaningless fact or those of self-styled "law," instead of insight; and he is quite right when he asks assistance in attaining it.

In many cases, to be sure, it is more than help that museum visitors ask: they want a sort of information capsule which will relieve them of the need to study the works before them. They can then go through gallery after gallery without seeing a picture, their whole attention being given to the docent, who tells his little stories, and otherwise dispenses "education through the ear." The listeners might as well be blind; as far as seeing the qualities of the pictures around them, they are blind.

The fallacy of such teaching is exhibited by the great philosopher,

Alfred North Whitehead, in *The Aims of Education*. Speaking of a subject closely parallel with the one we have been following, he says, "The literary side of a technical education should consist in an effort to make the pupils enjoy literature. It does not matter what they know, but the enjoyment is vital. The great English universities, under whose direct authority schoolchildren are examined in plays of Shakespeare, to the certain destruction of their enjoyment, should be prosecuted for soul murder."

Observers of people in museum galleries are forced to testify that the victims of the "soul murder" are, all too often, eager accessories to the crime. Let anyone begin holding forth on the art works, and he will soon have a flock of listeners. This is, of course, an indication of the public's unfamiliarity with art; it is likewise a proof that the work of the museum in America is not finished when it has made even such collections as are to be seen in our largest cities. Not only do they require increase and broadening, however; not only does the country need — and urgently need — more museums for the wide regions where none exist, but we must go immensely farther in our study of the use of museums.

We make a big step when we render them so attractive that they are frequented by large numbers of people. But the fact that quantity is less important than quality is very specially proved again when we consider the understanding as well as the number of museum visitors. By attractions of a sensational character, it might be possible to bring a million persons through the turnstiles for every thousand or even every hundred who now enter there. But, barring the accidental spark which would fire the imagination of this man or that, we should have accomplished little by the increase in attendance. With all due appreciation of what it means to inspire people unprepared for art experience, we need to learn more as to what we can do for those who are already interested, but puzzled and seeking for enlightenment. If they are susceptible to art and able to fight out its problems themselves, the one thing needed is logical and sympathetic arrangement of the exhibits. By such means, the visitor may be led from the known to the unknown. But not every one is ready for independent study. And here appears the opportunity for the infinite tact, understanding, and leadership of the museum as an educator. We are only at the threshold of such work, and must yet discover the best uses and proportion for the spoken word (in the gallery or the lecture room), the written word, and demonstration by reproductions, charts, and other means yet to be developed.

Acting on the good axiom that the education of a child begins with the education of its grandmother, and having been unable to educate the

51. China: Wei Altarpiece.
Courtesy of The Metropolitan Museum of Art.

grandmothers of most present-day people, museums are making a great effort for future Americans by educating their ancestors, male as well as female. To visit the Saturday classes for children at museums like Toledo and Cleveland, which have done most important work in this field, is inspiring. For the imaginative mind of the child responds with enthusiasm to the collections and to the opportunity for creating its own art works. Great numbers of the youngsters come spontaneously, often from considerable distances, and of course by sacrificing playtime. But the "play impulse," which enters into much of adult art activity, here expresses itself so naturally that the problem of the museum is largely one of finding room for all who want to come.

That need of the child, recognized intuitively by one of the great practical dreamers to whom we owe our public collections, was a chief part of the foundation on which the Toledo Museum was built. George W. Stevens, a man who delighted in entertaining — with music, stories, and pictures — saw that to get his community to support a museum when he started it, back in 1901, he must appeal to wider interests than those which artists or art collectors could offer. So that when he raised his first $1200 for the work which is so imposing today, he went to a hundred and twenty men for $10 apiece, and he argued largely on the basis of what his scheme would do for the children. Later on, when certain businessmen did not pay their contributions, Mr. Stevens would go on a house-to-house collecting tour, and again and again he carried his point home by saying, "If you don't see this as your museum, see it as your city's." It has been that to Toledo ever since, to a degree that one can find in few other places.

The question of service to our institutions by men of public spirit must wait for a later page. Our concern here is with a phase of educational work not undertaken by the schools. Certain students of children's work see in it very valuable qualities, and no one can deny its freshness of vision. Often in the presence of work of mature, even professional artists, it is possible to wish that more of the child's need of expression, and his instinctive response to form and color could endure. To make the most of the art instinct that we normally have in early years, the Metropolitan has set aside space for one of its charming features, the Children's Museum.

But life teaches that, with most people, such resiliency as we have been observing is a privilege of childhood, and that it disappears when we encounter the hard tasks of later years. So that since the natural course of events is going to take almost all people away from artistic pursuits, the next problem in this field is with older students. Here the Cleveland

Museum has done very distinguished work, and its findings, together with those of a number of our other institutions, have been published in quantity. Finally, there is the vast question of art instruction for adults. With New England's centuries-old belief in education, we would expect important activities from the numerous museums of the region, and they do not disappoint us. Far to the northeast, the fine museum of Bowdoin College has been mentioned in earlier pages; its art courses have been on a very high level. Harvard, with the Fogg Art Museum's unequaled equipment for the teaching of teachers, has dealt originally with the problem of adults, while at the Boston Museum, a particularly intensive inquiry is being made into the big question of bringing about a harmonious relationship between the work of our artists and that of museums, art experts, and educators.

New York's long-continued effort has placed upon the Metropolitan Museum's record an imposing list of authorities in every department of art, and they have contributed to the lecture courses. Among these, a special endowment has made it possible to aid workers in the applied arts. In this field, again, great services have been rendered by drawing on various commercial sources and giving exhibitions designed to promote the fullest co-operation between artists and manufacturers. As an example of the statistics encountered in art education, we note that the Metropolitan's lending collection of photographs and color prints runs to 43,000 examples; the lantern slides number 135,000, and the specimens of the applied arts, 181,000. They are in constant use; indeed it is often necessary to make reservations in advance, because of the demand for those materials for study and teaching.

With such figures before us, and with a reminder that this, the most important educational work of our museums, extends to almost all of the twenty-five hundred institutions in every part of the country, it will be evident that not even the barest summary of their work can be attempted here. The very bibliography of the subject is too extensive and specialized for a book like the present one.

Even the vital issues raised by the World War must not tempt us into discussions that are being held in hospitals, in centers for psychiatric research, and for those who are studying new careers of veterans. Take the single fact that of the enormous attendance at the Art Institute of Chicago, in the fiscal year 1944-45, ten per cent were service people, and it will be evident what effect our museums had at this period. Efforts that everyone will applaud have been made to give maximum benefits to the men and women of the armed forces. The docent service, which reaches millions in our galleries, has opened up great new vistas to many a boy or girl who had never been in a museum before. Special exhibitions have dealt with our war effort in terms of history and geography, and of the relation of art to technical developments, engineering, invention, aviation, and so on. The course of the fighting was mapped by photographs of cities and buildings of artistic consequence. This was, of course, entirely separate from the invaluable work of our institutions in drawing up lists of places which were not to be bombed or otherwise damaged; these data helped our officers in the field not only to spare the great things of the past, but also to set promptly to work at restoring those which suffered unavoidable injury.

The work of museums in their role as educators reaches out, evidently, to innumerable phases of human activity, and so art teachers have been given constantly more scope in directing our institutions. One city was so enterprising that it persuaded the head of the pedagogical department in an important college to give up her work there, and assume charge of instruction at the museum, where she has full rank as a curator. In fact, with so strong a tendency to stress the interpretation of art, we may need a reminder, in certain places, that as the Sabbath was made for man and not man for the Sabbath, art education must not be allowed to overshadow the original purpose of the museum. The individual teacher, lecturer, or writer has his own understanding of the significance of the collections; and when we add up such opinions, they command respect as representing an important part of the art ideas of our period. But the past saw art — through the glasses of religion, poetry, industry, and whatever — in different ways from ours, and the future is bound to view it differently again.

Indeed, today we must leave every person free to form his own convictions, and the way to do that is to concentrate on the collections themselves, allowing the masters and the schools to say their say, independent of interpretations by educators. As no one can have a love affair for another, so in the matter of the feelings aroused by art, no one can have or even transmit another's experience. What we need to do in the museums is to make people feel like coming frequently. Only by so doing will they have a full measure of the experiences open to them.

6. THE MUSEUM AND THE PUBLIC

A MOMENT AGO, we referred to the original purpose of the museum. In our desire to keep to fundamental ideas, we may make two further steps; one is to recall the private collections of the time before there were public ones (and, with them, churches, public buildings, and the homes where

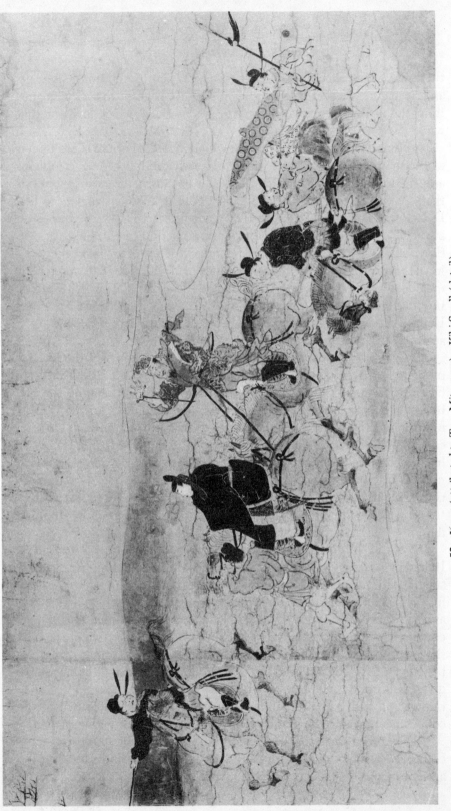

52. Japan (attributed to Tosa Mitsunaga) : Kibi Scroll (detail).
Courtesy of the Museum of Fine Arts, Boston.

there was no "collection" but where there were decorations, portraits and beautiful objects for daily use); the other is again to seek guidance from the artist's principle in creating his work, which is love for that work.

Fortunately, we have a document which includes both of these aspects of the matter, and it is basic in dealing with the last of the "problems and theories" to be treated here. As the document bears on questions that are vividly contemporary, I shall quote it at some length. When Delacroix was finally elected to the Academy, in 1857, the opinions on art which he had been writing down and sometimes publishing for over thirty years were given an official sanction, which was new to them. Collected in his *Journal* and in two volumes of his *Oeuvres littéraires*, they include a long letter to the Académie des Beaux-Arts, in which we read the following thoughts on a proposed dispersal of the Musée Napoléon III, a very great collection formed by Marquis Campana, and then acquired and developed by the Emperor.

"The particular impression I had was that a great part of the interest presented by that assembling of admirable objects resulted from the very fact of their assembling, and that the idea of reducing them, on the pretext of taking away secondary pieces, was quite contrary to the evident intention of the founder, and to the purpose of a true museum. Such a collection differs from that of an *amateur* who, passionate and exclusive, has his pleasure in admitting only the most select objects, among which rarity is often the only merit. A collection offered for study should be composed not alone of beautiful objects, but also of those less exalted things which still permit one to follow and judge the gropings of art in its rise to perfection.

"Nothing could be more instructive. The stimulating collection of Italian pictures in the Musée Campana has, in my opinion, been judged superficially and, in the main, condemned by persons who have not taken into sufficient account its importance in throwing light on the origin and progress of the Italian schools. Such instruction which, until today, could not be found anywhere in Paris, results from the juxtaposition of the pictures, and from the comparisons which thus naturally strike the beholder. Breaking up such an ensemble, and sending the works to divers collections, will destroy a reunion precious for the purposes mentioned; and such a course will not afford any notable enrichment of the collections to which the pictures will so unhappily have been dispersed.

"I venture to say the same about the magnificent gallery of terra-cottas, where one cannot weary of admiring the grace and variety of the antique genius. That variety derives, to my mind, from the frequency of the same motifs, repeated with almost insensible nuances, but yielding, upon study, the most interesting idea of the predilection of the ancients for certain subjects; at the same time one is made to realize how far the Greeks were from that reproduction of types which we see in the work of the machine; as opposed to it, the artist introduces into every piece he touches certain differences which, slight as they may appear to be, yet render in full the character he is expressing.

"I am quite aware of the incredible objection which has been urged: that the accumulation of so many examples would require too much space for their exhibiting. A strange objection, indeed, that of asking us to regret, in a way, that the collection is too rich. It is easier to find room for a classified group of paintings and statues than to discover and acquire so great a number of them, and such interesting ones. That is what Marquis Campana, with his care and taste, was able to do in that vast museum which bore his name; and imprudent mutilations, by dispersing the collection, will efface from it the name of its recent and august protector.

"The vases so delightfully painted, the majolicas, and the reliefs in faïence seem to me to give point to the same observations, and if I were permitted to add a wish to those which I form for the preservation and harmony of so rare an ensemble, it would be that we should see, included in it, the admirable works in plaster which M. Ravaison, with his intelligent zeal, had brought together for the same group of exhibits. I do not doubt but that soon, in case the museum is continued as it is, it will be enriched by gifts from a great number of amateurs jealous of the privilege of adding to its wealth and filling out gaps in it. To my knowledge, intentions of this type have been repressed and held in suspense since the time when fears of an approaching dismemberment have been inspired."

We have been seeing, in the present book, how American museums were built up. Now we see how France built up her wealth and culture. The voice of Delacroix is the voice of his nation. Scorning the idea that the public collections are too large, he tells how they can be made larger. (One would like to know what works in plaster the "intelligent zeal" of M. Ravaison had brought together.) At a later point in Delacroix's letter (he was away from Paris and took this means of speaking out in an emergency), he says that he is following the example of his "illustrious" colleague, M. Ingres. I have read the latter's words on this museum problem, and though they still ring with the warmth of his southern genius, their emotional quality deprives them of the logic through which Delacroix follows the tradition of the statesmen and great lawyers of his family.

People who speak of Delacroix as "the romantic" must mean that there is in him a certain preponderance of feeling over reason; they would do well to ponder his sharp distinction between the museum and the private collection. (Incidentally, those who see romanticism as indifferent to classical values must find food for thought in the painter's loving defense and analysis of the gallery of Greek terra-cottas.) But it is not to emphasize anew the greatness of Delacroix that I dwell on these points, nor even to show that he and his great rival fought as one man for museum collections. It is to point out that the supreme art center of modern times attained its position through building up her institutions on the sole basis of aesthetic merit. Let that dominate — say the French, with their centuries of experience — and the world will come to your museums; let your artists form themselves on such principles, and the world will eagerly acquire their work.

There have been persons who have tried otherwise to explain French success in the arts: France gives governmental support to its art, they argue; or France benefits from the immense propaganda due to her wine, women, and song; France has the organized power of rich and crafty dealers. But the most astute among the latter, Ambroise Vollard, told the secret of his success when he said, "You cannot sell pictures, they have to sell themselves." And I, for one, accept his statement at face value. When the public was not ready to buy the work of Cézanne, Vollard bought it. And when the public, convinced by the artists, from Pissarro and Monet to Prendergast and Arthur Davies, was ready for the great modern, the millions that Vollard made from cornering the market were not due to his salesmanship but to what one is forced to call his buymanship. (The word I have coined is a ghastly one, but it is needed for the idea it is meant to express.)

For people who think art is something really very nice, but who do not have too much confidence in it, especially for "the masses," museum policy is partly a matter of having good works, partly a matter of having safe, acceptable, popular works, and largely a matter of putting the thing across by means of publicity and educational features, and by support from the "better element" in society. That does not square with the record of America in our really great galleries. Read again the passages in Miss Howe's book on the early days of the Metropolitan and on its remarkable purchase in 1871; read again the story of Boston's carrying on of the old tradition of the Athenaeum, or of Chicago's buying its marvelous Rembrandt and those other treasures of the Demidoff collection, at a time when the city was completely new to such things: the record testifies consistently to the belief of Americans that works of art contain

53. Honduras (Copan, Maya art): Limestone Figure.
Courtesy of the American Museum of Natural History, New York.

important qualities and that we must have works of art. That is what I referred to before as the original purpose of our museums.

The fidelity with which that purpose has been respected is written in the history of the men who have supported the institutions. Statesmen, lawyers, financiers, merchants, and other men of prestige and wealth have furnished the money to build and buy, have given time from the busiest of lives to the details of management, and have stood as guarantors of value for the museum's work in days when, as we have seen, the public in general was not yet ready to support the institution. It still is not ready, and to turn our galleries over to governmental bodies (to politicians, that is) would at present spell disaster. The time for completely democratic control will come, and we must work for it. Meanwhile, the best preparation for this end is to orient our people so firmly to the best art ideals that no politician of a later day will be able to assail them.[1]

No one can foresee what government institutions will be in the future of this changing world. There may be a federal Ministry of Fine Arts, as in European countries. The idea is defensible for collective things like architecture, where intelligible standards, giving a basis of judgment to the whole country, might be an advantage. But for arts like poetry and painting, where the individual element is paramount, the influence of a cabinet officer or other authority could scarcely do anything but harm.

If Hitler succeeded in robbing the German people of one of its greatest treasures of Gothic art (the fourteenth-century *Virgin and Child* formerly in Berlin and now at the Cloisters, New York), and could do so under the pretext that it was French, if he could effect the selling to America, from the Frankfurt museum, of van Gogh's masterpiece, *Dr. Gachet*, by denouncing it as decadent, and could drive Max Liebermann from his position, because that admirable painter was a Jew, the fault lies partly with the German public. It had given at least partial, and certainly passive support to the rabble-rouser and his criminal ideas; but even before that, it had accepted the theory of governmental control of art. France had it also, and paid bitterly for it through the acts of officials who used art as a pawn in the game of politics, buying bad things because they were popular, and opposing the great artists until they were a success. Yet the feeling of the people for their heritage would never have

---

[1] An example of the present-day thinking of our legislators is furnished by the State Department's recall of an exhibition of American painting which had been sent abroad as part of the Good Will programme of cultural relations. The recall was caused by outcry in sections of the press which objected to the "modernism" of the work. It had been selected on a basis of art — which the political censors were, as usual, incompetent to judge.

permitted the sale of museum works. It is true that only for the limited time of the madness created by the Nazis could those fanatics attack Germany's artistic patrimony. Since the Germans never knew anything but acquiescence in the will of their rulers, we may not blame them in the present case. But we may learn to avoid their system for ourselves.

Often as we in America are tempted by the idea of an art supported by legislative bodies, national or local, we must reject it, at least till the time when private control has built up such general understanding that the ignorant officeholder would be powerless against it. To be sure, there have also been inferior men on our museum boards. Sometimes they have been merely egotistical, and desirous of using the institution for a private monument, as at the place where one reads, "Organized and incorporated to convert into a public museum and art gallery the former residence of Mr. X., and to preserve and exhibit his collection." Even this bid for immortality may become an asset to the community: "his former residence" may, in time, be rebuilt beyond recognition, and the same happy fate may befall "his collection." Balancing such an example is the record of a truly great benefaction; it is suggested by the unobtrusive label displayed in a gallery of Greek art: "All vases were purchased with income from the Rogers Fund unless otherwise stated." And those marvelous vases are but a small part of the acquisitions due to the old railroad man thus recalled.

With whole-hearted gratitude to the art lovers who have built up our galleries through their gifts of collections, money and administrative effort, with full admiration for the public spirit which has been their constant guide, one must still consider trustees and collectors as part of the museum's problem. The act of the Metropolitan in rejecting outright the assemblage of art works on which Senator Clark had lavished vast sums was hailed as a courageous gesture at the time; one of the daily papers commented on it in an editorial headed by the terse words "No Necropolis." For the magnate's will demanded that the paintings and other objects be kept together for all time. Had he, in planning his "monument more enduring than bronze," consulted the museum and made provision for showing his possessions, or parts of them, in a way to benefit the community, the drastic step of rejection need not have been taken. It was well worth while, however, as a warning to other men of wealth that our galleries had reached the stage of deciding their best policy, free from dictation by outsiders.

But we still have to think of the insiders, and here there exist complications resulting from great services to the museum and great knowledge of its needs, combined, at times, with arrogant refusal to accept the judgment of the professional staff, men whose study of special fields is not a matter of occasional thinking — that of the trustees — but of a lifelong devotion.

Most often the trustee, who may be a collector, and a good one, has professional advisers of his own. I do not speak of dealers, whose very real competence is offset by their interest in selling particular works or in defending things of the type they own against the allurements of other schools. The most dangerous enemy in the household is the bad artist. To give a single example, from the history of French museums: the work of one of the greatest painters of his time, Seurat, is contained in the six large works which chiefly represent his short career, and a certain number of smaller pictures. The masterpieces were in the hands of collectors who asked nothing better than to see them enter the nation's museum. One of these art lovers offered to France a whole group of Seurats, including one of his chief productions. The gift was rejected with contempt; and I am able to say from personal acquaintance with the official responsible for the act that he was merely continuing his policy in regard to the Cézannes, Renoirs, and other notable modern canvases with which he had previously dealt. Not an independent authority in his field, he was but carrying out the decisions of a council of museum men dominated by artists, but such artists as had made the phrase "official art" a synonym for about the worst things that the whole history of painting and sculpture can show.

Not many years later, every one of Seurat's masterpieces had been sold to collectors outside of France, and that country would, for all time, have been unable to represent the great man in his true quality had not an American, John Quinn, bequeathed the painter's last work, Le Cirque, to the Louvre. In doing so, Mr. Quinn was acting on his principle that a work of art is essentially owned by the country which produced it and where it can best be appreciated. He felt that we have no right to separate it permanently from the surroundings which saw its birth. In the case of the great Seurat picture, the whole atmosphere of the circus in a modest neighborhood, and the character of the audience and the performers are all intimately Parisian.

But Mr. Quinn was influenced by other ideas as well. Among his Seurat paintings was one — a marvel — that he had bought at public auction in New York, after its exhibition at the Metropolitan — which would have none of it. Indeed, he stated publicly that he disagreed with the museum for its apologetic attitude about the show in which the splendid work was included. It is now in the Tate Gallery of London, as part of the national collections, together with Seurat's earlier masterpiece,

54. Mexico (Aztec art): Basalt Figure of Corn Goddess.
Courtesy of the American Museum of Natural History, New York.

La Baignade, also rejected by New York on the advice of such artists as I have described in a book called *Ananias*. The spirit of that personage, so accurately analyzed in the Bible, is the chief cause of the loss by France of Seurat's work. And how much more has that spirit cost the world? Men like Corot, Cézanne, and Redon could go on through their years of neglect simply because their fathers had left them the money to live on. But what of van Gogh and Juan Gris, as two random examples of men dying before their time with superb work behind them — and every promise of greater things in the future so stupidly broken?

In our country, with all the good will of the museums, lack of judgment about the American masters prevented our record from showing anything near to proper support of Thomas Eakins and Albert P. Ryder. We have already noticed the obtuseness of our public galleries as regards Maurice Prendergast during his lifetime. The strongest painter among those who were my schoolmates, George McKay, was found dead of starvation in his room; it is true that the pictures he had produced were, according to museum criteria in that day, immature. But they were vigorous and fine. Had our galleries, for twenty years or so, consistently thrown their influence on the side of such ideals, instead of supporting the academic men alone, McKay's very able work would have found numerous buyers. His obscurity made that impossible. No individual can be blamed: the real culprit was the general state of knowledge at the time. With a thousand other matters to attend to, our institutions were not yet ready to cope with the problem of contemporary art.

If they now accept the challenge, it is because there is no middle ground between meeting it and restricting the museum field to scholarship and the past. Magnificent things are to be done there; yet, how we admire a Baudelaire when he speaks out for the talent of the men around him, especially one as fine as Constantin Guys! The fact that, for a long time, the poet alone saw the beauty of that artist's drawing tells us how difficult the question is. Since the case stood thus in a city as advanced as Paris, it is no wonder that an American, exactly contemporary with Guys, remained unnoticed. Yet the neglect of John Quidor most certainly resulted in loss, not so much for the artist as for the public. It cannot play Diogenes with his lantern: it looks to the museum to reveal to it the honest man. Many people are eager to know his work at the time it has its greatest value, and are only too happy to give him the means of continuing it.

It seems logical, at this point, to add to this record a statement about certain acquisitions which have come to our museums, not through their own initiative, but as gifts from a small foundation established to promote the welfare of American artists. It derives from the bequest of an old painter, Alexander Shilling, and is administered by men of his calling. Among the artists whose work it has bought and given to public galleries are A. S. Baylinson, George Constant, John B. Flannagan, M. A. Tricca, and others. They are all highly regarded in their profession and will, as time passes, unquestionably be better known and liked by the public at large. (Prophecies of this type are very dangerous, but in the present instance there would be the amplest confirmation for the foregoing statement.)

With every one of the artists just cited, the museum receiving his work was getting its first example of it; and in a number of cases, the painting or sculpture was the first by the man to enter any museum at all. Now, the significant point is that in every single one of these instances, the work of art was acceptable to the curator in charge of such productions, but again and again the question was raised as to the judgment to be pronounced by the trustees forming the committee on accessions. Here is one case — and it is one among many — where laymen and professionals held opposing ideas.

Although there has been marked progress in recent times, and boards of trustees allow their experts more freedom than formerly, the men who give the money or raise the money for our institutions still have so much the sense of authority that a curator in one of our chief galleries declared, only a few years back, "The museum belongs to the board." We are still far from the record set by one of our early trustees, Joseph H. Choate. That great lawyer, diplomat, and citizen was said never to have missed a board meeting when he was in New York, and never, in his many years of service, to have cast a vote on questions demanding artistic scholarship: those problems were, in his opinion, for the staff to handle. The reverse of his principle, the overriding of the convictions of experts, is what accounts for their "time serving," the word applied by one of them to the work which, on another occasion, he spoke of as giving him his daily bread. In the medical profession, we know that life-or-death decisions should never be affected by thought as to the specialist's tenure of office in his hospital; and in no case should his decisions be influenced by the financial or other power of trustees. Yet, that is the pressure constantly felt by museum men; and so they are apt to adopt a routine that avoids most risks — and most chances of brilliant success.

A stupendous Italian masterpiece went to a European gallery, where there were already many of its kind. To this day, in America, we have nothing like it, and there may never be one here. "Why couldn't we have had that picture?" was the question put to a prominent museum official.

"Well, you see, the family who owned that work really didn't need even the modest sum they got for it, I don't think they would have been tempted by a bigger offer, so we just did nothing about it." That is not the way, for example, that our oil men talk of a concession, even if its owners are not very keen on the money to be had from their property: far from doing nothing about a thing needed by the world, our people take vigorous steps to turn that idle resource into something real and creative. Our museum men need the energy that goes into "practical" activities, where the rewards of knowledge, originality, and enterprise are clear to all. Too often, such qualities are deadened, if a series of rebuffs by superiors has lowered the sense of initiative among the members of the staff.

This does not mean that museum staffs, given freedom and courage, would act infallibly. Curators, too, can get beyond their depth. And in cases involving more than the specialist's knowledge, the help of trustees may make all the difference between failure and success. A great collector may have come to distrust an institution, and decided to cut it off in his will. The irreplaceable paintings on his walls might still be saved for the community if men of wealth and standing, those who could meet that collector on equal terms and speak his own language, intervene and assure him that his possessions will be properly cared for. A curator might bungle this ticklish diplomatic job.

Or when the trustee has access to private galleries from which, in time, certain masterpieces are sure to reach the museum by gift or bequest, he may stand firm against the temptation to spend from a trust fund, even if the work offered for purchase is indubitably important and attractive. He may not be free to make public his reason for refusing the fine thing available, and impatient artists or art lovers may criticize the gallery for neglect of a brilliant opportunity. But the museum has time on its side: a few years more or less weigh but lightly in its calculations, whereas space on its walls is a limited commodity, and the money which would have gone for the "wonderful buy" may be used for some other fine work.

There may be legal difficulties to acquiring the object, and its price may not be recoverable if these matters cause the subsequent relinquishment of the painting or sculpture. Here again the curator, even when sure of himself on aesthetic grounds, needs the saving hands of the men of affairs who give to the museum experience and time that are simply beyond our power to reward.

And representing, as they do, a high average of general artistic intelligence (indeed, many are real connoisseurs), the trustees furnish a stand-

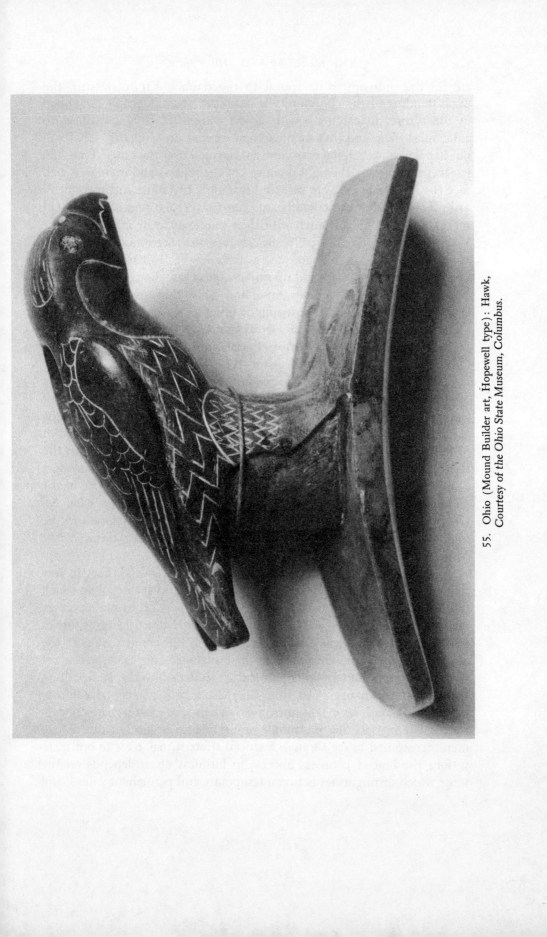

55. Ohio (Mound Builder art, Hopewell type): Hawk, Courtesy of the Ohio State Museum, Columbus.

ard for the museum in its appeal to the public. Far to outstrip the understanding of the community is impolitic: even if people are going, in the future, to catch up with expert judgment, it is a mistake to antagonize them and thus sacrifice their interest and support. That will not happen, however, if a wise course is pursued over the years. First, the trustees must secure the right members of the staff — and we may as well face the fact that there are plentiful instances of failure in this difficult task. Too many of our curators are even today, men of weak judgment on art, or are so out of touch with their public as to be ignorant of the kind of acquisitions that will really advance the interests of their museums. But supposing the choice of a staff member to have been a good one at the start, he can build up understanding in the community only if he can dispense with compromise, and refuse that easy success which so often turns sour with the passing of time.

Fashion sways the ideas of a great many persons, and it is the only possible explanation for monstrous fluctuations in the price of art works. One remembers the words of Oscar Wilde, "Today people know the price of everything, and the value of nothing." In 1860, a man buying a Murillo which was to go, somewhat later, to the National Gallery of London, paid nearly $50,000 for the picture, which today could not be sold for a tenth of the price it cost (though the Spaniard is coming out of the worst contempt he suffered, say, twenty years ago). At about the time when the great British gallery was acquiring the Murillo, Théodore Duret paid $8 for a Cézanne, and in the open market. The price of the Cézanne would today be some two or three thousand times what M. Duret paid for it; its value remains the same, and has no relation to the high price or the low one. The same is of course true in the case of the Murillo.

The question of the dealers has to be considered — and they are very influential men with the press, with collectors, and with the public which frequents their sumptuous galleries. As to numbers of people, one may say that they belong not to the school of this or that artist but of this or that dealer. I have already testified to the debt this country owes to the enterprising men who have brought us so many of our masterpieces; yet with the complicated exigencies of the art dealer's business and politics, the curator faces danger, also, from the masters of the trade. His absorption in art sometimes makes him an easy victim for persons who concentrate solely on securing maximum profits. Here is another case where men accustomed to see through financial strategy may offer to our institutions the best of counsel. Success in business often depends on the sense which distinguishes between temporary and permanent values; and it is, of course, necessary for our board members to have this sense in matters of art, to distinguish between fashion and enduring worth.

The trustee, finally, gives the community a sense of being represented in the governing of the museum. When J. Pierpont Morgan accepted the presidency of the Metropolitan, it was given an importance in the eyes of the country which only that leader of affairs could have conferred upon it. The whole world of art was strengthened by the prestige of the man whose concern for the collections immediately gave them a new meaning for people who had previously regarded them as outside the possible interests of a financier whose operations made him an international power.

It will be clear that, in a country where art needs every bit of support it can rally, to counterbalance the indifference or even hostility it still meets, the presence of distinguished and successful men on the board is in itself an immense asset for an institution. And a further result of this is a feeling among visitors that what they see on museum walls is right, even if it is difficult to understand. Suppose, instead of our present system, we gave to a director the authority that the Kaiser granted to Wilhelm von Bode. And suppose that the autocrat, in addition to the vast knowledge of ancient art possessed by Dr. von Bode, this time was able to judge modern art with the same success. His choices, backed by the great funds in museum treasuries, would be far superior to what our galleries have had, or are getting today.

And yet — paradoxical as this may seem — we should still maintain that the museum was not properly directed. For the acquisitions would be imposed from above, and would not call forth from their public the confidence now enjoyed by the gallery, as it develops under the guidance of men known to their communities as outstanding in their professions or businesses. Earlier in this book, I spoke of the weakness in our collecting which will persist as long as it gives the impression of being a series of one-man shows. We need to do things communally, and the road to such a result can be reached by way of public belief that our museums are wisely guided.

To inspire such belief, trustees must realize that their best policy — the one they are now following more and more — can be charted only by men chosen for their competence and encouraged to act without that pressure on their minds which comes of mistaking authority of office for authority of understanding.

An earlier period evolved the formula that "The King can do no wrong" and, down to World War II, certain pictures in the Louvre could not be moved to more appropriate galleries because Louis XIV had

ordered them to be placed as they still hung in 1939. Our democratic
period, if it is to equal the wisdom of Louis XIV and the other great
patrons of the past, must do so by drawing on the resources of men who
devote their lives to study of the museum and its contents, thus giving
the fullest supplement and direction to popular taste as expressed by the
trustees.

A strongly contrasting opinion on the matter is given by one of the
men best qualified to speak, Francis Henry Taylor, the director of the
Metropolitan Museum. In his recent book, *Babel's Tower*, he says that
"on the whole, persecution by trustees is isolated, if spectacular, and
sooner or later is solved by the mortality tables." As to the rarity of
"persecution," I can agree: it is indeed so isolated as to be negligible.
But a policy among trustees that leads to bad buying, or obstructs good
buying is to be seen in cases far from isolated.

Returning to Mr. Taylor's book, we read, in the paragraph previously
quoted, "If they [the trustees] ever really got the upper hand, the public,
whose cross section they represent, might question the omniscience of
the expert." But the expert, if he is at all worthy of the title, will be the
first to reject any thought of his "omniscience." In his dealings with
superficial critics, the curator may be top-lofty enough, but as regards the
great questions of art, he is apt to be decidedly humble.

The essential issue in Mr. Taylor's last-quoted words is that of the
public. It is of particular interest to us in the present chapter, since we
are here attempting to clarify the respective positions of the museum
and the people it serves. A more specific statement by Mr. Taylor
appeared, a few years ago, in an article published in *The Atlantic Monthly*
and reprinted in *The Museums Journal*. Its concluding words, addressed
to museum men, were these: "Had our colleagues in Germany and Italy
been willing to meet the man in the street half way, they might not now
be reduced to pimping for ideologies that destroy the very civilization
whose finest flowerings we are dedicated to preserve."

With our present knowledge of the mentality of dictators, we may be
quite certain that neither the policy recommended by Mr. Taylor nor any
other policy could save one of his colleagues who refused to obey com-
mands in totalitarian Germany, Italy, or Russia. Moreover, the fortunes
of Prokoviev and Shostakovich among the Soviets furnish a new example
of how a dictator promotes art merely as a means toward his own ends.
But to restrict the question to America, where is it that we are to "meet
the man in the street"? Must we go into the street and, for example, take
part in its battle of the Colas — Pepsi versus Coca — as they scream at us
from the billboards or from magazine covers? Latterly, an art exhibition

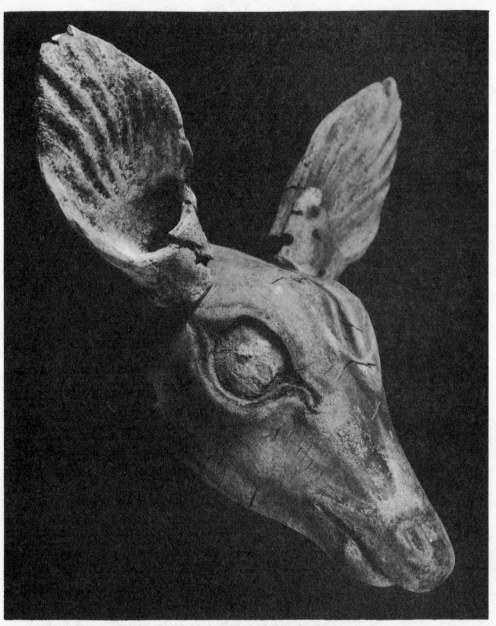

56. Florida: Deer's Head (Calusa wood-carving).
Courtesy of the University Museum, Philadelphia.

has contributed ammunition for their sniping, Pepsi having shrewdly enlisted museum aid.

The advertising field has recently been studied by that acute investigator of the effect of words, S. I. Hayakawa, of the English department at the Illinois Institute of Technology. He finds a common denominator between the poet and the ad-writer, for the task of both is to use language so as to put new thoughts into the mind of the people. But the two types differ in their purpose: the poet's is generous and disinterested; the ad-writer's, to quote exactly the professor's word, is venal. Schiller's *Pegasus im Joche* is as apt as in his own day: the poet who puts the yoke of commerce on the neck of his winged steed does a stupider thing than giving to that free creature a load it cannot bear — if its flight is hampered, its very nature is violated, and it soon becomes like any cart-horse — that humble servitor of the man in the street. The advertising agency can be a very alluring refuge for writers and artists after treading the hard pavement of the modern city; but they will forget at their peril that they enter there on terms laid down by its proprietors. At first, the concessions asked of the artist will seem small enough, especially in comparison with such payment for his work as he had never dreamt of obtaining. In the end (which usually comes pretty swiftly), his Pegasus not only has lost all desire for flight, but has lost the very power to lift its wings.

The intermediary between the advertising concern and the artist is usually a man who understands something of both sides of the question — the artistic and the commercial. This "art director" may have a quite genuine pride in the works he commissions: he often desires that they be worthy to rank with the fine things he knows at the museum. And so we find a popular cigarette being advertised by reproductions of paintings; very generous sums were paid to the artists who produced them. Some of the best-known American artists were invited to contribute to the series, with the understanding that the company desired them to work with complete freedom, and to paint only such pictures as would satisfy their artistic conscience. Naturally, a scene from the world of tobacco growing or selling was the most appropriate subject for their pictures, but that would allow latitude for any type of imagination. The sole stipulation — and it probably did not hamper the effort of any contributing artist — was that a tobacco leaf, itself a beautiful product of our fields, was to be shown, and to occupy a certain amount of space.

The motive behind the scheme may have been less a matter of advertising a product than of enlarging the contact between art and commerce, or even of creating for painters a dignified means of living by their work. But the results were lamentable. Some of the pictures were clear evidence that their producers never had been anything but commercial artists; others among the painters were like moths that shrivel at a touch of the flame which fascinates them but which is evidently not their element; still others were defeated by the difficulty — or the impossibility — of adjusting their work to the needs of the reproductive lithograph. This process always falsifies a painting, and the best things of the kind (like some of the old Currier and Ives prints, and others of their period) were done by lithographers working freely according to the beauty of their medium, and using the "original" — if, indeed, they had one — as merely a general guide or point of departure. Of course, the real masters of the art — like Toulouse-Lautrec, since he made posters of a commercial order — were men who handled the lithographic crayon as a means for new creation, and not to imitate the look of an oil painting or a water color.

"How could I ever know things like that?" asks one of the millions of plain Americans who would be willing to enjoy art, but who has given it up as a bad job after finding that the cigarette-advertising pictures, signed by nationally celebrated men, afford him no more pleasure than any other chromos. "How am I supposed to know about your masters of lithography? Where am I to see them?" The answer is, once more, that same one which we have already heard Renoir give in his tone of surprise, "Au musée, parbleu!" The museum will show you sheet after sheet of magnificent prints, some done merely for purposes of expression, some as political broadsides, some as advertisements — with names and addresses of firms, prices of commodities, and every other requirement of commerce. But the essential matter that makes these three types one is that they belong in the museum, and allow it to meet the man in the street where it should meet him: within the limits of its necessary principles. Instead of going into the street to meet him, it invites him into a building planned to the last detail for his pleasure and profit. In the long run, he will thank the institution for holding to the values that its long experience has proved to be the best.

Flattering the masses with promises of "strength through joy" and the other catchwords of the crooked ideologies was the characteristic means by which Germans and Italians were snared for the work described by Mr. Taylor as destroying "the very civilization whose finest flowerings we are dedicated to preserve." The man in the street may have a deep and sure instinct which will respond to those "flowerings"; the man in the museum, however, has given his life to studying and fostering such matters. In the confusion of values amid which the world is struggling, the man in the street may be so misled by the blare of loud-speakers and the dazzle of fierce lights that his chances of achieving good judgment and good taste are progressively endangered. Much of what he gets over the radio, at the movie house, and from posters, magazine covers, and the like is making his "street" always more unhealthy. In that case, the museum cannot go halfway in meeting him, as Mr. Taylor asks; it cannot deviate even one step from the course that concentrating on its problem has made it see as the right one.

Those necessary limits of museum principles mentioned before are not fixed by the walls of the building. John Cotton Dana, as we recall, proposed that our art works be displayed in the windows of vacant shops and even in the homes of people who would borrow them for a given time. Such schemes are often difficult to put into effect. The vacant shop and the art lover's home may call for a staggering amount of work on the part of museum employees; and the expenses for packing, transportation, insurance, surveillance, bookkeeping, and the rest may greatly exceed the benefits. Will the object shown under more or less imperfect conditions produce any good share of its proper effect? It was created for a certain setting, and we are thus always aware of its relation to the space around it, and to objects that strengthen or contradict its appeal. The phonograph record of even a fine song loses its value if heard in a noisy place, amid a babel of distracting words, or merely at a time when people's thoughts are on a wrong sort of things.

Following Mr. Dana in a general way, however, we are working out a better means of putting his idea into execution. It is a means that avoids the reproach of the "musée ambulant." That derisive phrase for light-minded loans from public collections was coined by Degas, who — as a defender of his beloved Louvre — was never a friend to the easy way in art appreciation. If he could wait and watch for years, as he said, in order to get a perfect proof of one of Delacroix's beautiful etchings, why should he send it around the country for careless people to pass it by after half a glance? Let them get their own prints. And let the national treasures of France be kept in safe places, where they could be seen by those who cared enough to go and study them. On the other hand, he would doubtless have approved of the branch museum.

This new intermediary between art and the public is particularly suited to big cities, where going long distances to the main gallery involves much loss of time. The parent museum will probably have ample material in reserve, and can fit out a neighborhood museum without loss to itself or placing inferior things at the branch. Sometimes, as with the Cloisters, in New York, or Alger House, in Detroit, the new gallery will have a character all its own, and the visitor to the parent institution will want to make a special excursion to the other one. Chicago is planning

57. Copley: Mrs. Seymour Fort.
Courtesy of the Wadsworth Atheneum, Hartford.

to reach racial or national communities within the city, and is planning exhibits most attractive to Negro or Polish citizens. The George Washington Carver School in Harlem, New York's immense Negro section, has done fine things with art classes (only one of the many attractions of its curriculum) and has made a start with a permanent collection. The idea, in each case, is to carry on the work of the big museums among people who, ordinarily, cannot get away from their work for more than an hour or so. But if they can drop in at the end of their day, or even at lunchtime, they get a new lift for their spirits, and their frequent seeing of art works provides the remedy that every experienced observer knows to be the only real remedy for the sense of strangeness — almost of hostility — that people often feel when first seeing master works. As that feeling melts away, our branch-museum public will furnish more visitors, and better-prepared visitors, to the central galleries.

If a city has the resources for more than one fine collection (as Boston, with Mrs. Gardner's house, New York, with the Frick mansion, and Washington, with the Phillips Memorial Gallery), it may enjoy the special quality of the small museum, which leaves brilliant memories of a limited number of particularly choice things. These smaller galleries can give the big museum a pointer in creating its maximum effect by carefully selecting and placing its resources. Of course, it must not be forgotten that the big museum, unwieldy as it sometimes seems, functions as a place of reference, somewhat along the lines of the great library.

To glance again at the important question of preparedness for enjoying art, let me quote Edith A. Abbot, one of our museum workers whose years of observation have given her a deep insight into people's needs. She places the branch museum high among the means for improving our service to the public. Her reason is that such an institution helps to overcome a very special enemy to pleasure in works of art and to benefit from them: that enemy is superficial observation, a result of haste in going through the galleries. Her analysis of the museum instructor's work derives from the same thought, and seems to me to go to the very heart of the matter. Herself an artist, Miss Abbot has found that even a fine talent needs time to achieve its effect, and that discovery, in turn, has also given her the secret of getting the best effect from a picture already done. Her description of the docent's task is convincing in its very simplicity: it calls for no more than holding the museum visitor before a given work of art until the master himself has had a chance to speak from his canvas or other medium. There is every likelihood that some of his words will hit home. None of us gets all of his message, but if the newcomer to the gallery lets himself rush on from one painting or sculpture to the next, he gets not a hint of what might have been his if he had given himself the joy of making one new friendship or perhaps two.

To be sure, there is a bit of a catch connected with Miss Abbot's idea of the museum instructor: he or she must really know which are the masterworks. Nothing is easier than to know names; they run on in a beautiful litany — Cimabue, Giotto, van Eyck, Antonello da Messina, Titian, Rubens, Rembrandt, Daumier, Ryder, and so on, "in centuries of centuries."

But too often, the docent, instead of appreciating the merit of the works, merely repeats what he has read up in the library (he spends more time there than in the galleries). In such cases, he will speculate on whether or not Cimabue ever existed, and the Giotto will furnish a pretext for one more retelling of the Vasari stories. Without any real convictions as to the genius of van Eyck, the docent may have made a "safe" remark about the technical brilliance of early Flemish painting a few years before, when the beautiful work by the founder of the school was still attributed to a minor artist; on the other hand, the "Antonello," in which a famous critic says he saw all the geometry of modern art, has to be rechristened by experts as the work of an insignificant provincial. It would be grotesquely unfair to ask a young museum instructor to have an opinion on questions of such extreme difficulty; but should he not know that the "Titian," an absolute ruin when it turned up, was given all of its "tone" and "modeling" by a restorer? If the docent has had any real experience with Rubens, should he not be able to tell his hearers that the work before them, while from the master's design, is merely one of those endless repetitions by his assistants? (Such pictures have been the small change of dealers for a good part of those centuries of art collecting.) Even his hours in the library should have taught our docent that the "Rembrandt" is simply a school work. And so, continuing the monotonous chant of praise to the masters listed above, our lecturer reaches Daumier; (the present canvas is of course not by that artist, but by one whose only merit was that he could simulate the painting of Daumier); and the Ryder is an outright fake. Since it is related to a good picture, it is still preferable to certain things one hears praised, even in museums. Let us note, however, that the other inferior works just mentioned, the near-Daumier, the near-Antonello and the rest, might be duplicated in European galleries; and they are growing rarer in our collections, where more real expertise is constantly being used.

Quite evidently, I am here entering into details which will be familiar only to persons well versed in art. But the general point which all these details illustrate is that even for docent service, real knowledge and insight are needed. Museum instructors have the easiest of tasks if they attempt no more than giving their public a pleasant hour with the masters. But the vital work of advancing America's realization of the profound value of our museums demands more than an application of the bed-time story technique to a knowledge of art history. An experience of which I cannot rid my mind will make clear the notion, too often found in Europe, of the superficiality of our country's acquaintance with pictures. To be sure, it affords a true idea as to a part of our public — and even as to some of our docents. But it does not hold good for all of us.

Once when I was testifying in court, the preceding witness was interrogated by the judge. He had grown impatient with the muddling of the district attorney's man, and suddenly cut in with the question, "Hasn't this portrait been repainted?"

Caught off his guard by the judge's sharp tone, the witness, an Englishman, in the pay of a picture dealer, stammered, "Oh no, Y'r Lordship, absolutely not, it was merely Americanized."

Hearing that little New York politician called "Your Lordship" was too much for the dignity of the courtroom. Lawyers, hangers-on, policemen, and the judge himself relieved the proceedings by various degrees of hilarity. But the joke was largely spoiled for me by that word "Americanized." It told too much about the practice of making pictures pretty and salable for our market, a practice evidently so general in London as to have given rise to that miserable expression among men of the trade.

To balance the account, I will simply reproduce the wording on the label of a sculpture in the museum of Providence, Rhode Island: "Greek(?), copy of the 1st Century A. D. of 4th-Century Greek Original." I say that that label represents the truer aspect of American connoisseurship because the Providence gallery has for years known that the way to do good work is to have a director with scholarship such as dictated that label. And the docent must not be any boy or girl who has "taken art" at college, but one who has really attained some sense of the difference between masterwork, ancient or modern, and its imitation.

Early in this chapter, I spoke of getting back to fundamentals by observing the attitude toward art of those two experts in enjoyment, the artist and the collector — the amateur, to recur to that exact word. The museum worker often combines qualities of both those specialists, to which he adds the conclusions he draws from his dealing with the public. Having mentioned some of Miss Abbot's ideas, I will quote one of her colleagues, in another city. Miss Himmelein, of the Detroit Museum, had said that the time would come when we should all be artists. The remark puzzled me, and I was beginning to tremble over the

58. Eakins: William Rush Carving the Nymph of the Schuylkill.
Courtesy of the Philadelphia Museum of Art, Philadelphia.

fate of the world. But far from seeing everyone equipped with chisels and stone, or brushes and paint, she merely meant, I am sure, that it would be within the reach of everyone to have the artist's pleasure in seeing, whether pictures or nature.

On a memorable day in my own experience, it really seemed as if the city where I found myself had reached the stage of development suggested, later on, by that Detroit student of museum possibilities. It was over forty years earlier that I first visited Dresden, the place in question. On one richly rewarded day after another, I explored the big picture gallery there. There was always a considerable attendance but, one morning, I found an unexpectedly large number of visitors. Apparently the same townspeople one saw in the streets, they quite filled the rooms. Finally I asked a guard, "Is today a holiday here?" He looked at me, surprised that even a foreigner did not know how those crowds happened to be in the museum, and then with a friendly smile, replied, "Oh yes, to be sure: it's the King's birthday!" And the capital was celebrating it.

In the afternoon, wanting a change from the Old Masters, I went to a big modern exhibition. The crowd had preceded me there, and seemed more numerous and more eager than it had been even before the master work it had so evidently delighted in, that morning. The exhibition was in a park, and when everyone had seen enough of pictures for one day, he went and walked under the fine trees, after which some took out refreshments to eat at the table of a beer garden, while others ordered dinner at the open-air restaurants. For all, there was gay light from festoons of bulbs, and good orchestras made music. People danced, or watched the gymnasts of various associations do their exercises with wands or Indian clubs. After four decades, I clearly recall thinking on that evening that the dancers and the athletes (young women as well as young men — and some not so young) were again giving me something of the pleasure of art that I had had from the pictures. Those people had gone to see the collections that had once been the private delight of old Augustus the Strong, the ancestor of the popular king whose birthday was thus fittingly observed. And the charming Saxon city, ending its festivity with music, dancing, and the gestures of bodily grace and prowess, gave testimony to the idea I was to hear, later, from that quiet museum worker in Detroit: that everyone can share in the pleasures of the artist.

The endless galleries of the Louvre doubtless show one a more sophisticated multitude: I recall two people discussing a great Byzantine ivory there, in a way that showed they were not special students of the art but just persons impressed with the grandeur of that noble object; I recall finding myself gently jostled by a nice old gentleman as the crowds concentrated at the exit, to which the guards urged us on with their warning, "On ferme, messieursdames, on ferme," and then, when my neighbor and I sat down on the stone bench outside, to take a rest before starting home, I remember his fine comments on what he had seen — and again they were words that showed him to be a completely non-professional visitor.

But why draw on memories of Europe? Every one of them may be matched by experiences that our enormous museum crowds can furnish on any day. At the beginning of this book, I said that the basic fact is that America wants the museum. Necessarily, in following its development, we had to think of collectors, trustees, and other benefactors. But the way really to prove the point is to mingle with the crowds and see what they get from their visits. One scholarly curator makes it a practice to do this, especially on Sundays, when plain, hard-working people fill the gallery. He tells me that, casually talking with strangers who have no idea who he is, he gets valuable information not only as to their enjoyment (which is obvious to any observer), but as to what they want. He sums it up in two words: serious treatment. That applies to themselves and to the museum. They sense and resent a publicity stunt almost as surely as does a competent newspaper man; they sense the effective arrangement of exhibits and respond to it. They may not have the slightest notion of the scholarship that Mr. Caskey used in displaying the Greek things in his charge, there at the Boston Museum, any more than they could imagine the infinitely complex preparation of a great orchestra leader in directing a symphony; but quite simple people can enjoy the results in either case. And they will realize that the man who produced these results knew his job.

That admirable curator of classical art just mentioned, was an example of American scholarship as fine as any in the world today. Though not all of our experts are on such a level, scholarship is, in general, high enough in this country for us to wish that the labors of such men could benefit a larger public. Even our most popular museum, the Metropolitan, with the impressive showing of 29,000 visitors in one day, could serve many more people than come to it. At Kansas City, an official told me that half of the residents of the town had never entered the building, though it is in a fine park, which should be an attraction in itself. To be sure, the collections, due to the bequest of a public-spirited citizen, were not opened until 1933, and one must allow the city more time to appreciate their value. The city government does not give enough money for upkeep; nor does it sufficiently help the staff to get the attention of the great numbers — in Kansas City and its environs — who might enjoy their extraordinary opportunities. To let these be known, resort has been made to such means as a G.I. dance, held in a great gallery that was cleared for the purpose. It was a success, for the servicemen and the rest soon went exploring the rooms round about — and were delighted with what they found.

Perhaps not even that last fact would be enough to convince old-time museum directors as to propaganda of that type. Especially in Europe, it would cause many men to raise their eyebrows. But we are going to meet our problems in our own way. It is a good way if it gets results. A city whose public collections are only twelve years old is different from one like Paris, which has had them for a hundred and fifty (indeed, it has had things which took their place, monuments, churches, and works of art in public buildings, during a couple of thousand years before that). And yet, one all too frequently hears people discuss American problems as if they were those of Europe. In one of the wisest discussions of museum problems that have appeared,[2] Dr. W. R. Valentiner draws on his experience of galleries on both sides of the Atlantic to show the necessarily different types of appeal used in the institutions of the Old World and the New. Yet, at the southwest corner of our country, the farthest one can go from Europe and the great ports pointing toward it, San Diego's vast new population of workers in the war plants came in great numbers to the museum, and showed the heartiest interest in painting and sculpture which artists produced in the presence of the public. Their ancestors had lived in Old-World places rich in ancient tradition and art, and if contact with that force was broken or diminished when they came to the New World, the essential thing, the instinct for it, remained as strong and eager as ever. It is not in the art of the collections that our museums must differ from those of Europe, but in their relationship with the people here.

The thing needed is to make them aware of the opportunities to satisfy their instinctive need for beauty. Whether among the new, uprooted crowds at the war plants or in Boston, with its long record of art activities, the museum must seize every opportunity to remind the public of the things offered to it: America is a busy place, and there is so much to solicit the attention of the public. The Metropolitan not only continues but adds to the free musical offerings which bring new visitors. The Museum of Modern Art owes much of its large attendance to its showing of motion pictures. It studies them as art, a natural corollary to

---

[2] As part of a volume on *New Architecture and City Planning*, published by Philosophical Library, New York, 1944.

59. Ryder: The Resurrection.
Courtesy of the Phillips Memorial Gallery, Washington, D. C.

its consideration of the men who, from Matthew Brady and those before him to Alfred Stieglitz and those after him, have applied themselves to photography with intensity and faith, those prime factors in the arts. We are pushing back the limits formerly set for the world of art, even as our scientists push back the frontiers of their domain.

Perhaps the cinema needs a new classification, since it has so much to do with the theater. Perhaps photography is to be classified among the crafts, since the image it gives was not formed by the mind of the man who released the shutter. To convince oneself of this, one has only to consider the many and impressive airplane views for which the camera was simply a mechanism set for a certain height and speed of the plane, and was quite independent of what the operator saw. The purely accidental results of the "candid camera," often most interesting things, are further evidence on the point; so that these photographs — and finally all photographs — are merely scientific reproductions of something in nature that already exists. The word "art" has to be reserved for the creation of things which did not previously exist. The works of the early masters of the camera established the range of its possibilities; but within them there was such latitude for the registering of individual interests, so much room for the craftsman's love of exact nuances in printing that the human eye alone can control, and so rich an opportunity to seize upon expressions of life and character that the way was open — and still remains open — for a limitless number of eager experimenters.

They and their vast public are given their place in the galleries. In fact, the whole public, as a creator of the institution, has its share in the work of the museum. The Muses, from whom it gets its name, presided over more fields than those we designate under the term "fine art." Evidently, to go on to the realms of Clio, Urania, Terpsichore and the rest, and deal with history, astronomy, dancing, etc., would call for buildings vaster than any we want to erect. But we can make allusions to all the activities in which man has expressed the finest of his ideas.

Something like that is implied in a recent sentence of John Masefield's. Thinking back to his early days on the sea, he still has the sense of its wide horizons. Still the sailor on the topmast, his mind leaps over intricacies of detail to make us heir to something of the sea space surveyed by him. And the wisdom of his later life permits his saying, "Surely all the generosities of the soul come from the arts." Such stimulus is what we have seen reflected in the faces of the happy crowds at the galleries of Dresden, Paris, and one after another of the cities of America. As we continue to strengthen our collections for their work of giving delight, more and always more people will see that John Masefield's definition of the arts is literally true, and they will turn to their museum in moods of thought or in festive moods, but above all, spontaneously, as we do with all the things that are the best in our lives.

CHAPTER V

THE MUSEUM OF THE NEW WORLD

IN THE INTRODUCTION to this book, I explained two senses of the term New World, the one denoting the different world that is so fast emerging, because of political, scientific, and intellectual change, and then the sense in which the words have so often been used, as a synonym for America. We must take note once more that America is — emphatically — a bigger place than the United States.

The bond between ourselves and Canada is largely one of language (though we must not forget that much of Canada speaks French). Far closer bonds hold the New World together. If Mexico and Brazil, especially, did important work in securing our southern frontier against the Nazi menace, and helped so much to protect us against the submarines of Germany and Japan, it was because, among all Americans, the same ideal of democracy is dominant, even if dictators are all too frequent in one country and another.

But we have not yet mentioned the greatest bond which makes of the New World a single place, and that is the land itself. A single chain of mountains, from Alaska to Argentina, gives a backbone to the hemisphere. The mountains change their name as they traverse different regions, but this is a man-made distinction. It is no more important, essentially, than the changes of name between the countries: Canada and the United States, Mexico and Guatemala, and so on. A hundred years ago, we took half of Mexico's territory after a war, but the earth there is the same earth, irrespective of its political frontiers.

Even after our centuries of city-dwelling, we must realize that cities are mere pinheads on the map, and that it is the country and its character that count. In Thackeray's novel, *The Virginians*, and in any number of other works dealing with the eighteenth century, we see how our people had become different from their blood relatives in Europe, even at that time, and the growth of civilization on our continent, since then, has accentuated the separation.

The great factor in this evolution has been our soil. It gave us wealth, and the desire for an equitable sharing of that wealth gave us our political institutions. But our way of life is more closely connected with

the soil than with political institutions. Outdoor sports, camping, hunting, and fishing — things dear to modern Americans (as they were to the
old peoples of this land) — are all intimately related to the character of
the land, and so determine very much of our character.

Since firsthand evidence is always the best, I do not apologize to relate
my experience as a one-man jury of admission for a show of painting and
sculpture. I had an almost uncomfortable sense of responsibility toward
the artists whose work came before me, and therefore scrutinized it with
more than ordinary care. The exhibition was one that Atlanta University
holds each year for Negro artists throughout the country. Even with the
cumulative effect of seeing so many works of one racial origin, I could
not avoid being convinced that their expression was identical with that of
white Americans — in idea, temperament, and accent. If the country
has done as thorough a job as that in naturalizing a people once alien, it
must be that there is an American character.

I conclude that it is logical for an American museum to take on
something of the character of this country. By that I do not mean doing
merely the external thing — giving special attention to American work
in the collections. That procedure goes without saying. The real expression of character in our museums will be marked, in time, by the general
tendencies of our people, no matter what type of art they acquire. It has
been observed, in comparing French and German museums, that connoisseurship in the former places manifests itself best in the works of a
Latin (and preferably French) tradition, while the German temperament
yields its strongest results with the production of Nordic artists, the
Flemish and Dutch, besides, of course, those which are specifically German. It should be added that, in recent times, the country's immense
scholarship made German acquisitions of Italian art decidedly better than
those of the French museums. In Europe, one often hears a dealer say:
"That is a picture for America; that other one — no." The question is,
of course, one of salability, but even that unidealistic standard tells something about taste and knowledge here. Sometimes they depend on the
degree of education we have reached as regards a given school or artist,
but sometimes the matter is one of inherent character — the thing we
have been considering in these last pages.

Too often, even today, people talk of work as American because it
represents some aspect of the American scene. That is to fall into the old
error of confusing the subject of a picture and its character; the chances
are that the same people who slip into that trap would recognize the fact
that a chromo of the Virgin and Child is not a religious picture and that
it is, in fact, enough to turn one against the very idea it is supposed to

support. Just possibly there would even be a realization of the essentially religious character in Cézanne. If they failed to hear the "music of the spheres" that lifts a still life by him wholly away from the everyday objects which were his point of departure, they would still be likely to feel the grandeur of his meditation on the mountain he so often painted; and the kindling green and blue in those solemn evocations of space and silence might come as the fulfillment of impressions left with them by a reading of Bryant's *Thanatopsis*, by a line or an image of Emily Dickinson's, or by some other memory of the old New England nature poets.

From those artists of words we receive, indeed, an expression of American character. It was natural that the great literary current we enter through our English blood should give us our earliest true expression. And yet, when we know better the character of our country, when we realize that its hills and plants and animals had already created great symbols in the art of the Indians, we shall perceive the essential quality of American writers as a thing not merely inherited from England or other parts of Europe, but evolved through contact with the new soil. Quite certainly, there were important points of contact between the ideas our settlers brought with them and what they encountered here, so that the development was, as I just said, one of evolution and not one of replacement.

There was no need for replacement, our ideas of the country being, in many cases, surprisingly like the ones held by our predecessors. Those men felt the character of our northwestern coast, from Alaska to California, and responded to it with the sculpture of the totem poles, whose sharp definition was calculated to have full effect in the misty atmosphere. How different is the art of Arizona and New Mexico! There the powerful sunlight, effacing sculptural form, led to a flat type of painting. The foregoing observations were first made by René d'Harnoncourt, who adds that the American artist of today may well study the work of those ancient compatriots of his for what it reveals of local truth, something that we need in our art today. A permanent element, it should concern us just as much as it concerned the pre-Columbian men who first registered the character of the country.

A society that had the enormous task of developing the idle resources of a continent, and that found individual property-holding its most efficient spur to effort, would naturally be at odds with the Indian and his inability to understand that a man, or a tribe of men, could own the land. For thousands of years, he had roamed it freely and had seen no cause to establish any fixed boundaries. Even when our early settlers moved into a land that had known a sedentary civilization — Ohio, for instance —

they were too much occupied with fighting the people they encountered to spend much time philosophizing on the noble spaces enclosed by the walls of the mounds. Yet, in some cases, the sites were respected, remained government land, and now, as parks, are public property again. As they were communal meeting grounds in the ancient times, places where the people assembled for councils, ceremonies, and games, there was here, even among economic and political traditions, a point of contact for the newcomers. The common or green of the New England village had carried on ideas dating back many centuries in Europe, where certain places were all-men's land, to coin a term suitable for communities doing things together.

In view of the almost unbridgeable divide between the forms of life of the Indian time in America and those of our time, it may seem that my talk of common ideas or sensations is pretty thin moonshine. The word is, however, by no means unfamiliar or frightening to people, who, for example, see a relationship between the quality of a Greek vase and that of a Chinese vase — things separated by as much of space and race as the ways of thinking I have been trying to relate to each other. Perhaps another connection will seem less tenuous — the feeling for animals that many white men share with the Indian.

When John Burroughs would pick up a bee and stroke it and roll it in his hand, to the apparent satisfaction of the little animal that would have rewarded a less knowing person with a fiery sting, the old naturalist convinced many an onlooker that there is some way to share in the instinct of the wild creatures. In our more primitive places, there are still numbers of men who seem to have a sort of speaking acquaintance with birds, raccoons, deer, and other man-shy beasts; the things they can do fill a city dweller with something like awe. I remember one old fellow in the Adirondacks who, in addition to his tremendous knowledge of the properties of roots, balsams, barks, and the other nature medicines, had what seemed like a veritable sixth sense for the hiding places of pickerel, the time when wild ducks would fly, and a hundred other mysteries that remained impenetrable even for the generality of men in those north woods. It is true that the old man was half Indian, but John Burroughs was not, and their powers are shared by any number of other Americans who have the same instinct for wild life. Even those among us who lack their extraordinary powers enormously appreciate the lore of nature.

At this point, it may seem far-fetched for me to refer to the popularity of Joel Chandler Harris and his *Uncle Remus*. But the tales of Br'er Rabbit, with which the old Negro held the little boy spellbound, have been connected by learned research with folk tales that go back far into man's memory of times when he was on more intimate terms with the animals. And the essential point is that they belong to ancient America as well as to Africa. Another American must ever be connected with those lovable stories. A. B. Frost, who came from a part of the country very different from Mr. Harris's Georgia, made illustrations for *Uncle Remus*, and earned admiration more important than that of Gérôme. The French Academician was impressed by the swift and incisive draftsmanship with which Mr. Frost portrayed his models. But to countless people in our country, the forthright realism of the drawings, in which the artist was aided by the example of his friend Thomas Eakins, meant more than a question of aesthetics. Americans knew and liked those "critters," which perfectly imaged the author's intentions.

This brings us to a matter of great importance, in considering American art. Much of its true quality would not be recognized by the public — and that was why I said it might have seemed far-fetched to bring *Uncle Remus* into the discussion. But if our people, on finding that what they admired was art, are as much astonished as Monsieur Jourdain when he learned that what he talked was prose, the more interesting point is that often the artist himself is unconscious of the essential thing in what he has created. That explains why many of A. B. Frost's drawings have to be called artless, with a double accent to the word. When we apply it to some fine piece of old American carving, pottery, or weaving, we use it with a different connotation.

To pursue this unconscious element in fine things — indeed, to turn now to very great things — I will recall a conversation I had with Diego Rivera about the relative merits of Tarascan and Aztec sculpture. (Both, incidentally, produced great masterpieces with animals as their subjects.) My own preference was for the mighty things of the Aztecs. Rivera loves the infinite fantasy, the utterly unself-conscious spontaneity of the Tarascans. He has a figure in beautiful, polished clay of a puppy curled up and looking at you with the irresistible eyes of a tired little animal. It is one of the tenderest bits of affectionate humor that man has ever produced. From this work, those very ancient people of the west of Mexico can turn to wild burlesques of fat women, or to the fiercest of fighting warriors. "The Aztecs, by comparison," said Rivera, "were too much the artists."

Word for word, that was what Delacroix said of Rubens and Watteau after seeing their pictures in a great Paris collection. One has to know the opinions of Delacroix, with their constantly returning admiration, indeed fervent admiration, for the two Flemish masters, in order to realize how startling is that passage in the *Journal*. For many people it is a favorite, even among the multitude of splendid things in that book, for it explains part of our love for the painter. He had enjoyed the Rubens and the Watteau, as usual, but then he came on a work by Ruisdael, and it is by comparison with the landscapist's humbly unself-conscious attitude before nature that Delacroix for once concedes that something could go beyond the work of those two idols of his.

Mr. Rivera's own group of Tarascan sculptures, probably the finest in the world, is generously sampled in Dr. Medioni's book on the collection. The drowsy little dog is shown in two good plates, which have delighted many people; but — as always in reproductions — only a faint hint of the beauty of the original is achieved. You will do better, if you live near any collection of old Mexican art, to go and see a few of the actual things, even if they do not reach the height of this one. Please do not neglect my Aztecs, when you do so. But — best of all — go to Mexico, and see the sculptures of the coyotes, snakes, rabbits, frogs, the marvelous grasshopper, and the "tigers" (i.e., jaguars or ocelots) that will thrill you, whoever you are.

Not equaling them, perhaps, in the quality of the colossal which marks their expressiveness, are some sculptures nearer home. I regret, for nonresidents of Columbus, Ohio, that the only way to see properly these effigies of the animals is to visit the museum there; but it is safe to say that anyone who does go will come away a better American. The old Mound Builders of the whole central part of the United States attained a climax of their art in southern Ohio, with related and still grand production in the neighboring states. But those animals now to be seen at the Ohio State Museum stand a bit apart from the rest, and have a very special impressiveness. They rank, I truly believe, with the fine things of Mexico — or of Egypt.

The "primitives" say their say without the least consciousness that their work is art. Homer's gods and women and warriors are not more directly presented. And so we hear again, as people look at the old animal pieces, that exclamation we have noted before, "How modern they are!" Take note whether or not you get that response from observers as they stand before the remarkable turkey, eagle, and other animals in the sculpture of Renaissance Florence. After people have seen the Mexicans and other old Americans, they will be a thousand times more likely to agree with you if you say of Pietro Tacca and other such Florentines, "They were too much the artists."

The illusion of modernity in the ancient work of our soil is, this time, of transcendent importance. The hawk, the otter with the fish in his mouth, and the goose so exactly observed that the ornithologist can tell its precise place in his realm, all these look as if they were made only yesterday. Then why can we not have such things today? Why not make them known to every American artist so that he may profit by this art, which is quintessentially his ancestral art? It belongs to us in the way that we belong to this country. Yet few of our artists know these works, and that grievous lack the Museum of the New World must remedy.

Its task is not merely one of exhibiting the art of our ancient peoples, but of discovering it, defining its extent, and letting us see how it relates to our present-day needs. People too often think of museums in terms of "end results," reference places to settle questions of names, dates, or even qualities belonging to the past. To do so is to forget the other and more interesting work done by the institutions. They have sent searchers to Egypt and other lands to dig up lost treasure, they have changed our conception of great masters, and, above all, they have provided to new masters a stimulus for which there could be no substitute.

Americans did a large part in restoring to the world some of the great cities of ancient Mexico, and that country is actively studying the problems and opportunities afforded by the wealth of the old arts. But their splendor must not blind us to the great things in our own land. The smaller objects, like those at Columbus, are not all we have to show. At Barrier Canyon, in Utah, there are cliffs where, on a space of rock sixty feet long, some forgotten race painted a multitude of human figures, strangely stylized, and receding into mysterious depths. A copy of the work, made by WPA artists, was one of the very grand features of the exhibition of Indian art held in 1941 at the Museum of Modern Art.

As with this painting, there is, in any number of sculptures, an intimate connection with the material from which the work emerges. A particularly fine one is the white stone effigy of an Indian personage, to be seen at the Field Museum in Chicago. Its "direct carving," an ideal of many sculptors today, would have delighted Rodin. Perhaps we might better say that it would have made him envious, for he is quoted as saying that he could never equal the vigor of the *Eagle Knight*, the Aztec portrait at the National Museum of Mexico. The great French sculptor owned a cast of the work.

Mention of it, just after that beautiful thing in Chicago, brings us to what may well turn out to be an essential characteristic of the ancient people of our country. In his monumental book on the Pre-Columbian art of Mexico and Central America (1944), Salvador Toscano traces the development of schools there, and uses the words "archaic," "classical," and "academic" that we know so well in their application to the arts of Europe. Perhaps, it is too soon to contrast the ancient Mexicans with the Indians of the United States; but data now available for forming an opinion point to an individualism in our part of America far greater than that usually found in Mexico. The high state of civilization in the southern countries and their relatively dense population permitted men to produce many more works than did our United States Indians. The presence of schools, as they may quite properly be called, never deprived ancient Mexican art of the degree of originality needed to make each piece live its own life, even where strong similarities exist. Many of these pieces are unparalleled, and will doubtless remain unique for all time.

But this is the prevailing quality in the art of what was the United States, previous to the advent of the white man. The people were largely nomads, which accounts for the scant remains of their art. Possibly, it found its chief expression in poetry, the drama, singing, and related activities. The rarity of sedentary cultures would also explain why individuals or, at most, groups would frequently have to make new beginnings, without the benefit (or hindrance) of models deriving from the past. There is a temptation to see in this a forecast of the inventiveness so marked in latter-day Americans, though here we are on pretty shaky ground. Yet, when we think of the high level of spiritual and literary achievement among our settlers at a time when their material conditions were still comparatively primitive, there can be thought as to a parallelism between the white men and those former inhabitants of the Ohio Valley. Of the latter, Dr. H. C. Shetrone, director of the Ohio State Museum, well asks, "What is it that caused these Indians, apparently no further advanced in their manner of living than others, to rise to such an extraordinary artistic height?" The question is only one of many that the Museum of the New World could help us to answer. And, quite clearly, accounting for this phenomenon would yield at least suggestions as to a finer culture for ourselves.

From another interview with the authority just cited (he is the author of The Mound Builders, the most notable document on the subject), I recall his pointing to a piece of stone from which some old-timer had flaked off pieces for arrowheads. Under Dr. Shetrone's guidance it was not difficult to imagine the deft, rhythmic strokes of the stone hammer that accounted for those bits of quartz, already beautifully shaped, which lay in the showcase beside the parent piece. In this testimony to the Indian's admiration for a thing precious to him for its utility but at the same time an aesthetic object, we have a note which, if by no means exclusively American, is one of those which make us feel, as human beings, very near to our forerunners on this soil.

We note the care they used in shaping and polishing their beautiful "banner stones," we see the same attention to things of daily use like knives and corn-grinders, for each of which an appropriate material was selected with exact judgment; and all this makes one think of good workmen we have known among ourselves, and the pride they have in their tools and the things made with those tools. More than that, the Indian's evident pleasure in the quality of a stone, a piece of mica or of copper, connects with our own enjoyment of things that nature offers us — a special tree, a boulder we always glance at again as we go along a certain path, or a bank of flowers that are "just no use, but kind of nice to see," as a countryman will often say. The old pantheism of America lives on in us of today.

Certainly, as our scholars have proved, pantheism is the basis of that extraordinary painting which we find among the Hopi and other Indians of our Southwest. Whether in mural work on the walls of their council chambers, or in the beautiful sand-painting which the Navahos still produce — their firm hands allowing a fine stream of colored earth to pour onto the ground and form clear lines and powerful designs — or again in the decoration of pottery and other objects, the basis of all of it is found in the shapes of the sun, the clouds, lightning, rain, and other manifestations of forces which, for the Indian, mingle the natural with the divine. A new respect is appearing among us for the people who have continued, through immense hardships, to bring forth their beautiful things in response to voices of the land, and perhaps we shall allow them to go on with their beliefs and their art. How much alive their art is, and how ready to offer new results, has been shown by the large number of young Indians in the Southwest who, on obtaining from white artists such materials as paper and water colors, have already done many pictures most authentically fine in quality. George C. Vaillant, in his pioneer book of 1939, *Indian Arts in North America*, speaks of these paintings as follows, "It is not too much to suppose that in this blend of the white world with the Indian is a conceivable point of departure for a national art. We have, in our own experience, seen the development of a Mexican national style, formed by a similar union of Indian design and balance with white skills in presentation."

These are, moreover, only the latest results of contact between the art of Europeans (or people of European descent) and of Americans of purely native descent. Again and again such contacts have produced new forms of value, indeed very high value. In addressing the graduating class of the School of the Chicago Art Institute, the director, Daniel Catton Rich, entitled his remarks "The Challenge of Art in the Americas," and

60. Prendergast: Landscape with Figures.
Courtesy of the Detroit Institute of Arts.

made observations on the point we are noticing. He said, "Not only will pre-Columbian civilizations appeal to you. For over three centuries Spanish settlers built churches, houses, and palaces, which for force of imagination and decorative power rival baroque and rococo architecture in Europe. The designs, many of them, were drawn in Spain or Italy, but the execution and materials were American. In those centers of early civilization, Mexico, Ecuador, and Peru, the native Indian workman took European designs, and unconsciously transformed them in the light of his own deepest inner feeling and symbolism. This was the slave's revenge, and it is a magnificent revenge. Today, such examples as the great Jesuit retreat at Tepozotlán in Mexico, and the Church of La Compañía in Quito, the capital of Ecuador, stand as imperishable American monuments — full of echoes of Aztec and Inca, blended with Spanish baroque into a highly original style."

Having heard from an Anglo-Saxon about the relationship between the artists of Europe and those of the older America, we may listen advantageously to a writer of Spanish descent. For the attitudes toward the Indian of the two great colonizing peoples were very different. Pedro Henríquez Ureña, born in Santo Domingo, secretary of the National University of Mexico, and later a professor at the University of La Plata in Argentina, until his death in 1946 deprived us of one of the great humanists, knew as did few others the civilization he told of in his *Literary Currents in Hispanic America* (Harvard University Press, 1945). It contains the following:

"In Europe, as we know, the first reports of the Aztec and Inca civilization were not even understood — Montaigne, as always, was the exception; but the men who actually saw them did understand. In the eighteenth century an effort at comprehension began, and it went on through the nineteenth: but it is only today that the conception of the individuality of the cultures is becoming an acceptable notion. Furthermore, we begin to discover that mankind has known scores of civilizations now buried under dust, that at many different times and at many different places, great cities have been built, great scientific discoveries made, great forms of art created. Many works that were formerly kept in ethnological or archaeological collections now migrate to art museums, and the sculptures from Cambodia or Ur of the Chaldees, from Guatemala or Cuzco, from Easter Island or from Central Africa, now hold their own side by side with the formerly unapproachable statues of Greece and Italy. We are not now ashamed to confess that any civilization may have been, in some of its aspects, as great as ours, if not greater."

A hundred years ago, the arts of Cambodia and Ur of the Chaldees, mentioned by Mr. Henríquez Ureña, were totally unknown. Even the greatness of Egypt was far from the appreciation it has today. A glance through the supplementary list, in this book, will reveal how many of our museums now give space to the arts of ancient America, also cited in the foregoing passage. But it is not enough to have splendid groups of them in places like the Museum of Natural History in New York. The whole psychology of such an institution, admirable in its own field, is wrong for works of art. The collection that Mr. and Mrs. Walter Conrad Arensberg have offered to the University of Southern California is a most appropriate one for a place which represents the humanities, and where art instruction is given. Moreover, the Mexican and other works of the Arensberg collection are associated in it with a splendid group of modern paintings and sculpture, and there is a connection between the two types of art. Yet, despite the fact that, as far back as 1841, John Lloyd Stephens set us far along the course of understanding the great creations of Yucatan and other parts of Middle America, our people are, in general, too much of the same mind as Benjamin Ives Gilman when he wrote, "Asia, the Levant, and in a minor way [the italics are mine] the Americas, still possess riches." After this grudging admission, we realize the progress that has been made when a man of Mr. Henríquez Ureña's learning and judgment can say that the ancient arts of this hemisphere hold their own beside those of Greece and Italy. As always greater numbers of people come to vouch for the truth of such a statement, the pioneer work of museums like those of Detroit and Harvard, in showing together the arts of all great races, will be followed by the institutions which still have not ventured to assume this necessary share in creating our collective Museum of the New World.

Whatever the wealth that France concentrates in the Louvre, or England in the British Museum and the National Gallery, we cannot see the art of the Old World in its fullness without visiting the places which can show the monumental works of Egypt, Greece, the Gothic time, and the Renaissance. Similarly, the most important arts that the New World has produced thus far will always have to be seen in places like Mexico and Guatemala. But as no European museum could think its work conscientiously done without including in it the fullest obtainable representation of the masters of its continent, American museums also will realize that their task and opportunity include the masterpieces of their continent. And for two reasons they may rejoice that this is so: in the first place, they will be showing some of the very great art of the world as a whole; secondly, they will be rendering a particular service to their public. The reason for this statement is again a double one; not only will they be telling us of "Our Ancestors of the Soil," my word for them in an article in The Virginia Quarterly Review, but as I wrote in the same magazine, a year later,[1] the ancient Americans can help us today, in the contemporary crisis of our own arts.

Beset with problems in which the aesthetic elements are often confused with scientific and social matters, the modern painter or sculptor has that need for guidance from the classics which we have previously noted as occurring at various moments in history. It is, perhaps, the natural thing for every period to see its difficulties as particularly big, or it may be that our time — with its enormous revaluation of values — is really faced with questions more complex than those of the past. Often as the great works of Greece and Rome have come to the help of artists who have consulted them, the "contemporary genesis," as Elie Faure called it, may demand answers from a wider circle of authorities.

The museum director needs prompting from his public, in some cases, to make him aware of such demands on his institution. Thinking at one moment of the use to give the material he has, he may talk of education and general service to the country. At other times, if he does not have a proper feeling for his opportunity to offer us the new inspiration afforded by ancient American art, he may fail to enquire whether or not a work proposed for acquisition is a good specimen of its type. For botanical collections, any one of a million leaves of a certain tree will be a fine specimen. But if the leaves are those of books — the ones adorned with fine prints, let us say — only one leaf in a million may contain the idea for which men are thirsting. The art museum, even if it needs reference material like the museum of science, has the duty to afford guidance to its public: it must take the responsibility of choosing the essential works from the myriads possible for it to acquire. It may not be passive; it must not follow, but lead.

Let us suppose, however, that our director is ready to lead, and competent to select works which will demonstrate the greatness of ancient America. Even so, certain new measures may be demanded. Mexico is very properly protecting her treasure against exportation, just as various countries of Europe have had to make strict regulations about the exporting of art objects; indeed, it is prohibited to remove those that governments believe essential for study and appreciation within their own borders. Yet, so much of the art of Greece and Italy had already left those countries in the past that the problem of the European classics is, in our museums, relatively simple. Of Mexican art, there are stupendous amounts in Mexico, much of it fixed in its place on buildings, and much

---

[1] The Virginia Quarterly Review, Summer number, 1944, and Summer number, 1945.

of it still to be excavated. Outside of the country, not enough of it is available to meet the needs of our collections. Here is an opportunity for the Museum of the New World to contribute to solidarity among its peoples. In various fields of art, a system of exchanges is already growing up whereby institutions rich in the work of a given school may share with those less fortunate in that respect, but able to reciprocate with material lacking in the other place. The Latin-American countries, properly approached, would unquestionably work with us in such civilized exchanges. In fact, by the loan to the Museum of Modern Art of the choicest material in the National Museum of Mexico, that country proved, in 1940, its willingness to co-operate.

And what material it was which gave us that show: "Twenty Centuries of Mexican Art"! And what material still remains to be shown! Or, if we can ever get people in general to look repeatedly at things they have seen before and to penetrate to their essence, instead of asking for novelties, what light on the whole enigma of the world we may obtain from the objects we already possess! For, they may tell us of certain conceptions of life and death that evolved in this half of the globe, and that remained unknown in the Eastern Hemisphere. We are horrified by the blood, skulls, and serpents of ancient Mexican art. But nature, in commanding its creatures to kill, and to eat one another, sets up her own standards. Our part of the world, like the rest of it, had a profound philosophy at the base of its art. When we come to consider this art according to its aesthetic qualities, and to make comparisons between Mexican sculpture and that of Egypt, Assyria, the Greeks, and the Gothic men, we see how high it stands.

Underlying it are mathematical laws directly related to those governing the movement of the heavenly bodies. A geometrical conception, like that of the other fundamental cultures, dictates the proportions of pyramids, temples, and monuments. From the enormous mass of the Pyramid of the Sun at Teotihuacán, a quarter of a mile long on each side, to the small clay heads found in countless specimens in the soil, runs the same sense of the finality of numbers. And with this abstract rightness goes a feeling for the life of men, animals, and plants that gives a romantic impulse to balance the classical element achieved by pure form. Representation may go to the limit of exactitude, whether the subject is a woman, a bird, or anything else in nature — like the wonderful life-sized squash in the National Museum of Mexico. In this work and others the realism of form and surface texture is complete. But in the pre-Columbian art of Mexico (I am not sure that the same can be said of the Peruvians), never is there a descent into mere imitation. Paralleling those great arts of the Old World mentioned just before, the American classics are always too charged with idea, as Plato called it, to be content with mere appearances. Indeed, one reason we of today can turn so readily to these works is that we are in a period which has seen the wisdom of Matisse and Picasso. Like the best of the moderns, the old Americans, employing an art made powerful by its expression of a whole people's thought, knew that the idea — again in Plato's sense of the word — may be expressed in forms having a semblance of nature or in forms very different from those of nature.

At times we are reminded of the perfections of Egypt, and indeed, it was by the same process of abrasion, the slow rubbing down of hard stone by sand and powder from harder stones, that the two civilizations produced their sculpture. At other times, the power of tigers, eagles, and serpents causes us to think of the mighty works of the Assyrians. Yet, the more we know this art, the more we think of it in relation to itself, no more justifying it by the example of Egypt than we would ask that land for authority to admire the art of Greece. Those two supreme products of the Old World have a relationship — and yet each can be used to condemn or, at the very least, to diminish the other. The art of the New World needs, in the same way, to be viewed as an independent achievement, complete in itself.

Having taken it away from philosophical considerations, and from the always odious field of comparisons, we may notice the character it shares with art in general, that of giving pleasure. Indeed, when one has got to the point of enjoying its quality, it may act like a strong liquor that causes other beverages to lose their flavor until one's palate has regained its normal sensitiveness. The old American arts do not affect us as they do merely because of their intoxicating strength, but because they give us the experience of sensations that the other arts had not let us know. There is a freedom in the work of this continent that is like fresh air to the lungs. Perhaps, it is something inherent, as many of us believe, or it may derive just from our not having known such a thing before.

And there is beauty, to take up the challenge contained in that word. We reserved it for the Greeks, at one time; later, we saw that it applied also to the art of the Dutch, to a gargoyle on a cathedral, or to a Chinese sculpture. All of these helped us to break with the superstition that beautiful subjects are necessary for beautiful art. Or, perhaps, we realize that the beauty of the thing or person portrayed is a relative matter, whereas the beauty of art is an absolute matter — since all differences of opinion on it disappear in time, as men come to agreement on one master or school after another.

If there is beauty in an archaic Greek head, then there is beauty in that Aztec head at the Fogg Museum. The ceramics of the Mayas at the University Museum in Philadelphia stand with the great things of their kind from Persia and China. As with the three Old-World arts just mentioned, we are equally drawn to the form and color, the aesthetic properties, and the human property of expression. In New York, at the Museum of Natural History, there is a little red stone corn goddess who has been in the collection for such a long time that we could no more question the permanence of our opinion about her beauty than we could doubt the *Mona Lisa* or a Delphic Apollo as beautiful. And our justification for saying so is the same in each case: the work has grown more wonderful to us with the passing of the years. Also (much as one dislikes to dissect), all of them possess the same equilibrium of appeal: there is, here again, the timeless harmony of lines and masses, on the one hand; on the other, that old American work bespeaks love of the girls who inspired it. The braids hanging down the back of the solid figure, and the chubby toes of the feet she squats on, are rendered with observation as intimate as the warm earth that bore her, and with sentiment as healthy as the corn she brings to men. A combination of form and content so beautifully balanced is what gives us the thing that is to be called "classical."

The American student today, harassed by the complexity of his period, is often uncertain whether it is to the world and life that he should direct his thought, or to the museum and its wealth. Asked about the latter source of guidance, Diego Rivera answered, "Of course, we should study the classics, our classics." For him, who has seen all that Europe has to show, both of her own art and that of other continents, there was no doubt but that it is the great American works which offer the best inspiration today, when the heritage of European tradition has been picked over so often that new light from it will be most difficult to obtain, and when the lassitude due to a war period begun in 1914 must make us doubt whether a new generation of Frenchmen or other Old-World artists will show the way to the new advance that is so much needed.

Such an idea is confirmed by the deeply considered book of a Spanish writer, Juan Larrea, now residing in Mexico. He knows the finest of modern art, and his erudition in Europe's past allows him to give, in his *Rendición de Espíritu*, a most striking interpretation of an ancient symbol. To the south, in his native land, Gibraltar looks across to a mountain in Africa, and together they form the Pillars of Hercules, beyond which, for antiquity, there was nothing. They marked the end of the world. But on the escutcheon of Spain, the Pillars appear again, with the words

Plus Ultra. The motto reverses the old command which said men might not go farther; Spain had indeed gone beyond, and had discovered the New World. Here, first in Peru and then in Mexico, Juan Larrea has sought a future that he does not see as possible in the Old World. Life and thought have, for him, shifted to this side of the Atlantic.

One wonders if that is so, despite the admirable things in the book, and they are many. More recently, Sr. Larrea has returned to his thesis, supporting it by some impressive quotations from Paul Valéry. Again an experience of my own seems to throw light on the question. In 1940, at the World's Fair in New York, the Mexican pavilion had a small theater where two sisters from the state of Oaxaca, one of the Republic's very old centers of culture, delighted large audiences by their rendering of native dances. Estela and Emma Ruiz had a wide knowledge of their country, having been invited to every part of it to organize fiestas in the ancient tradition that their city of Tehuantepec has maintained in great purity. The visit to the United States was their first in any foreign land, and going to the Metropolitan Museum, as they soon did, gave them a first sight of ancient art, save that of Mexico. It was therefore with extreme interest that I observed their reactions to what they saw that day. At one moment in it, their healthy and immediate enjoyment of the splendid things they saw took a really dramatic turn. That was when we reached the Egyptian sculpture of the girl bearing offerings, an excellent example of the type which gives us a culminating masterpiece in the beautiful *Porteuse d'offrandes* at the Louvre. Our own figure is fine enough, with its slow dignity, its grace, and its discreet polychromy.

The girls had been all eagerness, a moment before, each exclaiming over a new discovery and dragging the other (and myself) the length of the room to make sure we had not failed to see the latest wonder. But before that bearer of offerings, they simply stood still and silent, as if a spell had fallen upon them. Then, almost all together, they got back their speech, "Your gesture!" "My gesture!" And even I could see what they meant, for at once I recalled the dance of the *Zandunga* which Estela Ruiz had created from the traditional fiesta of their native place, and in which she came upon the stage with one arm raised to steady the bowl of offerings she bore on her head, using exactly that gesture of the Egyptian girl, thousands of years earlier. The similarity of externals was, however, less striking than the identity of sentiment: the noble dignity of the Mexican dance was closely akin to that of the Egyptian sculpture.

What shall we say, then, of Rivera's dictum, "Our classics?" The dance, in Mexico, is one of the great survivals of the classic period of the land, and here were two deeply initiated interpreters of Mexican dances

61. Constant: Waterlilies.
Courtesy of the Detroit Institute of Arts.

who, at the first glance, recognized their art in that of Egypt. The Pillars of Hercules no more shut us off from the Old World than they held back Columbus in his voyage to the New World. In an American museum, two artists, who were sent by their country to present its living past to the visitors at a great Fair, had seen the past of Egypt as living.

Could there be a clearer indication of the opportunity of our own artists, and of our museum of the New World? To the public, the museum affords such enjoyment as I saw thrilling those two dancers: to the museum, the opportunity is to create, or rather to develop what exists already, the capacity for enjoyment afforded only by the arts and their "generosities of the soul," as John Masefield calls them. Surely the institution can ask no finer chance.

The New World is still so much a-borning that we may not hazard a guess how strong will be its feeling for its museum. Yet, there are indications in a related field. With the great need, during World War II, of science, industry, and the like, the universities concentrated on technological studies for their remaining students. It was predicted that the coming of peace would accentuate this tendency. But instead, as the nightmare begins to wear itself out, educators in close touch with the public find it calling for a great expansion of the programme for the liberal arts. Moreover, the whole trend of interest in the museums, down to and even during the War, would seem to offer unmistakable evidence that the new period will more than continue the momentum which gave us our great collections. Without posing as a prophet, I feel certain that our problem in America will be one of finding material for the increase demanded of our museums, especially those called for in new places.

The problem of modern art and the problem of the American artist, to which we gave so much time, seem to disappear as the centuries and the oceans disappeared when those two Mexican girls, visiting our Egyptian collections, recognized themselves in the ancient thing from the distant country. The essential element in the whole matter was the art of the Old World — which turned out to be the art of the New World. It had simply been my good fortune to see, in reverse, what occurred at that great moment we have noticed before, when Dürer exclaimed in his delight on first seeing the sculptures, the gold, and plumed crown sent to Europe by Cortés.

But the range of art is a wider one than that fixed by time and space. It has also a defining power in terms of values. In the introduction to this book, we observed that material values, like metals, oil, and agricultural products, are limited by the soil which produces them; he who owns the land possesses its wealth. But in art, a thing without such limitation, we have values that are literally inexhaustible. They cannot be monopolized; it is obvious, indeed, that possession of them by one person does not prevent other men from having them also. On the contrary, the museum is an "all-men's land," to apply to it the term we took to cover things done in common; and as the sense that a great audience is enjoying a symphony enhances the pleasure of each person in that audience, so our enjoyment of painting and sculpture is increased if we see, by the intentness with which others study the exhibits, that they also are stirred by what is before them. No man who appreciates a fine work needs support for his idea of it from his neighbors; but man is a social animal, after all, and so we are pleased to be in the company of people who understand as we do. Stupid comments heard in a gallery irritate one, just as a concert hall with big expanses of empty seats is unfavorable to a performer in giving his best and to the people whose collective pleasure in the music is thus lessened.

It is not talking moonshine to say that immaterial rewards are often the most real ones. People who serve on hospital boards or school boards get more for the time they thus present to the community than they might have gained if they had given extra hours to business or other sources of material results. We cannot continue indefinitely to increase the world's store of wealth, however much is to be done in rendering equitable its distribution. But if we create for people in general a new set of values in which endless numbers can share, we increase the sense of well-being in a way that relieves the struggle for an impossibly large share of material goods.

A sinister charlatan like Huey Long, appealing to the mob in the way that Hitler did, could invent his catchword, "Every man a king," without being laughed off the map with reminders of the old joke about the regiment in which every man was to be a general. And there was a story in *Punch* about the scrubwoman who says, "We're all going to be equal, Maggie; me and you will be just the same as the grand ladies in their carriages; and we're going to have servants to wait on us." With conceptions of the future offering to the demagogue such material for his crazy structures, it is no wonder if we are plagued with imperialisms pretending to turn scrubwomen into grand ladies — with "the colonies" as the source of servants.

The New World, in the sense of the modern countries of America, began as colonies and, having seen that exploitation is a mistake, it demands a better formula for prosperity. Everybody knows the realistic way that our people put first things first. Food and shelter have got to be secured from the start, but we now possess the means to give necessary amounts of food and shelter to everyone, and prosperity demands more than those things. It is no last-moment statement on my part to say that the museum's contribution to well-being does not solve the problem for all men. On an early page, I spoke of the librarian whose experience had taught him that reading is not for all men. But for vast numbers of men, reading has been a source of new energy and of ideas on what to do with one's energy; or it may be a solace for days when physical activity is unprofitable. For numbers of people, the museum has a similar function. If Americans have made their great effort, over the last century or so, to give museums to their country, it is because their instinct as to the needs of the country told them that our people have an appreciation for art.

It was not to delude the masses with slogans like "Every man a king" that our museum builders gave us the institutions we have been considering. And yet, the lying words become truth when applied to the visitors at our galleries. In the larger ones, modern scholarship and resources for collecting have brought together such wealth as no king ever had in his collections. The Louvre, before the Revolution made it the property of the people, was already stupendous, exceeding in its quantity of paintings, for example, what we have in any American museum. But with the wider reach that the arts have been given in the last hundred and fifty years, the common man, in various of our cities, has possessions that the royalty of the past did not have. Of course, the common man has these things only to the extent that he makes them his own by enjoying them. Once more, we see the difference between material wealth and what, for lack of a better word, we must call spiritual wealth. There is no intrinsic value to the few square inches of old wood on which Raphael painted the St. George in the National Gallery, and the fragile paper of a Rembrandt etching would be of even less use. Yet, values as great as any in the knowledge of the human race are contained in those classics, call them intellectual, aesthetic, spiritual, or what you will.

"Our classics": that phrase of Diego Rivera's keeps coming back to mind. Directly after citing it, I showed, by the example of two other Mexicans, that the great things of the world as a whole are fully accessible to American appreciation. But we have been seeing proof of such an idea right through the history we have been following in these pages. It resides in the collections we have seen building up in this country; it is shown by the intuition of an old-time businessman like Luman Reed, who, having enjoyed pictures in his home, gave them to the city of New York. To the rule of a generous and idealistic attitude toward art and artists, established by men like Mr. Reed and countless others, it was necessary to note merely egoistical exceptions when considering the museum's problems, but such cases constitute a small minority. The magnificence and scope of our galleries offer clear testimony, also, as to the competence with which they have been directed. The classics of all humanity are, in sober earnest, "Our classics." Further confirmation on this point came to me in a conversation with that most eminent Mexican writer, Alfonso Reyes. Unconsciously paraphrasing the "*Homo sum*" of the old Roman, he said, "I am an American, and therefore nothing of our European heritage is alien to me."

As the best corroboration of the wisdom of American museum builders, there is the response of our artists. It is they who prove that this country's concern with the past is not to be connected merely with that conserving impulse which makes men unwilling to lose beautiful things, even if they have no faculty for producing more of them. On the contrary, we have gone from the naive work of our wilderness time, through the sturdy search of provincials, to a position where our men see eye to eye with the advanced workers of the older countries. The question is not simply of what they see, but of what they do. In the relatively brief span of our art history, we have produced work that is solid, original, and important. There is every promise that we are going further with it, especially as we become more conscious of our possibilities. The Museum of the New World can therefore render immense service in showing how our future will be built from our past, the long past on both sides of the Atlantic, which is revealed by our galleries. The American public believes in this future, partly through awareness that we share in the great traditions, and partly because of the achievement our artists have already reached, admirable results in the later time having followed the fine things of our apparently naive beginnings.

For if the museum shows, on the other hand, the "gropings of art in its rise to perfection," as we heard Delacroix say of certain early works, it shows also what we quoted from Egisto Fabbri, that the instinct for art, like the religious instinct, often rises at a bound to heights that no later time will surpass. Our continent brought forth primitives; and the line of descent from them, convulsively shaken as it was by the irruption of new peoples, was never broken. To invoke the ancestry of our soil is not to furbish out an ambitious and unreal genealogy, but to see the New World in the light of a past that gives new point to the words of van Gogh, "As long as men shall live, the dead shall live."

He spoke, of course, as an artist. But since this country has recognized the quality of his painting, it can recognize the truth of his words. The great things of the past continue to live in the minds of our people, and strongly enough, as we have seen, to let us enrich our expression by that of a race once as distant from us as the African. Negro spirituals are a part of American music in which we take an especial pride, and so we speak of "our Marian Anderson" and not of "a musician of African descent." Paul Robeson, singing "A Song for Americans" or playing the role of Othello, is, again, simply one of our artists. Shakespeare saw no anomaly in showing the Moor of Venice as a chief support of the country of his adoption, and we are on our way to such common sense, to deciding the value of our citizens solely on their merits. Even among Asiatics, we see that a contribution to American art is being made by a man of Japanese descent like Yasuo Kuniyoshi and by a Chinese like Dong Kingman. To say so is not to estimate the importance of these or other individual workers, but to recognize America's power to assimilate all the workers who live between the Atlantic and the Pacific.

Those two oceans are the boundaries of the New World, in the geographical sense of the term. Who will set boundaries for its achievement, if we think of that other sense of the words? Only the man who, at the museum, can set some limit of value on the art of the Old World. No man can do so; the boundaries do not exist. They will not exist here as long as we follow the course that life sets for us in its expression through art. That tells us to go constantly ahead.

We have been doing so for a long time, and under the steady influence of art. On the soil of the United States, as these pages recall, we have the impressive structures with which the Mound Builders enclosed the nobly proportioned spaces where their ceremonies were held. In the Southwest, we have glanced at the beautiful murals still decorating the walls of the council chambers. And, if we go beyond our political borders to see more of that larger America which is the New World, we may think of the Zócalo, the vast square at the center of Mexico City. In the ancient time, it was bounded by great buildings, just as today, when the cathedral occupies the site of the chief temple, and the palace of the President replaces that of the emperors. In this square, older than history, the Aztecs assembled for shows and festivities, as the Mexicans still do. For example, on the anniversary of the country's independence, each year once more the President echoes the "grito de Hidalgo," the cry of the old patriot priest who gave the signal for the Revolution. Thus announced from the balcony of the National Palace, the holiday soon fills another part of the same vast structure with visitors. That essential part of the government building is the National Museum, the place where the long past lives, for here are the works of art that tell the story of the land.

As the Dresden gallery was filled by a happy crowd on the holiday I

62. Flannagan: Monkey and Young.
Courtesy of the Addison Gallery of American Art, Phillips Academy, Andover.

told of there, so you will see eager people thronging the Mexican museum, and celebrating their freedom. In our part of the New World also, freedom and the art which expresses it enter strongly into the holiday spirit of the people. When 29,000 of them, as we have seen at the Metropolitan, in New York, go in one day to their galleries, they are keeping up an American tradition. That is what we do when we treat our museum as a chief center of normal, intelligent, and intense enjoyment.

Returning to a point previously made in these pages, we note that our museum visitors owe their enjoyment, in large measure, to the things we call American in the more restricted sense of the word. They are those things of the United States that lead to no thought of the land as it was before the coming of the white man, and to no thought of Europe. It is fortunate that our people recognize themselves in such productions and accept them as their own, because a sense of close relationship between ourselves and our art is essential if our artists are to have full support. Part of our strength is that we carry on with elements of the two cultures from which we are still evolving. We are uniting those two cultures. Some persons, as we have noted, have likened the masses of our big buildings to the constructions of the cliff dwellers; but quite as many others have thought of Italy, and seen our towers as a reminder of those of San Gimignano. Finally, Duchamp-Villon spoke of them with so European a phrase as "the cathedral of the future."

It is difficult, indeed, to find American expressions in which influences from the older cultures are not to be traced. This applies to our musical forms and even to our comics; Mickey Mouse has delighted millions of Europeans, who look on him as something distinctively original; but consider the marvelous animals of Wilhelm Busch, or those of the Indian sculptors, think of old-time New Mexico, with the Mimbres Valley potters who did the bowls ornamented with bats and rabbits: all tell us that the moment is not yet at hand, and perhaps will not be so for a long time, when we can claim that latter-day America has created anew in the arts, in the sense of producing that which the world had not previously seen.

Our purists, those who want our galleries to represent the art of the country only as it has been since the land was ours, will do well to consider the extent to which pre-Columbian and European factors determine numbers of things which we look on as particularly American. Baseball would certainly count as one of them. But at once we have to recall the old ball games of the Indians. They make our national sport only the more American, once more to interpret that word geographically; indeed, when we see the great ball courts of the ancient Mexicans, with tier after tier of stone benches rising high enough to accommodate audiences like those of the modern stadium, we feel just a bit more at home than we did before in the southern republic. One of the teams playing there would be the Tigers, a name we can duplicate among those of our major leagues, and if the Yankees fought under the name of their national bird, we should also have the Eagles, the other great organization of old Mexico. The ball game there, symbolizing the conflict of forces in the universe, had a religious significance; and with us the excitement over a world's series and the honors accorded to the heroes who defend or conquer the pennant tell that the spectacle has a real meaning for our people.

And baseball is no less American because we find that related forms of the game were played in Europe before the time of Columbus. Again noticing the emotional appeal of our own athletic contests, we are led to think back to what the Olympic games meant to ancient Greece, where events were dated as of this or that Olympiad, and where great champions were given such rewards as no Babe Ruth or Lou Gehrig has yet had among ourselves.

No, the very things which seem most typical of our country are but continuators of earlier things; and so it is with our art. A demand that it be one hundred per cent American, in the sense of a complete separation from Europe, and from the ancients of this soil, is too extreme to concern us. A more reasonable view of our art would show its gradual blending of the two strains in our heritage — the European and the purely American strain. A mingling of sources in other countries — Italy and France, for example — has, in the past, resulted in very great arts.

That our way is also to be one of evolving from separate sources will doubtless be demonstrated by the Museum of the New World. And in order to have the institution deserve that title and give us our means of recognizing the essential things in our character and direction, it must be satisfied with nothing less than the finest we can produce. It may exhibit lesser successes — we, like other countries, need time to decide on what *is* the finest. But by consistently keeping to the highest possible standard, it will create confidence in itself, and will be accepted as a guide and an inspiration.

Early in this book, I spoke of Ingres' understanding of the museum as the record of all that is best in humanity's achievement. We need to go beyond even that great claim. Indeed, we have already done so, for so American a seer as Thoreau has given us reasons to look upon our collections as pointing less to the past than to the future. He said, "For what are the classics but the noblest recorded thoughts of man? They are the only oracles which are not yet decayed, and there are such answers to the most modern inquiry in them as Delphi and Dodona never gave. We might as well omit to study Nature because she is old."

In quoting John Cotton Dana's reference to museums as "educational institutions," I did not register my strong objection to his phrase, which is inexact and gives a wrong idea of the feeling of those people who know best how to enter their galleries. For "education," I substituted the conception of Benjamin Ives Gilman, "culture," though — to repeat — the word has unfortunate overtones. Having cited three Americans, let me now give the floor to two men of that continent which, after all, tells us best about art. We have seen that it reaches its highest expression in Europe, as when, in the Ninth Symphony, Beethoven and Schiller unite to speak the final word in the Ode to Joy. The museum celebrates that serious and exultant theme in its own way. That our people understand the great chorus and want it to continue is witnessed by the convinced and eager activity that we have followed in these pages. They tell the story of an effort which has gone from modest beginnings to immense achievement, one whose success looks to still greater work in the future. We have earned the right to confidence in what lies ahead of us.

SUPPLEMENT

A LIST OF MUSEUMS OF ART IN THE UNITED STATES

Note: While care has been taken in drawing up the following list, it does not claim to be definitive. One reason for this is the speed with which things often occur in the United States: before this book emerges from the press, such additions might be made to an institution at present too unimportant to mention that it would take full rank as a museum; indeed, the opening of a great private collection to the public would automatically add another name to the list, and such events as the last-named have been frequent. Or when, as has been publicly announced, the Cone Collection, of Baltimore, is added to the Museum of that city, the character of that institution will be greatly changed. Doubts may arise, however, about the way students of the subject, as well as myself, have rated certain groups of paintings, sculptures, and works of the applied arts. I have been concerned with people who, in their travels, might be led to sacrifice time and money in order to see a collection, and who would feel that they had been badly advised if it had seemed not worth their effort. On the other hand, it has not been feasible for me to visit more than a certain number of the twenty-five hundred museums of the United States, and in selecting the ones worthy of study, I have had to accept some guidance from the printed word, in catalogues, hand-books, museum publications, etc. If an omission from the following list seems too serious to the persons who have given thought, care, or material contributions to the art collection of their town, I beg them to believe that I have acted without lack of good will. Should this book go on to later editions, more than one error will doubtless have to be corrected: the subject it treats is too extensive for me to hope that I have been right on every point.

Finally, there are, in certain places, isolated works or small groups of works so fine that one must regret one's inability to list the institution among museums, even when a number of inferior things surrounding the few of value fill more space than will be found in certain galleries men-tioned below. Or there are places as appealing as Kingston, N. Y.; its old State House contains a few works by Vanderlyn, though not of a quality to make one realize how very fine he can be. But if they were, it would still be yielding to a personal preference if I listed that historical relic with the institutions that are the subject of study here.

And I cannot include as museums such buildings as are notable, in the matter of art, only for their decorations. The murals by Puvis de Chavannes at the Boston Public Library are the last large-scale works of his career and, as some think, the masterpiece, collectively, of his whole life. They are therefore of the deepest interest to admirers of the man who did so much to restore the art of the wall to a place such as it had when the frescoes of Italy were painted. Again, however, one would be entering the province of Baedeker, Murray, and the *Guides Bleus* if that library were listed. And only because of my own lack of interest in so much of the mural painting of America should I then be avoiding mention of all sorts of public buildings that have been decorated at various times.

But the omission that I have hesitated about more than any other is that of Charlottesville, Virginia. No one who has made a pilgrimage to that delightful city has failed to see, in every drawing by Thomas Jefferson, the mark of a genius that might have specialized with success in the arts. The paintings, sculptures, and other objects that he acquired bear out this idea, which, of course, has its fullest confirmation in the architecture he produced. But basic as Monticello and, even more, "The Lawn" at the University of Virginia, are for understanding the art of our country, the home of this early American master has to be omitted from the following list:

CALIFORNIA

Los Angeles — *Los Angeles County Museum:* Permanent collection and extensive exhibition galleries.

Pasadena — *Pasadena Art Institute:* At present chiefly concerned with exhibiting and with art education, but working toward full museum activities.

Sacramento — *E. B. Crocker Art Gallery:* Paintings and one thousand and more drawings, including works by the masters.

San Diego — *Gallery of Fine Arts:* Varied collections, including fine Oriental art and European and American paintings; masterworks by men of the quality of Bellini, Giorgione, Titian, Caravaggio, Greco, Velasquez, Zurbarán, Goya, Bosch, Van Dyck, Steen, etc.

San Francisco — *California Palace of the Legion of Honor:* Notable for exhibitions (including some of superlative importance), and for the permanent collections, which contain Egyptian and Greek art, sculpture, furniture, and paintings of the Italian, Spanish, French, Dutch, British, and American schools.

M. H. De Young Memorial Museum: Sixty galleries used for contemporary exhibitions and for material accumulated in this pioneer museum of San Francisco, much of it uneven, although reflecting the eager enterprise of the founder; increasingly enriched by acquisitions of permanent value like the great Bronzino, *Vittoria Colonna.*

San Francisco Museum: Exhibitions and permanent and loan collections; important educational work.

SAN MARINO — *Henry E. Huntington Art Gallery:* British portraits and landscapes of great importance; outstanding tapestries; Italian and Flemish paintings; bronzes and objects of art; 250,000 printed volumes including important material for scholarly research.

SANTA BARBARA — *Faulkner Memorial Art Library:* Possesses 185,978 reproductions, photographs and clippings.

Santa Barbara Museum of Art: Until now mainly an exhibition gallery.

COLORADO

DENVER — *Denver Art Museum:* American paintings, Mexican pottery, art of the American Indian, etc.

CONNECTICUT

HARTFORD — *Wadsworth Atheneum and Morgan Memorial:* One of the old museums of the country, which has distinguished itself by its renewal of creative ideas, in its collecting, building, and public relationships (for example, in its reaching out to the allied arts: the theater, music, etc.). Superb examples of the earlier Americans (in painting and the allied arts), the group continuing to the men of today. Collections illustrating the production of various countries, as with Meissen (Dresden) porcelain. Admirable paintings of the European schools, especially the baroque; a masterpiece by Poussin, *The Crucifixion.*

NEW HAVEN — *Yale University Art Gallery:* Like the Fogg Museum at Harvard, of great importance for the students at the University, especially those at the large Yale Art School. The collections include Egyptian, classical, Babylonian, Assyrian, and Oriental art; also objects from the University's own excavations at Dura-Europos, on the Euphrates. The most notable among the European paintings are those of the famous old Jarves collection, with works by Daddi, Neroccio, Sassetta, Pollaiuolo, Titian, etc. The early American art is very fine and includes the unique group of works by Trumbull, also fine furniture, silver, and glass. Modern French and American painting.

NORWICH — *Slater Memorial Museum:* The Slater collection of casts, which exercised a strong influence on the early development of such material in various of our museums; Oriental objects, early American furniture, ceramics, etc.

DISTRICT OF COLUMBIA

WASHINGTON — *Corcoran Gallery:* One of the early large-scale museums of America; the original collection, including the great group of Barye bronzes but largely of American paintings, has been added to by the acquisition of large numbers of such works through purchase funds and bequests. The most important of these came from Senator W. A. Clark, whose extensive collections included works of the older European schools and certain extremely fine nineteenth-century paintings.

Dumbarton Oaks Research Library and Collection: Early Christian, Byzantine, Oriental, and ancient Mexican art of superb quality: paintings, among them an amazing Greco, other works of his period, and fine modern French art. With the important library, the old building was given to Harvard in 1940 as a research center for graduate students. In his last book, *Moyen Age,* Professor Henri Focillon gives a remarkable description of the Byzantine collection, and says of the culture there represented: "It lived, and one must see it live. For that experience, no setting is more favorable than Dumbarton Oaks."

The Freer Gallery: Oriental art of extremely high quality; extensive and important collection of the work of Whistler; a group of paintings by his American contemporaries.

National Gallery of Art: The collections given to the nation by Andrew W. Mellon and other donors (see p. 69) are so extensive and on such a high level that — as in the case of the New York and Boston museums — the proportions of this list scarcely permit mention of individual works. It must suffice to say here that the development of European painting is to be studied in its full span: the basic art of the Italian primitives can be appreciated, and the high Renaissance with an astonishing group of Raphaels (including that masterpiece, the *Alba Madonna*); also the character of Venice, marked by one of the very greatest works of Bellini, and continuing with Giorgione, Titian, and Tintoretto; the quality of Velasquez appears, together with the style of other Spaniards; a wealth of Northern painting has such culminations as van Eyck, Holbein, and Rembrandt at his greatest; other Dutchmen in magnificent examples (including several of the rare works of Vermeer), French, English and American painters, sculptures of the Renaissance, Chinese porcelains and other art objects, and prints of the highest quality, all combine to make of this collection, so suddenly revealed to the public in 1941, an astounding case of a museum created in its entirety by a small group of men. The planning of the National Gallery makes provision for its further development.

National Gallery of Fine Arts (Smithsonian Institution): Great collections of the works of the American Indian in various countries. Groups of paintings including those given by John Gellatly, whose bequest contains seventeen works by Albert P. Ryder.

Phillips Memorial Gallery: One of the real adventures of America in its search for the significance of art. The collection furnishes an opportunity for understanding the meaning of the modern movement, representing its triumphs with a supreme Renoir of the 1880's and fine works by Cézanne, following through with Gauguin and van Gogh, to reach a masterpiece by Matisse in his maturity, and an important group of Bonnards and Rouaults. Works by Derain, Picasso, Braque, Villon, and others carry on the evolution to its latest aspects; the visitor is reminded of the men who were the "moderns" of their day by fine examples of Delacroix, Corot, and Daumier (the latter in a number of remarkable examples). Albert P. Ryder is also represented by masterpieces, proving that the great modern movement was felt on our side of the Atlantic, where the work of Maurice Prendergast continues the story; the gallery is indeed particularly directed to the comprehending and advancement of American art.

FLORIDA

SARASOTA — *John and Mabel Ringling Museum of Art*: Italian, Dutch, and other European painting; many attributions have been questioned and are now (1947) being restudied.

WEST PALM BEACH — *Norton Gallery and School of Art*: One of several of Florida's new developments in art interest.

GEORGIA

ATLANTA — *Art Association and High Museum of Art*: Paintings, including some fine early American works; sculpture, and applied arts

SAVANNAH — Telfair Academy of Arts and Sciences: Evocative of the gracious living, good taste, and varied history of the city, rather than a major repository of art; some fine works of the applied arts of the older United States; paintings include a good head by Puvis de Chavannes, and contemporary American works of interest.

HAWAII

HONOLULU — Honolulu Academy of Arts: Founded only in 1937, it already has a considerable collection, including important Oriental works, Egyptian, Greek, and other objects to bring the history down to the present day.

ILLINOIS

CHICAGO — The Art Institute: Very extensive collections covering the arts of the world (though in an uneven manner — Greek art, for example, being far from adequately represented). The collection of European paintings is very notable, beginning with the primitives, going on to a group of magnificent Spanish works including a large Greco of almost unique importance, splendid Dutch pictures, French art with Poussin, Claude, the eighteenth century and the nineteenth with fine examples, culminating in an extraordinary group of Impressionists and one of Seurat's rare masterpieces. Twentieth-century painting is shown as in no other general museum in America. Other important features of the Institute are its Gothic collection (of an extremely high order), American collections, Chinese works, applied arts, and prints. The very large art school of the Institute is only a part of its educational work; and nowhere are museum problems being more eagerly studied.

INDIANA

INDIANAPOLIS — John Herron Art Institute: Paintings, sculptures, etc.

IOWA

DAVENPORT — Davenport Municipal Art Gallery: Paintings of various schools, the almost unique feature being a group of Mexican pictures of the colonial period.

KANSAS

LAWRENCE — *Thayer Museum of Art (University of Kansas):* Paintings, Oriental art; European glass, porcelain, pottery, furniture, and a collection of presepio figures from Italy.

WICHITA — *Wichita Art Society and Art Museum:* Paintings.

KENTUCKY

LOUISVILLE — *J. B. Speed Memorial Museum:* Paintings, sculptures, tapestries, ceramics, furniture, textiles.

LOUISIANA

NEW ORLEANS — *The Cabildo:* Old portraits, chiefly of historical value only.

Isaac Delgado Museum: Paintings, a collection of uneven merit.

MAINE

BRUNSWICK — *Bowdoin College:* Fine small collection, chiefly of European and American paintings, but also containing Assyrian sculpture, Greek ceramics, etc.

MARYLAND

BALTIMORE — *Baltimore Museum of Art:* Jacob Epstein collection (on indefinite loan), great works of painting; Mary Frick Jacobs collection, important paintings; Lucas collection, fine pictures of the nineteenth-century French school, lent by the Maryland Institute; Sadie A. May collection; Garrett collection of prints; other permanent features include mosaics from ancient Antioch, American paintings (especially fine ones by early artists), European art, etc.

Johns Hopkins University Museum of American, Oriental, and Classical Archeology: Large collection of Greek, Roman, Egyptian, Jewish, Chinese, and American antiquities.

Maryland Institute: Paintings, porcelains, George A. Lucas collection (see also the Baltimore Museum of Art).

Walters Gallery: Over 22,000 objects have been catalogued; Byzantine and medieval, Near and Far Eastern, Egyptian, classical arts; 1200 European paintings; ceramics; 700 manuscripts; 3200 incunabula and early printed books. The opportunity for enjoyment and study offered by this gallery cannot easily be over-estimated.

MASSACHUSETTS

ANDOVER — *Addison Gallery of American Art (Phillips Andover Academy):* Fine and creative collection of American art from the early days to the present, of great value in connection with the famous old school which houses it.

BOSTON — *Institute of Contemporary Art:* Largely for temporary exhibitions.

Isabella Stewart Gardner Museum (Fenway Court): A Venetian palace transferred, stone by stone, to Boston and there reconstructed. It is filled with art objects of all kinds, from painting and sculpture to furniture (the latter of a character generally appropriate to the architecture). One of the masterpieces of collecting in the late nineteenth and early twentieth centuries, even if little in the way of modern art was attempted by Mrs. Gardner. Her preference was chiefly for the Italian Renaissance, represented by Titian's *Rape of Europa* (which Rubens called the finest picture in the world), great works by Piero della Francesca, Raphael, Giorgione, etc. The Northern schools are also represented.

Museum of Fine Arts: Collections of very great extent representing the art of Egypt, the Near and Far East, Europe, and the United States, with examples which would be important in any gallery in the world. Particularly rich are the Chinese and Japanese collections; the Egyptian (with works of the all-important early period); Greek art: sculpture (including great masterpieces like the early fourth-century head mentioned on p. 88), and vases; European painting and sculpture: from an entire Romanesque chapel with its frescoes, through fine early and late Italian works, to a splendid showing of modern art; particularly rich and important group of paintings by Copley and other Americans of his period. Large galleries of the applied arts, with exceedingly well-selected examples. Fine prints.

After the Metropolitan in New York, the leader among our museums, both for theory and the wealth and quality of its exhibits.

CAMBRIDGE — *Fogg Art Museum (of Harvard University):* Although primarily used for the students of the university, above all those taking art courses (either general or professional), the museum is for the whole public and has some of the choicest collections in the country — its group of drawings by the masters being the finest we possess. The Grenville L. Winthrop collection brought to the museum extremely important nineteenth-century French works and a marvelous group of Chinese art, rounding out the very notable collections of it already there. Other outstanding exhibits are of Greek art, Romanesque and Gothic sculpture, medieval frescoes, and European painting, including great Italian works. Also from the Winthrop collection are superb Mexican sculptures, to which other examples from the Peabody Museum (of Harvard) are often added.

NORTHAMPTON — *Smith College Museum of Art:* Superbly developed college museum, containing examples of Egyptian, Greek, Gothic, and Renaissance art; European and American painting, the French school particularly represented from Poussin and Claude to the nineteenth century, with an outstanding masterpiece by Courbet, and works by Cézanne, Picasso, and other moderns. The museum did pioneer work in the study of Géricault.

SALEM — *Essex Institute:* Most various collection of old New England material; over 300 paintings, including a valuable group of portraits, chinaware, medals, coins, costumes, etc.

Peabody Museum (the remarkable Salem East India Marine Society, of 1799, combined with the natural history collections of the Essex Institute in 1867): Rich group of ship models, figureheads, and maritime art in general, paintings, curios, and ethnological material, Indian, Mexican, and, above all, South Seas — an amazingly impressive showing.

SPRINGFIELD — *George Walter Vincent Smith Collection:* On a large scale, what was formerly known as a "curio cabinet," the casual purchases of a person interested in art; even so, such old collections often contain interesting material and are useful as period pieces, in any case.

Springfield Museum of Fine Arts: Paintings, prints, tapestries, armor, furniture, Asiatic art.

WELLESLEY — *Farnsworth Museum of Wellesley College:* Egyptian and Greek minor arts; classical, Greco-Buddhist, Italian, and German sculpture; Italian, French, and American painting; tapestry, mosaics, textiles, Mexican art.

WILLIAMSTOWN — *Lawrence Art Museum (Williams College):* Egyptian, Greek, Etruscan, Peruvian, and Mexican pottery; Oriental art; paintings, drawings, etchings; sculpture, pottery, glass, furniture.

WORCESTER — *The John Higgins Armory:* Arms, armor, and the allied arts.

Worcester Art Museum: Egyptian, Greek, and Roman art; mosaics from Antioch; an ensemble of medieval frescoes; Romanesque chapter hall with twelfth-century sculptures; remarkable statue attributed to Jean Goujon; paintings by European artists, important early Americans, and men of the modern schools; fine Mexican sculpture; Chinese and Japanese art.

MICHIGAN

DETROIT — *Detroit Institute of Art:* A museum of the highest importance, having been developed with knowledge of the great classics — European, Oriental, American, and modern, the applied arts (notable textiles), and also the relationship of the collections to the public. Period rooms (still leaving possibilities of development in their difficult field) awaken the visitor's sense of the place of art in life, perhaps especially through the Renaissance exhibits at Alger House, a pioneer branch museum (in Grosse Pointe, a suburb of Detroit). The frescoes by Diego Rivera, painted on the walls of the museum, and showing the great industries of the city, have caused vast numbers of working people to come frequently to their galleries — which have also had active support from Detroit's men of wealth. Important showing of Egyptian, Greek, Roman, Chinese, Japanese, Hindu, Byzantine, Gothic, Renaissance, and modern art. Among the paintings, the Italian, Dutch, Flemish, French, and American sections are particularly important. The first great art museum in this country to include the Indians (especially the ancient Mexicans) on the same footing as the people of the Eastern Hemisphere.

MINNESOTA

MINNEAPOLIS — *Minneapolis Institute of Arts:* Important collections including Egyptian, Assyrian, classical, and Oriental arts (the superb Pillsbury Chinese objects on extended loan); European and American paintings (Titian, Greco, Patinir, Rembrandt, Poussin, Gauguin, Copley, etc.). Sculpture from the twelfth to the fifteenth century; a group of works representing pre-Columbian America; tapestries, textiles, porcelain, glass, jade, silver, furniture; fine prints.

Walker Art Galleries: Paintings — a large and uneven collection, including, however, some fine works.

MISSOURI

KANSAS CITY — *William Rockhill Nelson Gallery of Art and Mary Atkins Museum of Fine Arts:* Working with the art school and the University of Kansas City, the museum exemplifies the way an extremely inclusive collection may still be brought together — though at the expenditure of large sums, — and in a very short time. Egyptian, Greek, Roman, medieval, and Renaissance sculpture and applied arts; period rooms; textiles; ceramics; extraordinary Chinese and other Oriental collections; American Indian art; magnificent paintings covering the whole period of European and American production, and containing masterworks by the primitives, Titian, Greco, Goya, Poussin, Chardin, Hals, Rembrandt, and English and early American artists; drawings by Claude, Watteau, Ingres, Géricault, etc.; prints.

ST. LOUIS — *City Art Museum:* Mesopotamian, classical, and Etruscan art; medieval rooms; French Gothic portal; sculpture, tapestries, glass, ivory, bronzes; Renaissance marbles and furniture (Italian and French); period rooms (French, English and American); Ballard collection of Oriental rugs; Chinese ceramics; armor; textiles; paintings of various European old Masters, including a fine Holbein; modern European and American art; prints.

NEBRASKA

OMAHA — *Society of Liberal Arts, Joslyn Memorial:* Important paintings, etc.

NEW HAMPSHIRE

HANOVER — *Dartmouth College:* Paintings; the frescoes, painted for the college by José Clemente Orozco, the Mexican, are among the most important examples of mural decoration in the United States.

NEW JERSEY

NEWARK — *Newark Museum:* Archeological, Oriental, and applied arts; paintings. The scene of the remarkable pioneer work in museology and exhibiting evolved by the former director, John Cotton Dana.

PRINCETON — *Princeton Museum of Historic Art:* Established in 1888 with a collection of casts, it has evolved, in connection with the University's intensive teaching of art history, and has rich "material showing the development of art, from the earliest time, with emphasis on the Gothic" (illustrated, for example, by a stained-glass window from Chartres, and of the finest period). Paintings, prints, manuscripts, and miniatures; Greek and Roman art.

NEW MEXICO

SANTA FE — *Museum of New Mexico:* Southwestern archeology, history and art. Showing of New Mexico artists.

NEW YORK

ALBANY — *Institute of History and Art:* Paintings and applied arts.

BUFFALO — *Albright Art Gallery (Fine Arts Academy):* Important collections of sculpture, paintings, drawings, prints, etc.

GLENS FALLS — *House and Collection of Mrs. Louis F. Hyde:* Exceedingly choice group of art works, including a Rembrandt of the highest quality and other paintings by old and modern masters. A residence with admirable furniture, etc., where visitors are freely welcome; it is preferred, however, that they give some advance notice of their coming.

NEW YORK — *American Institute of Iranian Art and Archeology:* Very important collections illustrating the subjects given in the title.

Brooklyn Museum: Extensive and varied collections covering the fine and applied arts; important temporary exhibitions are held; permanent collections contain fine European and American painting (excellent early works of this country, and very inclusive group of our modern men); magnificent group of American Indian objects from the United States, through Mexico, to Peru and Ecuador; African art.

The Cloisters: This building, a branch of the Metropolitan Museum, at Fort Tryon Park overlooking the Hudson River, in uptown New York, is a remarkably successful attempt to recapture the effect of medieval art through the use of architectural ensembles, reconstructed as accurately as possible and used, as they were in the past, as the ecclesiastical or lay setting for sculpture and other works of the time, including the extremely important series of the "Unicorn" tapestries. Some of the individual works of Romanesque or Gothic sculpture are supremely fine examples, like the thirteenth-century heads high up in a chapel of the period, and the polychromed Madonna and Child of the fourteenth century sold by Hitler under the pretext that it was French art.

Cooper Union: Great collections of applied arts, especially textiles.

Frick Collection: Its distinguishing feature is its keeping to the highest level throughout. The paintings include such masterpieces as works by Duccio, Piero della Francesca, Castagno, Bellini, Titian, Greco, Goya, Rembrandt and Hals (the last named two at their best), Ruisdael, Vermeer, Hogarth, Constable; whole rooms decorated by Fragonard and Boucher; a perfect canvas by Chardin, a David, an Ingres, and a series of important Whistlers. The Renaissance bronzes are of great importance, as is a large terra cotta by Houdon. Fine porcelains, enamels, and numerous other objects.

Grolier Club: Devoted to the arts of the book, prints, etc. Extremely important exhibitions have been held here, and there are permanent collections along the lines indicated.

Hispanic Society of America: Collection of paintings, sculptures, drawings, etc., covering the subject denoted by the title; they include works by the great Spanish masters.

The Metropolitan Museum of Art: It has been said that of all the world's museums, no other covers the field of human effort in the arts as fully as does this one (although it still excludes almost completely the so-called barbarous peoples, including the early races of the Americas). The comprehensiveness of the collections is matched, in numerous fields, by their richness in works of very high quality. Of unequalled importance in America are the galleries of classical art, covering the whole development from an early archaic figure of more than life size to a series of frescoed rooms from Boscoreale (near Herculaneum), the latter being unique outside of Naples and Pompeii; unique also — and anywhere — are the prodigious Etruscan sculptures in stucco and in metal; extremely fine marbles of the best periods; a large number of admirable vases and figurines from the great centers for these arts; the Cesnola Collection of Cypriote antiquities is outstanding. The Egyptian collections are, in part, from the museum's own excavations. The assemblage of arms and armor is the finest in America. Extremely rich collections of the applied arts, with departments of silver, laces, textiles, ceramics, etc. The painting collections, though they have certain gaps, more nearly attain comprehensive representation than do those of any other gallery in this country. They include works of such importance as the large fresco by Pollaiuolo, paintings by Lorenzetti, Filippo Lippi, Mantegna, Raphael, Giorgione, Titian, Veronese, and Bronzino; the Spanish school, with numerous and fine works by Greco and Goya; magnificent examples of van Eyck, van der Weyden, Memling, Bouts, Bruegel, Rubens, Hals, Rembrandt, Ruisdael; French painting, from the time of the Avignon and Fontainebleau masters, through the seventeenth, eighteenth, and nineteenth centuries. The collections of English and American painting are very fine, and an entire wing of the building is devoted to the applied arts of our country as shown in period rooms. The department of prints and drawings is of the highest importance.

Museum of the City of New York: Many objects having, beside their historical value, the quaint charm of our early days. Certain very fine old American portraits.

Museum of Modern Art: Beginning in 1929 as a place for the exhibition of the latter-day masters and experimenters, it has already come to own a collection of fine works in its field, while continuing with exhibitions of the most important modern production, as with Picasso's *Guernica*, one-man shows of Rouault, Léger, Miró, and others, beside such great ensembles as "Twenty Centuries of Mexican Art" and the uniquely impressive showing of "North American Indian Art." Collections of moving picture films, photography, architectural material, and applied art.

Museum of Non-Objective Art (Solomon R. Guggenheim Foundation): Permanent collection centering around Bauer and Kandinsky, with other works of the type indicated by the title.

National Academy of Design: It has been holding annual exhibitions for over a hundred years, and possesses an extensive collection of works by its members, and portraits of them.

New-York Historical Society: Together with a multitude of objects appropriate for a body of this name, the Society has several galleries of paintings. Some are by the early Americans, and are thus more or less connected with its purposes, but others date from the days before New York had a permanent art museum, and these works, as also Egyptian, Assyrian, ancient Mexican, and other art objects, were given to the Historical Society before the time of our art museums. As with the Jarves pictures at Yale, it is heartening to find that our collectors of the earlier nineteenth century had the discernment needed for selecting the fine Italian primitives to be seen here, the Northern works (including a Rembrandt and a Rubens), good French pictures, like the Philippe de Champaigne, the Largillière, and others.

New York Public Library: Varied collections of paintings, including works by Turner, Reynolds, Copley, Stuart and others. Large collection of prints.

Pierpont Morgan Library: One of the great private libraries of the world; rich in illuminated manuscripts and other rarities of the book lover's domain; drawings by the masters (including an important group of works by Blake); a few fine paintings and objects of art.

Whitney Museum of American Art: It developed from exhibitions held at a club founded by Gertrude Vanderbilt Whitney, and still gives important exhibitions of contemporary American painters and sculptors. A long-continued program of support to our artists by the purchase of their work has given the museum a permanent collection; affiliated with the Metropolitan Museum.

POUGHKEEPSIE — *Vassar College Art Gallery*: Fine Italian paintings and sculpture, early and baroque; American and modern French painting; prints, ceramics, etc.

ROCHESTER — *Memorial Art Gallery*: Paintings (including a fine Greco), sculpture, prints, tapestries, textiles, furniture, vases, etc.

SYRACUSE — *Syracuse Museum of Fine Arts*: American paintings, Japanese prints, etc.

OHIO

CINCINNATI — *Cincinnati Art Museum*: The long history of art interest in the city is evident both in the high quality of certain Old Masters at the museum and in reminiscences of the "casts-and-copies" stage in our development. New vigor is however manifesting itself, as in the superb Derain recently added to the galleries. In fact, if I retain the foregoing sentences, based on the impressions of only four years ago, it is to confirm my statement as to the rapidity of change in our museums. A later visit (1948) found the "age of casts" so definitely left behind that magnificent original sculptures of the Egyptian, Greek, medieval and Chinese schools had completely replaced the older exhibits. A new architectural setting and ingenious ways of making the visitors notice outstanding works carried on the record of progress. The paintings include works by Tintoretto, Rembrandt, Van Dyck, Ingres, and many others. The American collection contains a unique group of works by Duveneck. There is a very rich collection of prints. Indian objects, in which southern Ohio is so rich, are shown, a remarkable one being an inscribed tablet dug up in the city itself.

The Taft Collection: Magnificent paintings by Hals, Rembrandt, Steen, Ruisdael, Reynolds, Constable, Goya, Ingres, Corot, Millet, and others.

CLEVELAND — *The Cleveland Museum of Art*: Although only some thirty years old, the Cleveland Museum has made a very special place for itself, not only by the extent and excellence of its collections, but by its forward-looking activity in the planning of the institution, in its relations with the public, and in educational work. It has fine works of Egyptian, Greek, Byzantine, Romanesque, and Gothic art, the examples from the "Guelph Treasure" of eleventh-century German and similar schools being of great importance. It has armor, tapestry, French-Renaissance works, the Holden collection of early Italian painting, and pictures by Holbein, Greco, Rubens, Rembrandt, Poussin, David, Copley, Delacroix, Redon, Renoir, and the older and latter-day Americans. Also, important drawings and prints, beside fine work of the ancient Peruvians, Mexicans, etc.

COLUMBUS — *Columbus Gallery of Fine Arts:* Sculpture, Oriental art, valuable collection of paintings; of especial interest for the American works.

DAYTON — *Dayton Art Institute:* As in so many recently founded museums, the emphasis is still on the impressiveness of the building (with its two Florentine doorways, Chinese garden, Italian-Renaissance cloister, etc.), rather than on the collections. Nevertheless, intelligent buying, to build up the galleries, gives promise for the future.

OBERLIN — *Dudley Peter Allen Memorial Museum:* Paintings, etc., intended chiefly as a reference collection for the students of Oberlin College, which has important art courses; exceptionally large collection of reproductions.

TOLEDO — *Toledo Museum of Art:* Very comprehensive representation of various important schools, with Egyptian and Greek art (including an exquisite fourth-century head); medieval and Renaissance work centering around an architectural ensemble; a most remarkable and complete collection of glass from all periods; fine bindings and examples of printing; the important group of paintings contains splendid representation of the art of Pesellino, Piero di Cosimo, Giovanni Bellini (a masterpiece, from which is derived the Giorgione in the Gardner Collection in Boston), Dürer, Holbein, Velasquez, Goya, Rembrandt, Hals, Clouet, David, Corot, Delacroix, Daumier, Théodore Rousseau, Millet, Manet, Cézanne, Gauguin, van Gogh, the English School (including Hogarth), and an interesting group of American painters; fine modern sculpture; admirable prints. The museum has been particularly happy in its relationship with the city; it has done outstanding work in connection with the public schools and in the teaching of art and music in Toledo.

ZANESVILLE — *Zanesville Art Institute:* Paintings, etc.

OREGON

PORTLAND — *Portland Museum of Art:* Recently given encouragement by receiving a fine and well-planned building, a new token of the city's long-continued interest in art. Chinese objects of fine quality, an important Delacroix, American art, and other bases for collections useful in the life of the region and its active educational interests.

PENNSYLVANIA

DOYLESTOWN — *Bucks County Historical Society:* 25,000 exhibits; applied arts of Pennsylvania.

PHILADELPHIA — *Historical Society of Pennsylvania:* Collection chiefly devoted to objects of historical interest, but containing a few fine portraits.

National Museum, Independence Hall: Portraits, many of them copies, but some originals by C. W. Peale, Sully, etc.

Pennsylvania Academy of Fine Arts: For well over a century, it has been holding exhibitions of current painting and sculpture by Americans, and has built up there an important collection of such work; also some European pictures.

Philadelphia Museum of Art: One of the outstanding museums of the country for the wealth of the collections and as representing the city's long record of interest in art. Medieval art includes an eleventh-century Romanesque cloister. Portals, chapel, and rooms further representing the Romanesque and the Gothic in France and Italy; rich group of contemporary objects appropriate to such a setting; Renaissance and later art of Italy, Spain, France, the Low Countries, and Germany, again shown in period rooms, and with fine examples of sculpture, ceramics, ironwork, furniture, leather, and other forms of the applied arts; period rooms also continue their valuable work in showing French, English, and American art as applied to decoration, the examples from the bequest of Mrs. A. Hamilton Rice being of a specially high order. Important collections of art from the Near East (a Sassanian portal, Isfahan faïence, carpets) and from the Far East (China, Japan, India); architecture, sculpture, painting, ceramics, etc. Rich collection of European paintings formed by John G. Johnson, covering the history of art from the Italian primitives to the latter nineteenth century; other groups round out these galleries, which contain, besides magnificent Giottesque works, examples of Lorenzetti, Masolino, Sassetta, Botticelli, Antonello da Messina, German, Flemish, and Dutch masters, including Bosch, van Eyck, van der Weyden, Rubens, Rembrandt, Steen, etc.; French painting, with a supreme Poussin; admirable nineteenth-century works by Delacroix, Corot, Daumier, and

Courbet, through the Impressionists, with a large Cézanne of his latest and finest period. Important paintings and sculptures by the earlier Americans; unique collection of the works by Thomas Eakins; French and American modern art; fine prints.

University of Pennsylvania Museum: Complementing the Philadelphia Museum by exhibiting the sculptures and other arts of the Mediterranean countries, Egypt, Babylonia, Palestine, Greece, Rome, etc. Exceedingly rich collections of the "primitive" peoples such as the Africans and above all, the ancient Americans of many regions, including superb Mexican sculpture.

PITTSBURGH — *Carnegie Institute, Department of Fine Arts:* Paintings, etchings, wood engravings, architectural models, and casts of sculpture. Important for its exhibitions.

RHODE ISLAND

PROVIDENCE — *Rhode Island School of Design Museum:* The work of an admirable director who could appreciate the first-rate classical, Gothic, and later objects seen here, and of a city drawing on its wealth of fine earlier American art (portraits, handicraft, etc.). The collection — with its splendid paintings, from the Old Masters to the moderns — is primarily for the use of the students of the School of Design and of Brown University, but forms a most delightful place for general visitors. Distinguished possessions in various fields.

SOUTH CAROLINA

CHARLESTON — *Carolina Art Association:* Collections of a general nature, illustrating the sciences as well as the arts. Our oldest museum.

Gibbes Memorial Art Gallery: Paintings, miniatures, etc., largely related to the city's historic past. The gallery also houses material connected with the extremely notable work being done to preserve Charleston's architectural wealth.

TEXAS

DALLAS — *Dallas Museum of Fine Arts:* Paintings, bronzes; the museum is of recent development, but it is important for the enterprising spirit shown by a number of Texas cities.

FORT WORTH — *Fort Worth Museum of Art:* An outgrowth of the library of the city: paintings, including the important Thomas Eakins picture, *The Swimming Hole.*

HOUSTON — *Museum of Fine Arts:* Fine and applied arts; as at Dallas, one of the most active Texas communities interested in art.

SAN ANTONIO — *Witte Memorial Museum:* Paintings; souvenirs of the older history of Texas.

VIRGINIA

NORFOLK — *Norfolk Museum of Arts and Sciences:* Painting, sculpture, applied arts; valuable support given to local production of original folk art.

RICHMOND — *The Virginia Museum of Fine Arts:* After a long period of inactivity, the great city of the Old South is emerging with collections of old and modern paintings that are setting an example to this section of the country.

WASHINGTON

SEATTLE — *Seattle Art Museum:* Paintings, sculpture, decorative arts, chiefly Oriental, among which are some important examples; center of very active regional interest in art.

WISCONSIN

BELOIT — *Beloit College of Art:* Anthropological and archeological collections; art of Europe and eastern Asia.

MILWAUKEE — *Leighton Art Gallery:* Paintings, chiefly illustrating the weaker type of nineteenth-century collecting.

Milwaukee Art Institute: Devoted largely to exhibitions and other educational work.

OTHER TYPES OF MUSEUMS CONTAINING MATERIAL FOR ART STUDY

IN ADDITION to the museums already listed, in which art of the "primitives" is shown together with that of other peoples (outstanding examples are the Fogg Museum at Harvard, the Detroit Institute of Arts, the Smithsonian Institution at Washington, the Cleveland Museum, and the University Museum at Philadelphia), mention is here made of places where such material is to be seen. Since I have not made professional studies entitling me to pass on the merits of the various institutions pos-

sible to note here, I have consulted Miss Bella Weitzner, of the American
Indian Department of the American Museum of Natural History, New
York, and thank her for the following list.

ALBANY, N. Y. — *New York State Museum*
ANN ARBOR, MICH. — *University Museum*
BERKELEY, CAL. — *University of California Museum*
BUFFALO, N. Y. — *Museum of Science*
CAMBRIDGE, MASS. — *Peabody Museum (Harvard University)*
CHICAGO, ILL. — *Chicago Museum of Natural History (Field
    Museum)*
COLUMBUS, O. — *Ohio State Museum*
DETROIT, MICH. — *Cranbrook Institute*
MILWAUKEE, WIS. — *Public Museum*
MOUNDVILLE (near Tuscaloosa), ALA. — *Alabama State Museum*
NEW HAVEN, CONN. — *Peabody Museum (Yale University)*
NEW ORLEANS, LA. — *Museum of Tulane University*
NEW YORK, N. Y. — *American Museum of Natural History*
    Museum of the American Indian (Heye Foundation)
PASADENA, CAL. — *Southwestern Museum*
SAN DIEGO, CAL. — *City Museum*
SANTA FE, N. M. — *Laboratory of Anthropology*
SEATTLE, WASH. — *State Museum*
WASHINGTON, D. C. — *National Museum*

NOTES ON THE ILLUSTRATIONS

ONE element in works of art is often difficult and sometimes impossible to judge from reproductions, i.e., the size of the objects. With certain other details, the following lines will note the approximate size of works, save for painted portraits of average dimensions. In selecting the illustrations, my aim has been to show the spread of the museum idea from coast to coast, as well as the importance of the works in America's public collections.

Frontispiece. Maya art of Mexico, polychromed clay statuette, height 8 ¾ in. In the case of paintings, color reproductions are almost always unsatisfactory, when not completely false. With sculpture, the problem is less exacting; and for most people it is important to have a reminder of the fact that large numbers of sculptures in the Egyptian, Greek, Gothic, and other great schools were painted. Those of ancient America were no exception to this rule.

1. First home of the Metropolitan Museum, 1872. Most of our early museums had to begin with the makeshift conditions incidental to housing in a private residence.

2. Central part of the museum's façade today. Thirty-two years after its founding, the Metropolitan was rapidly adding to the small building first erected for it in Central Park.

3. Project for the reconstructed museum. The Metropolitan, continuing to grow, looks to a building in which separate units will house the collections according to the nature of the various exhibits.

4. Hanging of pictures, old style. The walls crowded — with inferior pictures, principally. The earlier stages of museum development were dominated by the need to accumulate material; the fitting display of it was a secondary matter.

5. Hanging of pictures, new style. With increased insight into the quality of its possessions, the museum develops a new sense of the role played by spacing and light in giving to each work its fullest effectiveness. The essential progress we have made, and must still make is, however, immeasurably less a matter of presentation than of understanding.

6. Bust of Ankh-haf, 4th dynasty, life-size. Boston possesses a particularly notable group of works dating from the early dynasties, when the realistic power of Egyptian art was at its greatest.

7. Queen Hat-Shepsut, life-size sculpture. The long continued evolution within a narrow range of qualities was needed for Egypt to attain the perfections of its later periods.

8. Youth, ("Apollo type"), life-size. One of the most important examples extant of the early archaic sculpture of Greece.

9. Goddess, 4th century, life-size. Despite the damage to this work, it gives eloquent testimony to the continuance of the genius which, perhaps fifty years earlier, gave us the supreme art of the Parthenon.

10. Fresco from Boscoreale, about life-size. The Greeks, who, coming from Alexandria, founded Pompeii and Herculaneum, left in those cities almost the only works which today give us an idea of classical painting. After Naples and Pompeii itself, New York with its series of frescoes, offers far the best representation of this all-important art.

11. Engaged Capital, 12th century. Installed high up on a wall of the Cloisters, as it was when in its original setting, this sculpture, magnificent in itself, testifies also to the study which made possible the successful re-creation of a medieval interior.

12. Virgin and Child, 15th century, life-size, polychromed. The work from the Berlin museum referred to in the text as the finest Gothic sculpture in Germany.

13. Catalonian Chapel. An outstanding example of museum enterprise; the entire chapel has been set up to produce its original impression. An example of Byzantine art in Western Europe.

14. Giotto, St. Francis Receiving the Stigmata. Always conservative in its labelling of exhibits, the Fogg Museum is willing to let this great fresco be called "Workshop of Giotto." We have swung far — too far, in many cases — from the old way of making grandiose claims.

15. Hubert van Eyck, The Last Judgment (detail). The original is 7 ¾ inches in width; from the Hermitage Museum, Leningrad. The scholarship of Bryson Burroughs, former curator of the Metropolitan, permitted his attributing this masterpiece to the half-legendary elder brother of Jan van Eyck.

16. Franco-Flemish Tapestry, late 15th century. An example of America's progress in obtaining outstanding works — the Unicorn series being among the most important of tapestries.

17. Piero della Francesca, St. John the Evangelist, two-thirds life-size. Doubtless part of an ensemble, the other parts of which are lost, as far as is known.

18. Verrocchio, Lorenzo de' Medici, life-size, polychromed. *Il Magnifico* in a rendering that vindicates his right to the title.

19. Michelangelo, Study for the Libyan Sibyl. When a drawing or print is well reproduced in dimensions not too far from those of the original, as here, its loss of effect may seem, for the inexperienced, to be negligible. A look at the present study, not alone for the quality of the red chalk and paper, but for the whole magic of the work, will show this to be a fallacy. Strictly speaking, reproductions are merely imitations.

20. Raphael, The Alba Madonna; from the Hermitage Museum, Leningrad. Another example of the way that the world events of recent decades have caused America to acquire masterworks which seemed destined to remain in Europe for all time.

21. Bronzino, Vittoria Colonna. A particularly fine example of the portraits of the noble lady whose friendship and poetry meant so much to Michelangelo.

22. Caravaggio, Portrait of a Lady. The picture turned up in recent years; it was immediately accepted as a work by the great realist. Supplementing the plates after Verrocchio and Bronzino, the Caravaggio shows America's response to that marked interest which the Renaissance had in portraiture.

23. Giovanni Bellini, The Feast of the Gods. The great canvas, one of the final efforts of the master's long career, is an epitome of the poetic painting typical of the Venetian Renaissance.

24. Titian, The Rape of Europa, nearly life-size. Bellini's great pupil carries art to the point which made Delacroix say that if one lived to be one hundred-and-twenty years old, one would care only for Titian.

25. El Greco, Christ at Gethsemane. This large and very complete canvas looks backward to the Byzantine heritage of the artist, and forward to his effect on the moderns.

26. Velasquez, Man with a Wine Glass. Of the master's earlier period; it shows Spanish realism at a middle point between that of Italy and that of Holland.

27. Goya, Don Ignacio Omulryan y Rourera. One of the outstanding works of the rapidly created museum at Kansas City.

28. Dürer, Adam and Eve. This sepia drawing, of supreme quality in itself, takes on added importance through the light it throws on one of the greatest engravings.

29. Holbein, Lady Guldeford. When this picture in St. Louis became known, the attribution to Holbein of a similar portrait in the Metropolitan had to be abandoned.

30. Bruegel, The Harvesters. A work ranking with the masterpieces in Vienna, which place the Northern master in the same creative role as the greatest Italians.

31. Rubens, Isabella Brant. One of the most captivating portraits of the master's first wife; it was added to the collections at Cleveland only a few months before these pages were printed.

32. Frans Hals, Portrait of a Man. The name Admiral de Ruyter, probably indefensible, is at least a convenience in identifying what may well be the finest single figure by Hals.

33. Rembrandt, Man with a Beard. It should be a matter of legitimate pride with us that, sixty years ago, American collecting had risen to an appreciation of Rembrandt at his very greatest, as in this portrait.

34. Vermeer, Young Woman with a Water Jug. Like the Rembrandt just mentioned, this superlatively fine Vermeer came to us in the Marquand Collection.

35. Hogarth, The Lady's Last Stake. Our earlier collectors caused large numbers of fashionable English portraits to be brought to America; some of them are fine things. The growth of discrimination has shown the superiority of works like the delightful one here reproduced.

36. Constable, Stoke-by-Nayland. A letter of Constable's (1836) and preparatory sketches in various English museums are evidence of the artist's consideration of this large painting.

37. Jean Goujon, Diane de Poitiers, gilded wood, nearly life-size. France's new vigor, in the 16th century, carrying on the inspiration of Italy.

38. Poussin, The Triumph of Neptune and Amphitrite. One of Poussin's most splendid works, and one of the sensational acquisitions rendered possible by the epoch-making changes in Europe; from the Hermitage, Leningrad.

39. Claude Lorrain, Cattle at a Ford. After the long reign in America of the Romantic idea of landscape art, as represented in our very extensive collections of Barbizon pictures, the salutary influence of the great classical school, headed by Claude, will be evident.

40. Chardin, Lady with a Bird Organ. A work of unusual exquisiteness even for Chardin, contrasting with the 18th-century work of Spain such as Goya's, and showing that the graceful subject could yield a result of no less strength.

41. Houdon, Diana the Huntress. Houdon executed his life-size masterpiece in marble for Catherine the Great, and in bronze for other patrons. The present terra cotta is believed to be the example which he kept for himself.

42. Ingres, Mme. d'Haussonville. The master's studies, and contemporary letters by the sitter attest the importance of this work in Ingres's production.

43. Delacroix, The Lion Hunt. The subject, inherited from Rubens, an idol of Delacroix's, occurs repeatedly in his work. Dating from two years before the master's death, the present example is doubtless the culminating one of the series.

44. Courbet, La Toilette de la Mariée. A big canvas suitable for one of the great painter's most extraordinary creations. Prompt action by the Smith College Museum secured the work for America while European museums were hesitating over its acquisition.

45. Renoir, Le Bal à Bougival, about life-size. The most popular picture in the Boston Museum — and a proof that the finest type of painting can be popular.

46. Cézanne, The Bathers. The largest of all the master's works; it reveals his renewal of the genius which gave the Gothic arch to the world.

47. Seurat, Sunday on Grande Jatte Island. One of the six large canvases which sum up the painting of Seurat; as with the Cézanne, an architectonic quality is unmistakable.

48. Matisse, Studio, Quai St. Michel. Important for its size, period (that of the artist's most powerful works), but above all, for its quality.

49. Rouault, Portrait of Verlaine. The work of Rouault is so thoroughly impregnated with the spirit of the great poet who influenced numberless minds during the youth of the painter that it was natural for the latter to make his repeated efforts to create an enduring image of Paul Verlaine. The large canvas here shown, dating from about 1939, is doubtless his most important work on this theme.

50. Duchamp-Villon, The Lovers. The final version of this masterpiece, for which smaller studies exist. A turning point in the evolution to purely creative forms, but without loss of the beauty due to nature.

51. China, Wei Altarpiece. The small scale of this bronze does not prevent its retaining much of the impressiveness of the great stone images of the same period; dated (in the Chinese equivalent) 524 A.D.

52. Japan, 12th century, Kibi Scroll (detail), about 13 inches high, the entire scroll being over 80 feet in length. It depicts, in humorous fashion, the visit of the Japanese envoy to China.

53. Honduras, some of the finest of Maya art was produced, as with the present sculpture, in the city of Copan, at the time of the Old Empire, about the Eighth Century A.D.

54. Mexico, Aztec Corn Goddess, basalt, probably 15th century. The forceful simplicity of this shaft-like figure may seem rigorous after the tropical richness of Maya art, but more experience with the northern people usually brings about a preference for their direct approach to essentials.

55. Ohio, Mound Builder culture, Hawk, 3¾ x 2⅜ inches. The connection between Mexico and the United States in Pre-Columbian times is, of course, evident, but works like the present and the following one have relevance, also, for present-day Americans.

56. South Eastern Florida, Deer's head, 10¾ inches long, wood, with traces of paint. "The finest surviving creation of 15th-century Calusa wood-carving." The Calusa tribe is now extinct.

57. Copley, Portrait of Mrs. Seymour Fort. An example of the extraordinary heights attained by Copley during his earlier life, before going abroad.

58. Eakins, William Rush Carving the Nymph of the Schuylkill, 20⅛ x 26⅛ inches. The present canvas, dating from 1877, is probably the most beautiful rendering of the theme, for which there are many studies, and to which the artist returned thirty years later.

59. Ryder, The Resurrection. The imagination of our mystical painter could include within the few square inches of this picture a sense of the supernatural given only to the fewest of modern artists.

60. Prendergast, Landscape with Figures. As with no other painting in this book, we need to supplement the present monochrome reproduction by a memory of the artist's really extraordinary control of color.

61. Constant, Waterlilies. The timidity before new forms shown by our earlier museum officials is giving place to confidence in judging original work. The present large canvas by Constant, having been acquired by an important museum, augurs a great increase in our ability to recognize talent at the time when it appears.

62. John B. Flannagan, Monkey and Young, 15 inches high. Of particular interest for this book as showing the continuity on our soil of an understanding of animal life, (cf. Plates No. 55 and No. 56), as well as its expression in terms of important sculpture.

INDEX